El Salvador

INSIDE

El Salvador

Kevin Murray with Tom Barry

Resource Center Press
Albuquerque, New Mexico

Copyright © Interhemispheric Resource Center, 1995

First Edition, September 1995
ISBN 0-911213-53-8 : $11.95

Production and design by Christopher Givler
Cover design by Carolynne Colby-Schmeltzer / The Resource Center
Cover photo Copyright © Jim Harney

Published by the Interhemispheric Resource Center

Interhemispheric Resource Center
Box 4506 / Albuquerque, New Mexico 87196

A la hermanita de Roque,
Ana Xiomara

Acknowledgments

Five years of living and working in El Salvador leaves one with a long list of acknowledgments. A more decisive person could choose a few names from among all the Salvadorans and internationalists who cared enough to help me find my way from the first dazed and confused days just before the 1989 offensive to the heady, then challenging, days of peace and reconstruction. Since I can not list all of those people, I'll limit myself to a salute to the friends, coworkers, and teachers from the Center for Global Education and the Jesuit Refugee Service, the two organizations in which I spent most of those years. In 1993, an auto accident and a tragic illness took the lives of Mary Lynn Fields and Ann Manganaro, two women who taught volumes by example, as if to remind us that such sudden sadness was not behind us.

All the writing of *Inside El Salvador* took place in the United States as Ellen Coletti and I tried to find our way in a country that only faintly resembled the one we had left in 1989. As luck would have it, our first temporary home back in the U.S. was the house of Elisabeth Wood and Sam Bowles, and Libby freely provided her own research materials to get this project off the ground. Without even knowing it, Jack Spence and Katherine Yih convinced me that I could really do this. Jack also somehow found the time to read and comment on the whole manuscript (without getting any Darcy drool on it), while Katherine joined Garth Cheff, Mike Delaney, Peter O'Driscoll, Maggie Popkin, Christine Reesor, Laura Renshaw, Tommie Sue Montgomery, Bill Stanley, George Vickers, Lee Winkleman, and Libby Wood in trying to breathe life into one or another chapter. Don't blame them, though, for any problems: That's my department. Gene Palumbo, who one day must get his stories between the covers of a book, repeatedly went the extra kilometer to provide me with fresh information for this one, and Ken Ward helped out in that way, as well.

The Resource Center made the project possible. Debra Preusch got the ball rolling with a phone call before we even unpacked our bags, and she, Tom Barry, and the whole staff in Albuquerque were remarkably supportive, helpful, and patient throughout. Also at the Resource Center, thanks to Josette Griffiths for research assistance and Chris Givler for designing and producing the book. I wish the Resource Center a wonderful future in the move to a new home in Silver City, New Mexico.

In the end, however, Ellen made it happen. Not only did she spend countless hours kneading the ravings of a culture-shocked midlifer into sentences and paragraphs, but she also patiently accompanied him over and around the multitude of obstacles and hazards that challenge any attempt to return to this country.

Contents

Contents

Part 6: Social Organizations and the Popular Movement

Part 7: Ecology and Environmentalism

Part 8: U.S.-El Salvador Relations

Reference Notes

Acronyms

Bibliography

Chronology

For More Information

Figures

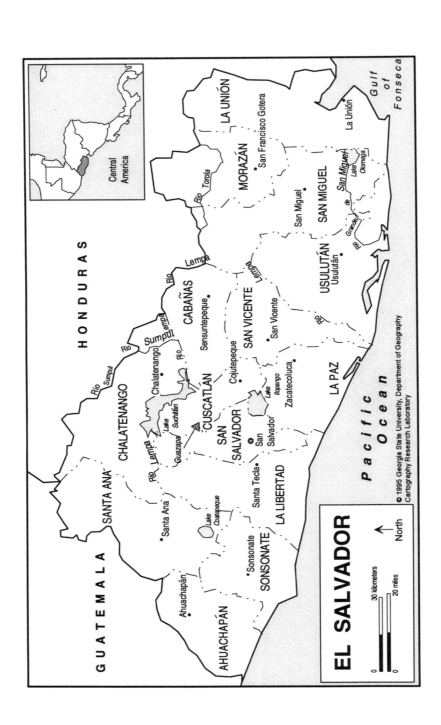

EL SALVADOR

Introduction

This book describes and analyzes the key social, political, and economic forces shaping Salvadoran society in the mid-1990s. The path to this goal is clearly marked. It begins with the tragic turning point in Salvadoran history represented by the 1989 offensive and the killing of the Jesuits and their companions, continuing on through the signing of the Peace Accords in Chapultepec, Mexico, and the 1994 elections. The path ends amid great uncertainty with the departure of the United Nations Observer Mission (ONUSAL) in April 1995.

By presenting the historical roots of the war and the experience of the 1980s from various angles, the stage is set to follow El Salvador along that path. At the end of the path lies a series of questions concerning the long-term viability of ARENA's economic model, the recomposition of Salvadoran political parties and popular movements, the impending environmental catastrophe, and the Salvadoran people's ability to sustain the peace process in the absence of ONUSAL. The answers to these and similar questions will determine the range of possibilities open to Salvadoran society as it enters the twenty-first century.

In the search to shed light on the "big questions" facing El Salvador, another path also needs exploring. This second path is less traveled and at times a machete is needed to clear the way. It, too, has deep historical roots, but takes a sharp turn with the rural crisis of the 1960s and 1970s when the landless population increased from 12 to 41 percent of the total rural population.[1] From that difficult beginning, this path winds its way through the Christian base communities and other organizing efforts of the 1970s, past the violent repression and massacres of the early 1980s. At that point, during a time of mass displacement and life in refugee camps, the path all but disappears. It reemerged in the late 1980s with the resettlement of rural communities even as the war continued.

This second path is, of course, the experience of those who have suffered most throughout the country's tortured history—the poor majority. It, too, passes by the offensive of 1989, the signing of the Peace Accords and the elections of 1994; but by 1995 it has reached a point quite different from the ceremony marking the departure of ONUSAL.

At journey's end, we rest in a wobbly chair at the only table in a small wooden house with a dirt floor. This house is in the community of Santa Marta, Cabañas, but could be in any one of many similar places in rural communities or in the "marginal" areas around the big cities. We wave our hands in a vain attempt to keep the flies away from our lunch of beans, a small piece of salty cheese, and two tortillas, with salt.

The questions here are different from those at the end of the other path, and we can ask them directly of the woman who has just served us lunch. How are the people who have traveled this path living today? Has the journey of the past two decades been worth the pain and sacrifice? Our challenge in this book has been, simply, to describe national and international trends shaping Salvadoran reality without forgetting the look in the eyes of the woman at the end of this second path.

El Salvador: Country and People

Almost exactly the size of Massachusetts, El Salvador ranks as both the smallest and most densely populated country on the American continent. The "little thumb of Latin America" gained international prominence in the 1980s when its brutal civil war placed it at the center of East-West geopolitical conflict. When hundreds of international correspondents filled luxury hotel rooms beyond capacity to cover the 1984 elections, El Salvador drew the eyes of the world as never before. Eleven years later, the world scarcely noticed as the United Nations observer mission shipped off the last of its Toyota Land Cruisers and moved out, leaving the protection of the peace process to the Salvadorans themselves.

El Salvador contains three distinct geographical zones. A narrow plain runs along virtually all of the 120-mile Pacific Coast. Immediately inland from the coastal plain, a volcanic ridge traverses the country in a remarkably straight line from east to west. The capital city, San Salvador, sits nestled among the volcanoes in the Valley of the Hammocks, near the spot where El Salvador's indigenous inhabitants located their pre-Colombian spiritual and commercial center. A taller, more rugged mountain range traverses the northern third of the country.

The Lempa, Central America's largest river, cuts El Salvador in two and forms a formidable natural barrier between the traditionally isolated eastern area, and the more populous and economically developed central and western sections. Hydroelectric dams located on the Lempa provide most of the country's electricity. The two main highways—the Coastal Highway and the Panamerican Highway—cross the Lempa at large bridges, both of which were blown up by the guerrillas during the war.

The war caused major population shifts in El Salvador. As many as one million Salvadorans left the country, at least half of them emigrating to the United States. With the war and market conditions limiting income from El Salvador's traditional exports like coffee and cotton, people quickly became the country's most important export. Dollars sent back home by Salvadorans living abroad fueled the postwar economic expansion, and made U.S. immigration policy a paramount concern for any government in San Salvador.

Within the national borders, huge numbers of people moved south and west to avoid the fighting. Those shifts left three-quarters of the population living in the southwestern section of the country, including the capital. San Salvador, alone, now contains over a quarter of the nation's people. New population patterns increased pressure on land and water resources, aggravating already serious environmental problems.

War and Peace

Since the arrival of the Spanish in the early sixteenth century, a small group of people have extended their control over El Salvador's primary natural resource, its land. This economically and politically powerful class—often referred to as the "fourteen families"—transformed itself over the years but continued to hold the reins of wealth and power in El Salvador well into the twentieth century.[2]

The civil war, which began in earnest in 1980, is best understood as one in a long series of protests by those excluded from that small circle of economic and political influence. The war's primary protagonist, the Farabundo Martí Liberation Front (FMLN), traced its heritage back through its namesake, Farabundo Martí, who fell before a firing squad in 1932, to the indigenous leader, Atlacatl, who left his arrow in the leg of the Spanish invader Pedro Alvarado four and a half centuries earlier. Frustrated by the electoral frauds of 1972 and 1977 and the repression that followed them, the FMLN formed to take control of the state by military means and restructure the economy for the benefit of the country's poor majority.

Eighty thousand Salvadorans lost their lives in the war, a large percentage of them unarmed civilian victims of state repression. Salvadorans did the vast majority of the killing and the dying in the conflict, but they did not do it on their own. Other countries like Cuba, Mexico, and Nicaragua influenced the course of the war; the United States, however, exerted influence of an entirely different order. The only external actor that could have forced a resolution of the conflict in its early stages, the United States not only failed to encourage such a resolution but fueled the conflict for more than a decade with its military and economic aid.

By the late 1980s the war reached a military stalemate that many feared would drag on for another decade, yet 1989 proved a turning point in Salvadoran history with the breaking of that stalemate. Faced by what it saw as an ARENA government of the extreme right, the FMLN planned a major military offensive. Some saw the offensive as a final attempt to incite an insurrection and topple the government, others understood it as the only way to push ARENA to negotiate seriously for peace.

With the guerrillas occupying large areas of the capital, the Army ordered aerial bombardment. Although the military leadership was criticized for bombing urban neighborhoods, another decision proved much more damaging. The High Command gave the order for a team of elite commandos to murder the members of the Jesuit community at the Central American University. That single act spoke with unparalleled eloquence of the impossibility of professionalizing the Armed Forces. The Jesuit murders, combined with the military lessons of the offensive, turned many of the main actors in the war—including the Bush administration, the FMLN, the Salvadoran government, and an important sector of the country's economic oligarchy—into supporters of a negotiated solution.

Although the Salvadoran civil war was primarily a product of social and economic injustice in El Salvador, international forces set the limits within which the conflict developed and helped bring it to an end. The Esquipulas II agreement initiated the Central American peace process that sought negotiated solutions to all the region's conflicts. An international tour in 1988 convinced guerrilla leader Joaquín Villalobos that the international balance of forces had turned against the FMLN as an armed movement. CNN could hardly find time to report on the 1989 offensive because it occurred precisely as German activists began knocking down the Berlin Wall.

The end of the Cold War robbed El Salvador of its geopolitical significance and increased the U.S. stake in ending the war as opposed to winning it. Months after the fall of the Berlin Wall the Sandinistas lost the 1990 elections in Nicaragua, leaving the FMLN without its key diplomatic and military ally in the region. Neither the government nor the FMLN crawled to the negotiating table as a defeated force but both had important reasons to seek an end to the war. A complex web of local and international forces created a powerful momentum behind a peace process that finally yielded an agreement on New Years' Eve, 1991.

The Chapultepec Accords

A series of carefully crafted agreements put an end to the Salvadoran conflict. These began with an agreement reached in May 1990 on an agenda for peace negotiations and culminated with the signing of comprehensive Peace Accords in Chapultepec, Mexico on January 16, 1992. From the beginning, the United Nations played an active role in support of the negotiations, a role that often involved direct pressure on both sides to move the process beyond several sticking points.

In essence, by signing the Peace Accords, the FMLN agreed to stop shooting and, eventually, to destroy its arms in return for a long list of constitutional, institutional, and procedural changes designed to demilitarize and democratize Salvadoran society. The FMLN recognized both the Constitution of 1983 (with amendments) and the ARENA government in return for the assurance that it would be able to participate in the legal political process. Aware of the importance of some sort of national reconciliation, the negotiators agreed to establish special commissions to deal with past human rights abuses by the military and other actors.

Specific provisions reduced the size of the military while others constitutionally reduced the scope of its functions. The Peace Accords placed public security functions in a new civilian police force and created an independent government office led by an ombudsman with broad powers to monitor respect for human rights. Further constitutional reforms altered both the judicial and electoral systems in the hope of making them function more efficiently and equitably.

Although structural economic problems initially caused the FMLN to take up arms, the Peace Accords contained few commitments for concrete economic changes. Rather than attempt to legislate socioeconomic transformation, the negotiators agreed to create a more open, democratic political system through which economic changes could come later. The government remained adamant throughout that its neoliberal economic model was not up for negotiation.

The implementation of the Peace Accords proceeded along a rocky path, full of slippery spots and narrow ledges. Marrack Goulding, special envoy of the UN General Secretary, regularly flew in and out of San Salvador with his translator to defuse numerous crises that threatened to derail the peace process. Surviving several such crises, the implementation process lurched toward its built-in litmus test, the 1994 elections.

The complicated election schedule mandated the election of the president, the eighty-four deputies of the legislative assembly and all of the country's 262 mayors in 1994. With the FMLN participating in elections for the first time, all the ingredients were in place for the "elections of the century."

The elections occurred with the participation of the FMLN and without the kind of overt massive fraud that characterized the balloting in 1972 and 1977. Augusto Ramírez Ocampo, head of ONUSAL, gave the first round of elections his seal of approval even before anyone cast a ballot. Technical fraud and other irregularities were so widespread, however, that other observers saw the elections in a different light. Because they viewed the irregularities as more the rule than the exception, observers at the Central American University described the elections as the "fiasco of the century." Fraudulent or not, the elections left ARENA firmly in control of executive power for the rest of this century.

The Challenges Ahead

The FMLN did not set out to become one more party engaged in the business of winning elections. The resolution of the war, ironically, threatened to put the Frente in exactly that position. If, as the RAND Corporation concluded, U.S. policy in El Salvador failed because it set out to crush the FMLN, then the revolutionary project of the FMLN, similarly, must be judged a failure (See U.S.-El Salvador Relations). While the Peace Accords, and the struggle to implement them serve as the backbone of this book, another important theme involves the political future of the Salvadoran left as it tries to decide how best to transform society, if not by revolution.

Important questions about the Salvadoran economy remain to be answered. Triumphant press conferences announcing more healthy economic statistics became the order of the day in El Salvador during the early 1990s. Land and housing values skyrocketed and more cars jammed the already crowded streets of San Salvador. New fast food franchises and convenience markets seemed to be going up on every corner.

The popular movement and the FMLN shouted that the prosperity was not reaching the poor, but the most potent opposition to the Cristiani government's economic program came from more surprising places. Ex-soldiers and civil defense members, earlier the heroes of public order, threatened the economic celebration with memories of street violence of the 1970s and proved their capacity to make good on their threats if their demands for major severance benefits were not answered. But the most serious questioning of neoliberalism as practiced by Cristiani came from the Calderón Sol administration itself. After months of indecision, Calderón Sol announced a package of economic proposals designed to put structural adjustment on a new track through a radical opening of the Salvadoran economy to foreign investment and commercial competition. The outrage of the business community caused Calderón Sol to tone down his plan, but his announcement exposed the structural weaknesses of the current economic model.

All political and economic plans may be in for a shock if the ecological crisis is as bad as some environmentalists say. Seldom mentioned during the war, ecological concerns are working their way onto the national agenda as the interrelated issues of deforestation, erosion, pesticide poisoning, and water quality and availability begin to pose concrete and absolute limits to social and economic development. These issues await the political movement or party that will put them before the Salvadoran public in a compelling and effective way.

With the violence of war behind it and three years of reconstruction and reconciliation under its belt, some suggest that El Salvador in the mid-1990s stands at the edge of a long period of relative stability and growth. A closer look *Inside El Salvador*, however, suggests that, while there is reason for hope about the country's future, the social and economic problems that caused the violence of the 1980s remain fundamentally unsolved despite the dramatic transitions of the 1990s. If those in power mistake the military demobilization of the FMLN for a signal to renew past practices of ignoring these problems, growth and stability will remain distant dreams.

Part 1

Politics and Government

© Edgar Romero

ERP's Joaquin Villalobos greets ARENA's Gloria Salguero Gross, May Day 1994.

Constitutions, Oligarchs, and Lieutenant-Colonels

While the negotiators of the Chapultepec Accord avoided a frontal attack on the Salvadoran economic system, they did give serious attention to transforming old political institutions and creating new ones. Legal political participation was opened to new players and, with the help of the United Nations (UN), the electoral process was altered to modernize it and make it more democratic. Carrying these changes through to their conclusion meant not only a challenge to traditional patterns of political exclusion and military rule but required a complete restructuring of political relations at all levels of society. No political institution was immune to these changes.

Two powers—the oligarchy and the army—have historically stood behind the democratic facade erected by a series of Salvadoran constitutions. Political competition among elite groups has occurred, while the armed forces assumed the mission of guaranteeing the stability of the system by repressing any active disaffection among the masses.

Within these parameters a number of political variations were possible. Governments were sometimes one-man dictatorships, and, at other times, institutional regimes with civilian leadership and respect for constitutional formalities. The military governments more often than not served the interests of the oligarchy, yet favored the military's own institutional interests when they occasionally deviated from those of the oligarchy.

Repression of opposition was at times brutal and total, yet often highly selective or even interrupted by short periods of populist-oriented policies. These varying levels of repression resulted from the ebb and flow of opposition politics as well as the ongoing debate—both in the Salvadoran oligarchy and the military—over the relative strategic merits of absolute repression versus cooption.

For example, the historic popular uprisings of 1931-1932 grew out of frustrated hopes and deepening economic misery. A reformist civilian president, Arturo Araujo, was unable to deliver his promised social benefits because of the depression-induced collapse of the world coffee market. When the Communist party called for an insurrection based on the protest of rural workers, the Armed Forces, commanded by Gen. Maximiliano Hernández Martínez, crushed the poorly organized revolt and with it all forms of organized opposition. Diverse vigilante bands formed by local oligarchs also participated in the violence, remembered as the *matanza* of 1932.[1]

The *matanza* represented a watershed in Salvadoran history for two reasons. On the one hand, its indiscriminate violence silenced opposition in the countryside for almost two generations (See Social Organizations and the Popular Movement). At the same time, the establishment of a military government under Hernández Martínez represented a new division of labor in which the oligarchy withdrew to social and economic concerns, leaving the stability of the political system to the military and the corrupt class of venal politicians that prospered at its side.

The Martínez regime endured twelve years but could not withstand the epidemic of hope for a new world of democracy that broke out as World War II drew to a close. A national strike supported by military dissidents overthrew Hernández Martínez in May 1944. Three military coups between October 1944 and December 1948 kept the Casa Presidencial in constant upheaval. With Major Carlos Osorio, who led the December 1948 coup and ruled the country until September 1956, military and economic elites unsuccessfully sought to stabilize Salvadoran politics through a military-led reformist regime. Recurring military coups and fraudulent elections characterized the period between 1956 and 1979. Hope for democracy blossomed in the early 1960s with a promising break in military rule, but the familiar reassertion of military control ended that short-lived experiment.

In 1972, a strong opposition movement ran José Napoleón Duarte and Guillermo Manuel Ungo for president and vice-president, respectively. Although Duarte appeared to have won the election, the military installed Col. Arturo Molina as president, leading to mass demonstrations and violent repression. The same scenario was replayed with even more violent results in 1977 when the opposition actually chose a retired military officer as their presidential candidate. The frustrations of these two major elections convinced many Salvadorans that the peaceful path of electoral politics offered no solution to their country's staggering problems.

In each of the several democratic "openings" since 1932, Salvadorans relied on one set of military officers to curb the excesses of military rule. Each incoming set of military "progressives" would attempt some moderate social legislation—a minimum wage, a public-health program, even a land reform. But resistance from the oligarchy, frequently expressing itself through factional maneuvering within the military by pro-oligarchic elements, limited the effectiveness of any proposed changes while removing any threat to the dominance of traditional elites.

The same script was replayed during the military coup that took place in October 1979, but not all the actors were willing to assume their traditional roles. During the 1970s increasingly militant and radical popular organizations developed alongside an incipient revolutionary movement. The repression and corruption that characterized the regime of General Carlos Humberto Romero (1977-1979) closely resembled political life in Nicaragua under Anastasio Somoza—an analogy which made some army officers uneasy.

Against the backdrop of rapidly broadening social protest and brutal military repression, a reformist coup was organized by a group of young officers who hoped to head off a revolutionary turn of events like that in neighboring Nicaragua. The coup had the passive support of the United States.

Upon taking power, the young coup leaders made quite a dramatic proclamation pledging to remove the military from politics and implement profound social reforms including agrarian reform and a nationalization of the financial system. To initiate this process, they turned power over to a mixed military-civilian junta that included two colonels (Adolfo Majano and Jaime Abdul Gutiérrez) and three civilians (Ramón Mayorga, Guillermo Manuel Ungo, and Mario Andino).

In a sense, this "first junta" represented another chance at the reformist option blocked by the electoral frauds of 1972 and 1977. The coup placed power in the hands of a reformist military-civilian junta but hard-line forces within the military under the control of Defense Minister José García moved almost immediately to undermine the younger officers represented in the junta. These conservative forces countered the junta's attempts to introduce social reforms, restore respect for human rights, and bring to justice those engaged in the repression of the Romero years.

It soon became clear that the junta was ineffectual, and it began to be referred to as the junta of *chompipes* (turkeys) who would be cooked and eaten by Christmas. In fact, the junta lasted less than three months. In the first week of 1980, the civilian members of the first junta resigned, having failed to receive assurances that the armed forces would recognize civilian control and stop the slaughter of the popular movement.

A second junta was formed in which the three civilians of the first junta were replaced by Hector Dada and José Antonio Morales Erlich, two leading members of the Christian Democratic Party (PDC), which had held itself aloof from the first junta, and José Ramón Avalos, a virtual political unknown. Dada resigned in March 1980 and was replaced by José Napoleón Duarte. The United States, which had found the civilian members of the first junta too closely allied with left-leaning popular organizations, favored this coalition. Despite the inclusion of the less progressive PDC leadership, the extremist elements in the military still felt that the second junta was much too reform-minded. A second coup under the leadership of Major Roberto D'Aubuisson, planned for the end of February, was forestalled by the vigorous intervention of the U.S. chargé d'affaires, James Cheek.

The repression of the popular movement and scourge of death-squad killings that caused the withdrawal of the civilian members of the first junta intensified under the second junta (January 1980-April 1982). The assassination in March 1980 of Roman Catholic Archbishop Oscar Arnulfo Romero—planned by Major D'Aubuisson himself—made it clear that the hard-line faction of the military was clearly in control.[2] Political and economic reforms were introduced, but they were too little and too late. The reformist leadership that many Salvadorans had hoped for soon proved corrupt, inefficient, and subservient to the U.S. embassy and Salvadoran armed forces.

By October 1980, five revolutionary organizations had initiated the coordinating body that would become the FMLN. In January 1981, the new guerrilla front called on the population to support a "final offensive" to overturn the military regime. The final offensive, timed to coincide with the inauguration of Ronald Reagan as President of the United States, failed to unseat the government but did signal the beginning of all-out civil war. In the early 1980s, against the backdrop of the widening war, constitutional government by elected civilian authorities became institutionalized. The transfer from military to civilian rule and the scheduling of regular elections began with the Constituent Assembly elections in 1982. The newly organized Nationalist Republican Alliance (ARENA)—under D'Aubuisson's leadership—won effective control of the Assembly.[3] In May 1982 the Assembly selected Alvaro Magaña as provisional president and proceeded to write a new constitution for the country. A presidential election was held in 1984, followed in 1985 by mayoral and Assembly elections—with the Christian Democrats under Napoleon Duarte winning both times. ARENA dominated the 1988 mayoral and Assembly elections and went on to win handily the presidential election of March 1989.

This series of elections was intended to consolidate civilian government. El Salvador's first peaceful transfer of power from one elected civilian to another in more than 50 years occurred in 1989. As long as the FMLN and their supporters existed as a belligerent force actively opposed to the system and in effective control of an important part of the country, this U.S.-backed democratization was partial at best. No solution to the armed conflict was possible without changes that enabled the political participation of the FMLN and its supporters.

Government Structure

The three major centers of governmental power in the country as set forth in the 1983 constitution are the presidency, the Legislative Assembly, and the Supreme Court. Like most other Central American countries, El Salvador has a unicameral legislature whose 84 members are elected every three years. Sixty-four of the deputies are elected as representatives of El Salvador's 14 departments (administrative units similar to states or provinces) with each department represented by a number of deputies in rough proportion to its percentage of the national population. The other 20 deputies are elected nationwide on a proportional basis.

The country's complicated proportional system offers good possibilities of representation to small parties. Members of the Assembly can be elected to unlimited consecutive terms while the president must leave office at the conclusion of a five-year term. A run-off is held for the presidency if no candidate receives an absolute majority in the first round.

As a result of the Peace Accords, members of the Supreme Court are elected by a two-thirds majority of the Legislative Assembly from lists of candidates selected by the country's lawyers and by a special National Judicial Council selected by the president for this purpose. (See Justice, Human Rights and Public Security). Local judges are appointed, evaluated, and, if necessary, removed by the Supreme Court.

Departmental governors and deputy governors are appointed by the president. Voters directly elect their mayors in each of 262 *municipios*. Run-offs do not occur in municipal elections; a plurality of votes assures victory. Prior to municipal elections, each contending party must present a full slate of officers for the municipal council and that entire slate takes office with the victorious party. This structure hampers local efforts at consensus building and leads to the characterization of local elections as "winner-take-all" contests.[4]

During the late 1980s this system of local government was seriously disrupted as mayors were identified by the FMLN as vehicles of government counterinsurgency and labeled as military targets. Several mayors were assassinated and many more were forced to leave their *municipios*. As a result of the Peace Accords, the "exiled" mayors were allowed to return to their posts. Although the transition was not peaceful in all cases, municipal elections were carried out in all 262 *municipios* in 1994.

Political Parties and Elections

The militarization of Salvadoran politics caused a weakening of the country's system of political parties. When elections threatened to alter the country's balance of power, they were simply overruled, as in 1972 and 1977.

From its inception, the U.S.-supported plan to defeat the FMLN insurgency combined an effort to rehabilitate El Salvador's system of political parties and promote the image of democratic elections with an effort to defeat the guerrillas militarily.

This plan began with the Constituent Assembly elections and continued through the 1980s, despite the active opposition of the FMLN. Strong political parties like ARENA and the PDC gained prominence in the context of that system. With the signing of the Chapultepec Accord, the government acknowledged the need to make important changes in the political system as it had evolved since the writing of the 1983 constitution, and the FMLN accepted the legitimacy of the system with those changes. The conversion of the FMLN into a political party dates from the Chapultepec Accord.

The deep, internal transformations of the postwar period spared no political party. The profound recomposition of all political parties and alliances was the essential political characteristic of that period.

ARENA: *Patria Sí, Comunismo No*

A shadowy group of right-wing military officers, paramilitary operatives, and conservative members of the traditional oligarchy formed ARENA in September 1981. The key figure in the organization of that group and its maturation into one of the strongest political parties in Central America was Major Roberto D'Aubuisson.

In May 1980 D'Aubuisson, a former military intelligence officer, was arrested for planning a coup against the Duarte-led junta.

D'Aubuisson had once worked under Gen. José Alberto (Chele) Medrano, the founder of the National Democratic Organization (ORDEN), a paramilitary network of informers and enforcers organized by the security forces to crush political discontent in rural areas. His coup attempt having failed, D'Aubuisson used the contacts he developed through ORDEN and his activities as an intelligence officer in the National Guard to lay the foundation for a new political party.[5]

D'Aubuisson first made a public splash in 1980 when he began appearing on television flashing documents and photographs of "suspected terrorists," warning them that they "still had time to change their ways." Such broadcasts preceded death squad killings such as the one that took the life of State Counsel General Mario Zamora, brother of Rubén Zamora, then still a member of the PDC. Prior to his departure from the Salvadoran National Security Agency (ANSESAL), D'Aubuisson had removed the intelligence files accumulated by the security forces and used these files for his "anti-terrorist" campaign. Even after the Major returned the files, the support of high-level Defense Ministry personnel for his denunciations assured that he had access to all the secret information he needed.

The new party broadened its base around a program of virulent anticommunism and nationalism. The party gained force in the 1980s as a defensive alliance of those who felt the nation was under attack by a conspiracy of terrorists, socialists, liberal academics, and soft-headed reformers. Although the U.S. embassy and others dismissed ARENA as a marginal group of ultra-right extremists, the party was founded with substantial support from the oligarchy. D'Aubuisson played a critical role in the organizational development of the party and expanded its base by convincing many wealthy Salvadorans of the need to answer the political challenge posed by the leftist threat.

Although it initially had opposed the elections for Constituent Assembly scheduled for March 1982, ARENA later decided to enter the electoral contest and won 29 percent of the vote. A charismatic campaigner, D'Aubuisson electrified many voters with his macho image and fiery speeches. The PDC, which co-governed the country with the military from 1980-82, was burdened by a sagging economy and capital flight, a drooping coffee industry, high unemployment, and its inability to control the armed forces.[6] It, nonetheless, polled the most votes in the elections.

Joining with the National Conciliation Party (PCN), traditionally the party of the military, ARENA formed a rightwing coalition in the new Assembly, which elected D'Aubuisson Assembly president. Only pressure from the United States prevented the Assembly from naming him provisional president of the country. In 1984 D'Aubuisson ran against Duarte for president but lost in the run-off election. The following year the PDC also won control of the Assembly.

From the beginning, ARENA had an ambivalent relationship to the United States. The party's extreme nationalism translated into anti-U.S. sentiment that rivaled that of the FMLN, and the U.S.-sponsored reforms of the early 1980s only heightened those sentiments. Nonetheless, not even the most virulent nationalists could deny the importance of U.S. support to the war effort or the need to construct an image that could play better in Washington.

Seeking the Center of Power

After its defeat in the 1985 Assembly elections, ARENA began a process of party strengthening in preparation for the 1988 and 1989 elections. The essential task at hand was to broaden the party's political base by reaching beyond the oligarchy and extremists to members of the middle and lower classes who were frustrated and disgusted with the performance of the Christian Democrats. Critical to this broadening of ARENA's support was the effort to shed the party's death squad and extremist image without losing the large number of supporters who were drawn to that image. The resounding victory of ARENA in the 1988 elections demonstrated both the success of this effort and the degree to which the PDC had fallen out of favor with Salvadoran voters.[7]

D'Aubuisson began grooming Alfredo "Fredy" Cristiani as a symbol of the new public image of ARENA in 1985 when he suggested that Cristiani be placed on the party's executive council. The next year Cristiani became party president although D'Aubuisson retained his position as "Maximum Leader." The position as the party's presidential candidate was D'Aubuisson's if he wanted it, but D'Aubuisson chose to step out of the electoral limelight in 1989, aware that his unsavory reputation as a death squad organizer would undermine chances for international acceptance of an ARENA government.

The collapse of the Christian Democrats had left the U.S. foreign policy of supporting the political center orphaned and discredited. Cristiani, with his Georgetown degree, perfect English, and no known death squad connections, proved the perfect candidate for the United States. Cristiani also proved to be a popular candidate among Salvadorans, winning the presidential elections in the first round. His victory consolidated ARENA's gains in the legislative and municipal elections of 1988 and gave the party almost total control of the Salvadoran state.

As president, Cristiani surprised many with his apt handling of the reins of power. He was particularly adept at convincing the U.S.

Congress of the sincerity of his reform agenda and the advisability of continued congressional support for the war effort. After a very difficult first year in power that saw some of his closest aides assassinated by the FMLN and a guerrilla offensive that shook the foundations of his power, he showed himself to be committed to walking the tightrope between the recalcitrant right wing of his own party and the Salvadoran people's desire for peace.

The most serious crisis of his presidency involved the military's killing of six Jesuit priests, their housekeeper, and her daughter during the 1989 offensive. Although no direct connection could be firmly established between the president and the order to carry out the killings, he was repeatedly criticized for not telling the Salvadoran people all that he knew about the affair and for failing to press for the punishment not just of the killers themselves, but of those who planned and ordered the action.

Economic successes notwithstanding, the major achievement of Cristiani and the ARENA party during the period 1989-94 was a peace agreement with the FMLN. Although he did not directly participate in the negotiations until the final stages, Cristiani was able to project himself in the media as the architect of the agreement. His leadership was suspect at many points in the process; many analysts believe, however, that only an ARENA president could have withstood the heavy pressure from the right to limit concessions to the guerrillas.[8]

D'Aubuisson, while remaining dominant in internal party politics, publicly converted to a more conciliatory position in the early 1990s. His speech on the occasion of the tenth anniversary of ARENA's founding emphasized that the party unconditionally supported the president's peace initiative and welcomed the FMLN into the democratic system.[9] Central American University rector Ignacio Ellacuría, just weeks before his murder in 1989, said "D'Aubuisson is no longer responsible for the death squads because he understands the necessity of moderating his party to be able to win the elections." [10]

D'Aubuisson's death from cancer at age 50 in February 1992 was surely the most traumatic moment for ARENA during the Cristiani years. Although ARENA supporters hailed the passing of a hero who they believed had almost single-handedly saved the nation from communism, those in El Salvador's political opposition shed no tears over the death of the man they saw responsible for the death of Monseñor Romero and so many others.

ARENA's opponents saw D'Aubuisson's death as the harbinger of serious divisions as the various factions of the party struggled for supremacy. With the broadening of the party in the mid-1980s, several factions developed. These groupings expressed themselves in two main tendencies: a conservative tendency of military officers and business people linked to the domestic economy and the traditional export crops like coffee and cotton, and a more politically moderate group linked to financial and industrial capital and more sensitive to international political and economic concerns. Cristiani's selection as presidential candidate, with the surprising support of D'Aubuisson, signaled the ascendancy of the latter group.

The traditional sector opposed President Cristiani on nearly every concession made to the guerrillas in the peace talks, and continuing support for the death squads comes from the fringes of its ranks. This is the ARENA of nationalist fanaticism, of fist-to-heart salutes, and the neofascist appeal to God and Fatherland. The more pragmatic ARENA wears tailored European business suits and speaks flawless English. This latter sector saw that peace and some democratic reforms would be good for business, even if it meant concessions to the FMLN. The pragmatists have a powerful institutional expression in The Salvadoran Foundation for Economic and Social Development (FUSADES), an U.S. Agency for International Development (AID)-funded foundation that has spent millions of dollars promoting trade liberalization and the overall neoliberal agenda.[11]

D'Aubuisson's death set the stage for an intense struggle along factional lines for the leadership of the party. Armando Calderón Sol had been an ARENA member since its founding and had close historical and political ties to D'Aubuisson. Despite these ties, and Calderón Sol's impeccable rightwing ideological credentials, he did not fit neatly into either of the two leading factions. As mayor of San Salvador, Calderón Sol had formed strong relationships with moderates, including Cristiani. During his second term as mayor, he assumed the powerful position of elected leader of ARENA's executive committee with the support of both Cristiani and staunch conservatives like Assembly President Roberto Angulo.

The modernizing faction of the party was unable to field a convincing presidential candidate to oppose Calderón Sol. The likely choice was Roberto Murray Meza, a millionaire industrialist who had presided over the Social Investment Fund (FIS) during the Cristiani years.[12] An attractive candidate electorally, Murray Meza's lack of ties to the history of the party (i.e., to Roberto D'Aubuisson) made him suspect to long-time ARENA supporters. A prominent figure in ARENA signaled Murray Meza's difficulties when, during the period leading up to the party convention, he confided to a journalist that, "Calderón Sol's woman has more balls than Murray Meza." Despite holding degrees from Harvard and Yale, Murray Meza apparently lacked the macho charisma necessary to be an ARENA leader. More importantly, he lacked Calderón Sol's ability to hold the various party factions together.

In March 1993 Calderón Sol easily won the party's presidential nomination. After a long internal debate, the moderate faction was able to push through the nomination of Jorge Borgo Bustamante as vice-president. The political distance between Borgo, the CEO of the highly successful TACA Airlines, and Calderón Sol is measured by Borgo's reported participation in a "Stop Armando" movement within the party during the run-up to the convention.[13]

During the election campaign, the Salvadoran political class debated whether or not the mellowing of the party's public image reflected real changes or opportunistic illusions that would give way to the traditional ARENA policies after the elections. After the predictably wide swings of campaign demagoguery, Calderón Sol punctuated his first statement as president with a commitment to faithful compliance with the Peace Accords. He then flew to New York to assure the UN Secretary General of that commitment.[14] In his inaugural address, however, he assured the Armed Forces that its position was secure in his administration, and he promised the country an "authentic" ARENA government (as if the Cristiani administration had been something else).

Notwithstanding these predictable contradictions, the actions of the early months of the Calderón Sol presidency projected more a tone of continuity with the Cristiani administration than a departure from its policy directions. Nonetheless, during the massive ARENA celebration on the evening of April 24, both Calderón Sol and Cristiani stood arm-in-arm on the stage and led the screaming crowd in the chant that makes it hard for Salvadorans to forget the ARENA of the early 1980s...¡Patria Sí, Comunismo No!

The convincing ARENA electoral victory carried Calderón Sol into office in June 1994 on a wave of euphoria. The euphoria, however, was extremely short-lived. Within the first six months of the new administration, the old division between party traditionalists and the modernizing element associated with Cristiani reappeared with a vengeance. The pushing and shoving threatened to overwhelm Calderón Sol's ability to act as an effective bridge between factions. In October 1994, ARENA held a convention at which an outward showing of unity papered over the worsening internal tensions.[15]

At the same time, the party was wracked by charges of corruption coming not from the left but from Dr. Kirio Waldo Salgado, a leading intellectual of the extreme right. Given Salgado's public notoriety and his access to the media, the charges caused a public sensation, leading directly to the resignation of two cabinet-level members of the Calderón Sol administration.[16] During the 1994 campaign, Salgado's

Freedom and Democracy Institute (ILYD) had strongly supported Calderón Sol's candidacy with a well-orchestrated publicity campaign attacking Rubén Zamora and his FMLN-supporters as terrorists.

Salgado chose the fifteenth anniversary of the 1979 military coup (and the moment of the October 1994 ARENA national convention) to launch his Liberal Democratic Party (PLD). For Salgado, the PLD seeks to "rescue the nationalist principles of Roberto D'Aubuisson."[17] While a good number of former ARENA members were said to have answered Salgado's call, the PLD was unable to attract any well-known ARENA leaders.

The divisions in ARENA, by 1995, appeared to be qualitatively different than at any previous time in the party's history. A range of observers concurred in the vision of the Calderón Sol administration as a car careening out control with no one at the wheel.[18] The difficulties encountered by Calderón Sol as he attempted to deal with delicate issues of national policy in early 1995—such as crime, overall economic policy, and the demands of former members of the Armed Forces—only added to this feeling.

ARENA did not, therefore, escape the pressures resulting from the changes wrought by the Peace Accords that challenged all Salvadoran political institutions. Although, as of mid-1995, ARENA had been able to avoid the outright splits that had occurred in other parties, it faced significant internal tensions. Without leadership from the president to unite diverse party interests, these tensions can only be expected to increase. In the post-electoral period, some analysts suggested that the dimensions of ARENA's victory in 1994 represented the establishment of the "hegemony" of its social and political project for El Salvador. Others went so far as to warn of the danger of the establishment of a "one-party state" of long duration, like the PRI in Mexico which seemed invincible in mid-1994.[19]

Although so far kept within certain acceptable limits, the divisions and difficulties outlined above suggest that it is difficult to speak with certainty of an ARENA project that could serve as the basis of such a one-party state. Furthermore, the government's own proposal to deepen the structural adjustment of the Salvadoran economy points to the limits of the pre-1995 model, and to the temporary character of its undeniable successes (See Economy). Finally, although ARENA has shown itself to be strikingly adept at coopting all opposition from its right, the formation of Kirio Waldo Salgado's PLD, in the long term, may represent a higher-profile opposition that will succeed at attracting significant numbers of defectors from the party's right wing.

ARENA is unlikely to self-destruct as the Christian Democrats did so quickly in the late 1980s, but the party and its national project is not without its vulnerabilities. Whether or not the opposition can exploit those weaknesses and present an alternative project of its own is quite another matter.

Christian Democrats: An Endangered Species?

In 1964 the newly founded PDC became the first opposition party to win seats in the legislature since the repression of the 1932 uprising. The party soon became dominant in the national capital, regularly winning the San Salvador mayor's seat. During the late 1960s and early 1970s, the PDC was also the center of opposition to military rule at the national level. Its presidential candidates, José Napoleón Duarte in 1972 and Col. Ernesto Claramount in 1977, were deprived of victory only by fraud.

The party follows the classic principles of Christian democracy: a denial of the necessity of class conflict, and populism and reformism that do not threaten established social and economic structures. The PDC has been composed primarily of rising middle and working classes in urban areas, as well as people of all social levels in the countryside. Although progressive in tone, the party's position was never anti-imperialist, nor even clearly anti-military but consistently has stood for the principle of civilian control.

Its reformist reputation, combined with the flexibility and the prestige of its leader, Duarte, made the PDC an ideal civilian partner for the military in the 1980s. The party's right wing assumed the formal reins of government with the formation of the second military-civilian junta in early 1980.

The party's small but highly visible left wing split off in early 1980, disgusted with the party's willingness to join the military-civilian junta. Thrust into national office in 1980, the party became the willing, although at times uncomfortable, instrument for the U.S. counterinsurgency project for most of the decade. Rather than taking advantage of its position as the ruling party to push through reforms and build on its popularity, the PDC chose to maintain a close alliance with the military. Duarte was also careful never to stray out of favor with the U.S. embassy, even to the point of kissing the U.S. flag on one of his several trips to Washington.[20]

Once in office Duarte made little effort to maintain his support among the U.S.-backed unions and peasant associations whose votes had been critical to his victory. Instead, the U.S. foreign-policy priority—defeat of the FMLN—became the government's top priority. This lust for victory in the war swept aside earlier promises to push forward economic reforms and pursue peace negotiations. Under constant pressure from the U.S. embassy, Duarte's economic policy became increasingly oriented toward the private sector, leaving the poor majority to face deteriorating socioeconomic conditions (See U.S.-El Salvador Relations).

The Duarte government did carry out the reform package decreed by the coup leaders in 1979, but manipulation and corruption disfigured the reforms to such an extent that, by 1987, they were easy targets for ARENA's attacks. In fact, corruption reached new highs during the Duarte administration, with several top public officials caught red-handed pillaging public resources. While government officials enriched themselves, living standards for the poor kept falling, and human rights abuses against labor leaders and social activists continued.

Disgusted with the subservience, corruption, and internal factionalism of the PDC and weary of the economic decline that had become the hallmark of the party's rule, many voters responded to the rightwing appeal to push the Christian Democrats out of office. Duarte fell ill with terminal cancer in 1988 and could do little to stop the party's downward slide. ARENA swept to victory in the 1988 elections, gaining control over the Legislative Assembly and a clear majority of the municipalities.

Divided and demoralized, the PDC had no chance to hold the presidency in 1989. Its candidate, conservative technocrat Fidel Chávez Mena—Minister of Planning under Duarte—ran a lackluster campaign that could only muster 36 percent of the votes against the ARENA steamroller. To make matters worse, soon after the election, the majority of the PDC legislative delegation bolted to the breakaway Authentic Christian Movement (MAC). The party that had seemed invincible five years earlier was reduced to the role of a weak opposition force. In each election since 1982 the number of votes cast for the PDC has dropped—from 590,000 in 1982 to 216,000 in the first round in 1994.

Whereas the Christian Democratic government had refused to negotiate seriously with the FMLN "terrorists," the defeated PDC now limped to the side of the FMLN to join its call for a negotiated settlement to the war. The party sharply criticized the neoliberal economic policies of the Cristiani government, accusing it of "being against everyone"—inverting the FMLN slogan of "everyone against ARENA."[21] Party officials began to talk publicly about a "confluence of interests" with the FMLN, and the National Union of Workers and Campesinos (UNOC), a PDC labor-campesino coalition, joined the anti-government opposition alongside the leftist National Unity of Salvadoran Workers (UNTS) alliance. Christian Democratic campesino leader Amanda Villatoro joined Chávez Mena and several militant speakers from the UNTS on the podium at the giant May Day 1990 rally in San Salvador.

In the Legislative Assembly elections of 1991, the party presented to the public a candidate list that included several members of UNOC and related organizations. This move acknowledged the PDC's awareness that it had to do something to respond to the challenge from the left being posed by the Democratic Convergence (CD). The changes were not sufficient to stem the decline of popular support. On election day, the PDC finished a clear second to ARENA, but it actually lost its position as the second electoral force in San Salvador to the CD. In 1991, 42,000 fewer Salvadorans cast their votes for the Christian Democrats than in 1988, even though total votes cast increased by 100,000.

During the 1991-94 legislative term, the PDC worked as part of the generally ineffective effort to oppose the neoliberal program being implemented by ARENA. The ruling party formed a majority coalition with the PCN and the MAC that held together on nearly every important issue. The legislative opposition was slightly more effective when it came to pressuring the government to seal a peace accord with the FMLN. Although they had no direct participation in the peace process until the final stages, the PDC took credit for proposing compromise solutions on several key issues as the negotiations neared conclusion.[22]

The signing of the Peace Accords demanded of the PDC a strategic response to the entry of the FMLN into legal politics. This challenge became yet another occasion for internal divisions. Many party members were convinced that the party had a bright future as a modernized, progressive alternative to the extremes offered by the FMLN and ARENA, but only with major leadership changes. A "rescue movement" arose with the expressed goal to democratize the party internally and the unspoken goal of assuring that someone other than Chávez Mena would lead the party in 1994. Former Foreign Minister Ricardo Acevedo Peralta, an early proponent of this reform movement, was expelled from the party for his trouble.

In early 1993, the reform effort began to coalesce around the candidacy of Abraham Rodríguez. Rodríguez, a jurist, wealthy businessman, and a founding member of the PDC, gained national attention in 1992 through his participation in the Ad Hoc Commission to investigate the human rights records of military officers. He was also the preferred candidate of a sector of the FMLN who favored an opposition alliance to defeat ARENA over a candidate clearly identified with the left.

To its credit, the PDC had established a primary system for the nomination of its candidates, and Rodríguez supporters presented him as an alternative to Chávez Mena in the run-off held on May 23, 1993. Rodríguez lost the nomination in a close race. In any case, the choice of Chávez Mena doomed the PDC to a mediocre showing in the March 1994 elections. Internal divisions turned into a series of expulsions and court cases that became the subject of nightly TV reports. In addition, Chávez Mena was turned down by several possible vice-presidential candidates until Atilio Viéytez accepted the post just before the registration deadline.

Given its dismal results in pre-election polls, many analysts were surprised that the ticket polled over 15 percent on election day. The party suffered a drastic decline in San Salvador, but important pockets of die-hard supporters voted PDC in the countryside. That support allowed the party to win nearly twice as many municipal races as the FMLN (29 to 15) and to secure 18 seats under the proportional system for electing Assembly candidates. For the second round, the PDC declined to offer its support to either of the two run-off candidates.

In the wake of the 1994 elections, party activists attempted to negotiate an orderly transition in the leadership of the party. Although the party was able to stay together on issues like the election of a new Supreme Court, profound differences persisted between those who had supported Chávez Mena and those advocating party reform. As always, part of the problem revolved around old personal rivalries within the party, but the groups also differed concerning the most practical direction for the party—regardless of who might occupy its leadership.[23] These differences surfaced and became irreconcilable over the issue of who would represent the party on the Supreme Electoral Tribunal (TSE).

Although the majority of the party's legislative deputies were in the reform group (*abrahamistas*), the *fidelistas* controlled the majority of the party's governing council. When the latter group imposed Eduardo Colindres in August 1994 as its selection for the TSE, the reform group saw no alternative but to add its name to the list of parties formed by splits in the PDC.[24] In November 1994, the *abrahamistas* created the Social Christian Renovation Movement (MRSC) and immediately began talking with other opposition formations about the creation of a broader opposition project.[25]

The PDC has been without its own political project since it became wedded to the U.S. counterinsurgency project in 1980. After the departure of the MRSC, the bleak future of the PDC is perhaps best described in the following *Proceso* report:

> "...the PDC could, in the best of cases, end up being one more party in the political system, reproducing itself through the inertia of cautious votes. In the worst of cases, it could follow the steps of the PCN, subordinating itself to the ARENA and,

thereby, assuring itself a slow, inexorable death as a political institution. The other alternative, rejected by the current leaders of the party, presumes the realistic search of a policy of alliances with the FMLN and the other opposition parties with an eye toward the formation of a political coalition with real electoral appeal." [26]

FMLN: From Insurrection to Elections

One of the key trade-offs of the Peace Accords was a commitment by the FMLN to respect the constitutionality of the elected government in return for government pledges to allow the Frente to become a legal political party. The transition from political-military movement to political-electoral party was a complex one with many implications for national politics. The main public steps along this path are clear:

- January 1989: A FMLN proposal to participate in the 1989 presidential elections if they could be delayed to allow them to organize their campaign.
- January 1992: The signing of the Chapultepec Accord in which the FMLN recognized the legitimacy of the Salvadoran state.
- December 1992: The announcement by the Supreme Electoral Tribunal that it had accepted the FMLN's proposal to become a legal political party.
- January-April 1994: Participation in the electoral campaign and the elections of March 20 and April 24.
- May 1, 1994: The formal investiture of the victorious legislative deputies and mayors of the FMLN.

Ironically, it was on May 1, International Workers' Day 1994, that the culmination of this long process signaled the crisis in the FMLN as a political party. The smiling embrace between Gloria Salguero Gross, ARENA leader and president of the new Legislative Assembly, and Ana Guadalupe Martínez, former commander of the Revolutionary People's Army and now Assembly vice-president representing the newly renamed People's Expression of Renewal (ERP), stands as an enduring image of that day. How that embrace between an ARENA hard-liner and one of the FMLN's best-known leaders came to occupy center stage on May Day 1994, and why it caused so much rancor among the ranks of the FMLN, fairly well tells the story of the early stages of the Frente's postwar transformation.

Origins and Constituent Groups

In the aftermath of the 1969 war with Honduras and frustrated by continued electoral fraud, several leftist groups decided that armed struggle was fundamental to changing the country's repressive and unjust economic and political structures. These structures recruited new members and developed military capacity throughout the 1970s. When repression intensified in 1980, the Communist Party also chose to join the armed struggle, and the stage was set for a higher level of unity among the guerrilla groups. The FMLN was formed in October 1980 on the eve of the declaration of a "final offensive" against the Armed Forces and the Salvadoran government. The following five organizations originally constituted the FMLN:

Popular Liberation Forces (FPL)

The largest of the FMLN groups, founded in 1970 by Salvador Cayetano Carpio and other dissidents of the Communist Party of El Salvador, the FPL had strong links with the Popular Revolutionary Bloc, a large popular coalition formed in the mid-1970s. Internal political and personal disputes led to the murder of top party leader Melida Anaya Montes in 1983 and the subsequent suicide of Carpio. A former schoolteacher, Leonel González, led the FPL into the postwar period.

The People's Expression of Renewal (ERP)

Founded in 1971 by leftist student leaders as the People's Revolutionary Army, many considered the ERP to be the most radical member of the Frente. The postwar Truth Commission charged the ERP with the killings of several mayors in the late-1980s who refused FMLN demands that they resign. The ERP took responsibility for the killings, but protested that they had been singled out because they were the only ones who gave complete information to the commission.

At its party congress in 1993, the ERP, then still the second-largest organization within the FMLN, officially changed its name and unveiled a new, social-democratic orientation. In late 1994, the ERP joined the RN in formal withdrawal from the FMLN. Ana María Guadalupe Martínez and Joaquín Villalobos remained the primary leaders of the ERP.

National Resistance (RN)

Founded in 1975 through a division of the ERP after that party's leadership ordered the killing of the beloved poet, Roque Dalton, the RN has, ironically, shown the most affinity to the ERP's positions in the postwar period.[27] During the war, the RN emphasized building mass political support and established links to several strong organizations in the capital. Fermán Cienfuegos remains the best-known RN leader.

The Communist Party of El Salvador (PCS)

Founded in 1930, the PCS is by far the oldest of the organizations of the FMLN and was the last to heed the call for armed struggle in El Salvador. It participated in the war through its military arm, the Armed Forces of Liberation (FAL). Jorge Shafik Hándal, a veteran of decades of party organizing and the first General Secretary of the FMLN as a political party, heads the PCS.

Central American Revolutionary Workers Party (PRTC)

Founded in 1976 as the Salvadoran component of a proposed regional guerrilla army, the PRTC was the smallest of the FMLN armies. The PRTC gained notoriety in the U.S. for its involvement in the 1985 Zona Rosa attack in which five U.S. marines were killed at a Salvadoran nightclub. Francisco Velis and Mario López, two of its founding members, were assassinated in the months just prior to the 1994 elections. Legislative deputies Francisco Jovel and María Marta Valladares are its primary surviving leaders.

In the face of the massive repression of the late 1970s and early 1980s, the FMLN moved fairly quickly from being loosely organized groups of people trying to defend themselves with revolvers to one of the most effective guerrilla armies in Latin America. Only a massive military and economic intervention by the U.S. on behalf of the government kept the guerrillas from seizing power in the early 1980s. They combined advanced military tactics with popular support to expand their "zones of control" throughout the decade. By the war's end, they had fought the Armed Forces to a stalemate and exerted effective control over nearly one-third of the national territory.

Differences always existed between the various groups of the FMLN: differences on the proper strategic path to victory, the correct forms of popular organization, the handling of international relations, and any number of other questions. The aforementioned cases of Roque Dalton, Cayetano Carpio and Mélida Anaya Montes are only the best known of the many situations where differences were resolved by fratricidal violence. As the FMLN itself admits, the differences between the five organizations, particularly ideological squabbling, was one reason why the revolutionary forces were unable to seize power in their 1981 offensive.[28] During the course of the 1980s, the struggles within the FMLN often boiled down to intense competition between the FPL and the ERP. The government's effort to exterminate it taught the FMLN to prize its points of unity, and the alliance learned to keep internal conflict within manageable limits.

"New Thinking" and Postwar Political Definition

In 1987-88, after the failure of peace negotiations with the Duarte government, a qualitatively new debate began to emerge. Many in the FMLN began to question whether or not an armed victory over the government was possible—or, if possible, would be worth the social costs. This "new thinking" led to intense debate within the FMLN and a long series of meetings that Ignacio Ellacuría called the guerrillas' "Vatican II." The FMLN's dramatic proposal to participate in the elections of 1989 was an immediate result of those discussions.[29]

Neither the Salvadoran right nor the U.S. government was ready to accept such a proposal but it was clear that the FMLN had come to think differently about the war that was still being fought with great intensity. On the eve of the 1989 elections, the FMLN released a proposal to the Salvadoran government based on the new goal of a "democratic revolution" that no longer required the armed overthrow of the government. The FMLN advanced this proposal even as they prepared for a major military offensive.

The road from this proposal to a negotiated solution of the conflict was not a smooth one. Many in the Salvadoran Armed Forces and the ARENA party, and some leaders in the FMLN, still saw military victory as the only dignified solution to the war. While the Bush administration had shown signs of an interest in a negotiated solution to the conflict, it had not yet advanced a coherent policy in support of negotiations (See U.S.-El Salvador Relations). When the first series of negotiations with the Cristiani government was shattered on October 30, 1989—by the bombing of the National Federation of Salvadoran Workers (FENASTRAS) headquarters in which 10 people were killed—the FMLN responded with the massive military offensive that it had been planning for at least a year. By all accounts, the 1989 offensive marked a turning point in the war. The offensive cost the FMLN dearly in terms of loss of life, but its ability to mount such a nationwide action ended all talk of a quick military victory for the government.

As hundreds of civilians fled the luxurious Colonia Escalón at the height of the offensive, a well-to-do businessman told a U.S. journalist, "They should either kill them all or negotiate. This thing has to end...We need a solution." [30] Precisely because it led to attitude changes like this one, many in the FMLN see the November 1989 offensive, which cost the Frente hundreds of lives, as the critical turning point in the negotiation process.[31]

Many young Salvadorans died in the two years of often-intense warfare between the November offensive and the 1992 signing of the Peace Accords, but the momentum was clearly on the side of a negotiated solution. From the perspective of the development of the FMLN, the Peace Accords represent a concrete expression of the Frente's decision that the country would be best served by a democratic revolution carried out within the confines of Salvadoran constitutionality. In addition, the signatures of the FMLN General Command on the final document indicate that it was worth the personal and political risks to come down from the mountains to pursue such a revolution.[32] Those signatures did not, however, mean that the Frente's differences were safely behind it.

Soon after the signing of the accords, major differences began to surface between two major groupings: not surprisingly, the ERP led one group and the FPL the other. Different views arose over how to dispose of the surface-to-air missiles under the control of the Frente. Many in the FMLN protested when Joaquín Villalobos appeared, without party sanction, in the middle of the contentious negotiations between the powerful Poma family and the members of El Espino cooperative. Perhaps most dramatically, in a face-to-face meeting with Cristiani, the ERP openly expressed its disagreement with the FMLN's majority decision not to negotiate with the government over the list of names of military officers to be purged from the army for human rights violations.[33]

Differences on these issues turned on varying interpretations of the role of the Peace Accords in the democratic revolution. The RN and the ERP maintained that the Peace Accords had radically changed the political landscape of El Salvador, making it imperative that the FMLN adopt a new position, more ready to adapt to the "rules of the game" and negotiate with the "modernizing" faction of the business sector represented in the ARENA party.

They envisioned the possibility of a strategic alliance with the modern sector of private enterprise as a key underpinning of the democratization of the country. Having accepted the system, they argued, it no longer made sense to adopt "anti-system" positions of principled opposition. In early 1994, the ERP formally declared itself a social democratic party in the tradition of social democracy in Europe and Latin American countries like Chile.

The FPL-PCS-PRTC alliance within the Frente agreed that the accords represented a break with the past but believed they had left many tasks dangerously unfinished. To complete these tasks, the FMLN and the left in general had to prioritize the organization of the traditionally excluded sectors of Salvadoran society into a powerful legal opposition. Only the pressure created by the presence of such an opposition could be expected to lead to alliances across class and ideological lines that would advance the cause of democracy. The FPL and the PCS maintained some democratized form of "socialism" on the utopian horizon while they fought for the democratic revolution in the short run.

The need to pick candidates for national office accentuated these differences. The ERP-RN group insisted that the only way to defeat ARENA was to run someone like Abraham Rodríguez as coalition candidate of a broad opposition that included the PDC. The FPL-PCS-PRTC was divided on the ERP proposal, but Rodriguez's defeat in the PDC primary unified the three parties behind a Rubén Zamora candidacy.[34]

Unable to reach consensus on this and other decisions, the FMLN fell back on the party-based "majority rules" system adopted during the war, with each party allowed a single vote. Zamora became the presidential candidate and Francisco Lima, an aging lawyer with historical ties to the PDC and the PCN, was chosen as his running mate.[35] The choice of Zamora as presidential candidate signaled a decision to form a coalition with the CD at the presidential level. The Frente also joined in a complicated patchwork of coalitions for the legislative and municipal races.[36]

The lack of harmony in the Frente surely affected the electoral effort. The ERP and the RN accepted the choice of candidates but never devoted major resources or energy to the campaign at the national level.[37] Perhaps more importantly, the FMLN did not consistently project a positive image of its campaign in the media or directly confront the negative image of it presented by ARENA.[38] Even a perfectly orchestrated campaign would have had a hard time competing with the volume of resources available to ARENA.[39] The FMLN also had to continue devoting considerable resources to the struggle to get the Peace Accords fully implemented and faced the political problem of getting its youthful base as interested in winning an election as it had been in winning the war. These and other factors influenced the outcome of the elections, but the FMLN still made a reasonable showing for its first electoral foray, clearly establishing itself as the second leading political force in the country.

Yet another difficult decision faced the Frente as their fifteen mayors and twenty-one deputies prepared to take office. The outgoing ARENA-controlled Assembly had altered the rules concerning its Executive Committee so that ARENA would be assured a majority on the Executive Committee of the incoming Assembly. The ERP-RN group wanted the Frente to assume the two seats set aside for it on the committee, while the FPL-led group insisted that the Frente stay off the committee in protest of ARENA's manipulation. After a long discussion, the issue was finally decided in favor of the FPL position on the familiar 3-to-2 vote.

The next day, under the glare of television lights, Ana Guadalupe Martínez and Fermán Cienfuegos defied the party decision made the night before by taking the FMLN seats on the Assembly's governing council. After the swearing-in ceremony Martínez shared her famous embrace with her ARENA colleague while the other FMLN delegates seethed in their chairs. In a matter of days the other parties de-authorized Martínez, Cienfuegos, and the other five deputies of the ERP and the RN, declaring that they no longer represented the FMLN.

Over the next few months, cooler heads sought to prevail, but the momentum was clearly in favor of a definitive split in the FMLN. By October 1994 divisions reached the point where Joaquín Villalobos of the ERP accused the FPL and their allies of inciting ex-soldiers to hold 27 Assembly members hostage in an attempt to get their demobilization benefits from the government. The hostility and mutual recriminations accumulated until December 1994, when the ERP and the RN formally withdrew from the FMLN, demanding the Frente's dissolution as a consequence. The split was not a clean one. Eugenio Chicas of the RN stayed with the FMLN and predicted that many RN members would do the same. The Democratic Tendency, a group of former ERP members, also remained part of the FMLN. Villalobos summarized the reasons for the split saying, "The Frente is not viable as an electoral instrument and should pass on to become part of history."

Even as the FMLN was falling apart, questions remained about the significance of real political differences between the factions. The old problem of the struggle between the ERP and the FPL for hegemony over the Frente was at least as much of a factor as concrete differences in political approach.[40] Ensuing events suggested that the differences were not simply cosmetic.

At their convention in late 1994, the remaining parties of the Frente decided to maintain the FMLN as a three-party electoral alliance with shared leadership gradually moving toward the formation of a single party as proposed by the FPL. A more radical proposal presented by FPL leader Facundo Guardado that would have quickly formed a single party was defeated by a majority of the votes of the convention.

A few months after their departure from the FMLN, the RN and the ERP joined with the MNR in the formation of the Democratic Party (PD). The PD steered a course of opposition to the government through early 1995, and joined the surprising vote against ARENA's proposal to increase the size of the value added tax (IVA).[41] The PD then shocked many political observers by reportedly proposing, and then signing, the San Andrés Pact with ARENA on May 31, 1995. The pact committed the government to a few policies championed by the opposition in exchange for the support of the PD on the issue of the increase in the IVA. The bill to increase the IVA to 14 percent passed the Legislative Assembly shortly after the signing of the pact. A new alliance was born and ARENA no longer had to rely on the votes of the PCN in order to get its policies through the Assembly.

The FMLN could not have expected immunity from the redrawing of the political map of El Salvador in the wake of the war and the 1994 elections. Whether or not it is true that the differences emerging in the FMLN in the mid-1990s had always existed, it was clear that many of the factors of unity holding the FMLN together during the war did not exist in the postwar period. The division of the FMLN surely leaves the Salvadoran left in a weakened position. More important, however, than the ability of the five organizations that formed the FMLN to maintain their wartime coalition, is their ability to maintain sufficient coordination to enable them to act as a catalyst for the formation of a new national project of opposition—an alternative to ARENA's neoliberal one. The apparent fragmentation of the traditional forces of the FMLN and the decision of the PD to move closer to ARENA surely questions the viability of such a project.[42]

Smaller Political Parties

Nine parties or coalitions sought voter support in the 1994 elections. Three parties—ARENA, the FMLN, and the PDC—received the lion's share of the votes. In the legislative elections, where party preferences were perhaps clearest, the three major parties received just under 85 percent of the votes with the other six parties dividing 15 percent among them. Of those six parties, only three received the 1 percent of the votes necessary to retain their certifications as political parties: the CD, the PCN, and the Unity Movement (MU).

Democratic Convergence

For most of the 1980s the unarmed political left had denounced elections as part of a counterinsurgency strategy to put a democratic front on a repressive state apparatus. It reversed this policy in 1988 and decided to participate in the 1989 election campaign. Democratic Revolutionary Front (FDR) leaders Guillermo Ungo and Rubén Zamora returned to the country for the first time since 1980 and helped forge the CD. Three political parties composed this new electoral coalition: The National Revolutionary Movement (MNR), the Popular Social Christian Movement (MPSC), and the Social Democratic Party (PSD), which was formed in 1987.

Given its lack of infrastructure, the ongoing repression, and the time constraint of its late entry in the race, the CD had no hope of winning the 1989 election. According to Zamora, "We don't have an electoralist position. Our participation seeks to improve the possibilities for reaching a politically negotiated solution to the crisis."[43] Even though the CD never harbored any illusion of winning the election, it did hope to do better both in the vote count and in the realm of popular mobilization. It had projected winning 10-15 percent of the vote but collected only 3.8 percent, placing a sad fourth. Its showing was dramatically affected by the FMLN's call to boycott the elections after the government spurned its offer to participate in return for a delay in the process. The difference of opinion on electoral participation caused hard feelings between the CD and its former allies.

In the period between the elections of 1989 and 1991, the CD protected the space it had opened for the unarmed left despite considerable repression. In October 1989 the homes of MPSC leader Zamora and Democratic Nationalist Union (UDN) leader Aronette Díaz were bombed by unknown attackers, presumably because of their strong support for a negotiated settlement to the war.[44] Three members of the MPSC were killed around the same time, and Héctor Oquelí, a key leader of the MNR, was assassinated in Guatemala by a Salvadoran death squad.[45] The CD received another blow in February 1991 when Guillermo Ungo, its Secretary General, died after a long illness.

The CD ran a much more successful campaign in the 1991 legislative campaign. The coalition won eight deputy seats at the national level and managed to place second behind ARENA in San Salvador. Rubén Zamora was named vice-president of the Executive Committee of the Legislative Assembly. Although concrete legislative victories were few, from their position in the Assembly the CD deputies were able to give voice to their left-of-center agenda and press the government to reach a negotiated settlement to the war.

In the wake of the murder of Oquelí and the death of Ungo, the traditional differences between the two largest parties of the CD, the MNR and the MPSC, had developed into serious tensions. After the 1991 elections, Victor Valle took the MNR (and with it the support of the Socialist International) out of the CD. Ironically, the Peace Accords and the constitution of the FMLN as a political party also weakened the Convergence, by placing a large, popular force alongside the CD on the political left. As part of the postwar reshuffling, the UDN joined the CD in late 1992, but the coalition entered the 1994 campaign much weaker than in 1991.

The choice of Convergence leader Rubén Zamora as presidential candidate of an FMLN-CD-MNR coalition gave the CD a certain visibility in the campaign, but it was clear from the start that many of the people who voted CD in 1991 would be Frente supporters in 1994. Internal disagreements over candidate choices within the CD made matters worse. These problems surfaced publicly in January 1994 when the Convergence was unable to muster enough agreement to present a list of candidates for at-large legislative deputies.[46] This failure cost the CD a deputy in the balloting, but cost them much more in terms of their public image. The 4 percent they polled on March 20 was only marginally better than the 3.8 percent they received in the wartime elections of 1989. Jorge Villacorta was the lone CD deputy returned to the Assembly. Six months after the 1994 elections, the Convergence succeeded in fusing its constituent forces into a single party and named former deputy Juan José Martell as General Secretary.[47]

National Conciliation Party (PCN)

The PCN was the military's chosen vehicle for governance during the 1960s and 1970s. With the exception of an occasional reformist program, it represented the status quo of coexistence between military and landowners in the days before the country became dominated by the dynamics of revolution and counterrevolution. The PCN managed to survive the dramatic events of the 1980s, with ups and downs in its support, sometimes in alliance with ARENA and sometimes cooperating with the Christian Democrats. After holding 12 out of the 60 legislative seats in the 1985-1988 session, it had dropped to 4 out of 84 seats by 1994.

Its fourth place showing in 1994 was a testimony to the grip of tradition in El Salvador. Many observers expected the party to disappear entirely after it was racked by internal scandals during the entire pre-electoral period, and its chosen presidential candidate, former Air Force chief Gen. Juan Rafael Bustillo, withdrew in frustration with the leadership just months before the election. Party leaders managed to stay out of jail and found Colonel Roberto Escobar García, another retired military man, to take Bustillo's place.

Although the PCN won relatively few seats in the Assembly elections of 1991 and 1994, it held the balance of legislative power during both sessions. The 4 seats won by the PCN in 1994 were enough to give the right wing the slimmest of Assembly majorities. In addition, its standing as the third largest bloc in the 1991-94 Assembly entitled the PCN to representation on the Supreme Electoral Tribunal, which it used to become a dominant force in the shaping of the 1994 elections.[48]

It is difficult to envision a bright future for the PCN unless a significant sector of the country's right wing—the military, for example—becomes seriously disillusioned with ARENA.[49] Nonetheless, the party has carved out a niche for itself within ARENA's plans to dominate national politics. As long as it can prove itself useful to the governing party, the PCN is likely to remain a minor, but persistent actor on the national stage.

Evangelical Parties: The Unity Movement and the National Solidarity Movement

The period before the 1994 elections saw the formation of two new parties with close ties to the country's large evangelical population—the National Solidarity Movement (MSN) and the MU. Although El Salvador remains a predominantly Roman Catholic country, its evangelical churches grew explosively in the 1980s, often with the financial support of their brother and sister churches in the United States (See Religion). These churches had remained nominally apolitical, but most analysts believed that the evangelicals voted in large numbers and gave the ARENA party the bulk of their support. Perhaps encouraged by the success of the Solidarity Action Movement (MAS), which elected Jorge Serrano as president of Guatemala in 1991, Salvadoran politicians with close links to the evangelical movement decided that there was space for a political party making a direct appeal to evangelical Christians.[50] Separate groups formed the two aforementioned parties in 1992.

Jorge Martínez, a former Vice-Minister of the Interior under Cristiani, became the presidential candidate of the MU and brought several evangelically oriented local leaders of ARENA with him. The work of the MU was focused in the eastern part of the country in areas where political disenchantment with the Roman Catholic Church opened a space for evangelical growth. The party was built by inviting recognized local evangelical leaders to take on leadership roles in the MU.[51]

Although Martínez turned out to be an ineffective media personality and the party had a comparatively small TV budget, the MU did surprisingly well in the elections.[52] It parlayed Martínez' connections and organizing skill into 2 percent of the votes cast and a seat in the Legislative Assembly.

The MSN named Edgardo Rodríguez Englehard, a newcomer to national politics, as their presidential candidate. Despite having a much larger budget than the MU, it failed by 500 votes to garner the 1 percent of votes cast necessary to continue as a legal party. The party protested that it had been denied the needed votes through a combination of fraud and mismanagement of the electoral rolls by the Supreme Electoral Tribunal (TSE), but to no avail. The TSE decertified it shortly after the election, along with the MNR and the MAC.

Both the MU and the MSN went to great pains to steer an independent course during the elections. The MSN consciously sought to establish itself as a moderate option for those who would seek a morally unimpeachable alternative to the excesses of the right and the left. Martínez did not hesitate to criticize the Cristiani administration of which he had been a part, and he pledged that his party would be in no one's pocket. During the first major post-electoral challenge, MU appeared to be keeping their pledge, siding with the FMLN, the CD, and the PDC to deny ARENA's efforts appoint a Supreme Court over which it would have decisive influence.

Elections '94: Negotiated Revolution Goes to the Polls

The elections of 1994 were universally billed as the "elections of the century." The scheduling of elections in the 1983 constitution mandated a simultaneous general election of president, deputies, and mayors only once every fifteen years. In 1994 that happened for the first time since the drafting of the new constitution. More importantly, the signing of the Peace Accords made 1994 the first postwar elections and perhaps the first time in Salvadoran history when the entire political spectrum of the country would be represented on the ballot.

Amid much international fanfare, elections took place on March 20 with a second round to decide the presidency on April 24. When the final results were tallied, Armando Calderón Sol, the ARENA presidential candidate, had decisively defeated his second-round opponent Rubén Zamora, candidate of the left-of-center coalition made up of the FMLN, the CD, and the MNR. ARENA had won 39 of the 84 seats in the Legislative Assembly (the same amount it won in the

1991 legislative elections), and perhaps most surprisingly, ARENA swept to victory in 207 of the 262 mayoral races. By establishing itself as the country's second electoral force, the FMLN made a respectable showing, but the elections were a resounding victory for ARENA.

The FMLN polled quite well in San Salvador, especially in poorer sections such as Soyapango, Mejicanos, and Ciudad Delgado. In rural areas, however, the Frente did surprisingly badly, losing by large margins even in the northern and eastern zones where they had exercised considerable influence during the war.

Besides winning the presidency and 80 percent of the mayor's races, ARENA, in coalition with the PCN, maintained majority control of the legislature. In addition, its showing assured a powerful ARENA influence over the choice of the Supreme Court. Coming on the heels of ARENA's victories in 1988, 1989, and 1991, the 1994 elections led some analysts to begin to speak of ARENA's hegemony and the danger of the establishment of a one-party state.

Free and Fair Elections?

The elections of 1994 were observed and analyzed by more than two thousand international observers. The United Nations fielded the largest group of observers through ONUSAL, although the United States Citizens Elections Observer Mission (USCEOM) also assembled a team of more than five hundred observers.

When it came to evaluating the elections, beauty as always was in the eye of the beholder. Everyone acknowledged the problems of the registration period and the major "irregularities" dominating the first round, many of which went uncorrected for the second round. As usual, differences arose over the question of what importance to assign the problems. Official groups, including the United Nations, tended to downplay the irregularities while citizens observation groups offered more substantial critiques.

The accumulated irregularities in the voting did not alter the outcome of the presidential election and probably made only a minimal difference at the legislative level. Given the closeness of so many municipal races, however, the combination of voting problems likely decided a number of local races.

USCEOM acknowledged that the elections "marked a step forward in the peace process, since 1.4 million voters went to the polls on March 20 without serious violence or massive ballot-rigging." [53] Nonetheless, primarily because of the "disenfranchisement" of thousands of voters, the balloting "did not achieve the level of democratic involvement and participation expected in a 'transitional election' meant to move the country from war to peace." [54] The Central American University's documentation center CIDAI went a step further, insisting that the undemocratic character had transformed the "elections of the century" into the "fiasco of the century."[55]

In essence, the electoral reforms carried out as a result of the Peace Accords failed to create a sufficiently democratic environment for a "transitional election." The accords had called for the creation of a Supreme Electoral Tribunal (TSE) to replace the hopelessly corrupt and politicized Central Electoral Council (CCE).[56] In 1994 traditional politics retained its grip on the TSE and the tribunal's "willful incompetence" denied electoral credentials to over two hundred thousand Salvadorans, many of them residents of the former zones of conflict where the FMLN enjoyed wide support.[57] To make matters worse, on March 20 another large group of Salvadorans showed up at the polls with their electoral cards and were unable to vote because their names were not on the rolls, the data on their cards did not match the voting rolls, or the polling place was so poorly organized that, unable to find their assigned voting booths, they gave up and went home. No one will ever know the exact size of this group, but the 25,000 claimed by ONUSAL appears to have been a gross understatement.[58] The failures of the TSE were quite consistent with an apparent consensus among its pro-government members that major expansion of the voting population could only benefit the opposition.[59]

In addition to the active and passive blocking of willing voters from exercising their right to vote there was a high level of abstentions. At least a third of the potential electorate either never bothered to get a card, or received a card but did not vote. In total, barely half the eligible electorate voted in these historic elections. Given the experience of the 1980s, this low level of participation was predictable, but the massive funding for the promotion and administration of these elections and the supposed broadening of the electorate to include the political left led many to expect a higher turnout. The optimistic pronouncements of the FMLN on the morning of March 20 suggested that even they had been led to this conclusion.

Explanations abound for the apathy with which so many Salvadorans viewed the elections. Whether it was the extremes of the country's poverty, a lack of vision in the campaign, the absence of faith in the credibility of the election, or the fear campaign generated from ARENA's right wing, the lack of electoral participation stands as a huge obstacle to any effort to democratize the country.

Why the ARENA Victory?

Neither the machinations of the TSE nor the apathy of the Salvadoran public can explain the fact that ARENA, a party clearly linked to the mass violence of the early 1980s, received the votes of almost 800,000 Salvadorans when it faced the FMLN in the 1994 presidential run-off. Among the most important factors contributing to ARENA's victory were the following:

- Economic growth experienced during the Cristiani presidency, whether or not the result of temporary factors, clearly benefited the ruling party.
- ARENA had the resources to mount a huge publicity campaign.
- The party made a real move toward the country's political center.
- ARENA achieved this shift without losing the support of the large number of supporters of the anticommunist nationalism upon which ARENA was founded.
- The ruling party effectively projected the idea that, if elected, the FMLN would not be able to govern, and that a vote for the FMLN was a vote for more instability.

For a first campaign, and given the tremendous amount of resources that the FMLN was still devoting to assuring the fulfillment of the Peace Accords, the coalition ran a credible race, but the ARENA victory was also aided and abetted by some notable deficiencies in the opposition effort. These included the following:

- The coalition could not shake the history of divisions and sectarianism that has traditionally plagued the Salvadoran left.
- Specific errors, like the Convergence's inability to present a list of at-large candidates for the Assembly, increased ARENA's advantage.
- An inconsistent policy of alliances within the coalition resulted in many missed opportunities to defeat ARENA at the local level.
- Inexperience and a lack of resources left the coalition at a great disadvantage in the all-important publicity war.
- The coalition was unable to convince people of its ability to govern the country through consensus-building negotiations with both business and the popular sectors.[60]

The 1994 elections were characterized by a systematic effort to limit the entry of new voters into the system. This effort was complemented by a large degree of voter cynicism, especially among poor Salvadorans who did not see the election as a vehicle for real improvements in their living conditions. In that context, ARENA's well-oiled electoral machine was able to win a decisive victory that will leave it in control of El Salvador's executive-oriented system through the end of this century. That Salvadoran political institutions were transformed in the wake of the Peace Accords is undeniable; that the stage has been set for a stable democracy is much less certain.

The FMLN demobilized as a military opposition and gained constitutional recognition as a political one, but many of its followers were systematically disenfranchised in the preparation for the 1994 elections. Furthermore, the past echoed loudly in the wave of assassinations on the eve of the electoral campaign (See Justice, Human Rights and Public Security). Internationally supervised elections successfully transferred power from one civilian leader to another, but the electoral system still contained many of the imperfections which had helped plunge the country into civil war fifteen years earlier. Former guerrillas occupied one-fourth of the seats in a much more representative Legislative Assembly, but local politics in El Salvador remained the autocratic domain of systems of power rooted in sixty years of dictatorship.

The first experiences of peace confirmed the popular wisdom that democracy means much more than seeing one's favorite party on the ballot. That one-half of Salvadorans eligible to vote stayed home for the "elections of the century" might be seen as normal from the vantage point of the United States, but in El Salvador, it raised a red flag of warning about the fragility of the democratic process.

Military

Army and Politics

The inauguration of President Armando Calderón Sol on June 1, 1994 was a triumphal celebration of the ARENA party's sweeping election victory. Calderón Sol's acceptance speech was interrupted repeatedly by the applause of his jubilant followers, the loudest applause reserved for his announcement that the place of the Armed Forces of El Salvador (FAES) was assured in his administration.

But just what did the new president mean by this pronouncement? Civilian rule had been formally established in 1982, and Calderón Sol's inauguration marked the second consecutive peaceful passage of executive power between civilians. The end of the war had robbed the military of its primary function during the 1980s—the search to eradicate the few thousand guerrillas of the FMLN by force of arms. Furthermore, the agreement that brought the war to a conclusion called for a sweeping transformation of the military and its submission to civil authority. Was Calderón Sol assuring the FAES of the limited place assigned it by the Peace Accords, or was he signaling his intent to undermine the accords by maintaining military influence in Salvadoran society?

A coup by General Maximiliano Hernández Martínez in 1931 commenced a half-century era of nearly uninterrupted direct rule by the military. In October 1979 this period was brought to a close by a reformist faction of young officers which forced Gen. Carlos Humberto Romero out of the presidency. For two and a half years, until May 1982, the country was ruled by a military-civilian junta. Between March 1980 to May 1982 this junta was headed by José Napoleón Duarte.

With the selection of Alvaro Magaña as provisional president in mid-1982 the transition from military to civilian rule was complete. Two years later, the election of Duarte as president further institutionalized civilian government and installed the president as the commander-in-chief of the armed forces. But the switch to a civilian government did not weaken the military; instead, its power increased as its budget and ranks expanded with the injection of U.S. aid. The civil war militarized Salvadoran society as never before.

Despite over $1 billion in U.S. military aid and substantial clandestine support by U.S. intelligence agencies, the Salvadoran military never became the professional army its U.S. sponsors hoped it to be. It remained a highly corrupt institution with little respect for human rights and without the capacity to defeat an underequipped insurgent army fighting in terrain highly inhospitable to traditional guerrilla warfare.

The November 1989 offensive by the Farabundo Martí National Liberation Front (FMLN) highlighted the shortcomings of the military. Despite many signs that the FMLN was preparing a general offensive, the army was taken unawares by the breadth and intensity of the FMLN's campaign. The offensive demonstrated the army's inability to wage a counterinsurgency war in the cities. Only by relying on aerial bombings of poor neighborhoods was the military able to drive the guerrillas from their urban strongholds. The offensive shattered the belief that the military had the upper hand in the war and the FMLN was in the process of disintegration. The military's difficulty in turning back daring advances by the FMLN seriously damaged its prestige while aggravating tensions within its ranks. The offensive isolated those voices still insisting on a military solution to the war and strengthened the hand of those who saw the necessity of political negotiations.

The November offensive also served as the FAES' Waterloo in a more profound way. When the High Command decided, on the fourth day of the offensive, to use the martial law conditions as a cover for carrying out the assassination of six Jesuits, their housekeeper, and her daughter, they saw themselves acting against the intellectual progenitors of the guerrilla movement. Rather than striking a blow against the guerrillas, however, the murder of these eight unarmed civilians achieved the isolation of the Salvadoran military on the national and international stages in a way that a decade of human rights violations had not done.

By circling its wagons and engaging in a total institutional cover-up of high-command planning of the act, the Salvadoran military was able to avoid prosecution of all but a pair of unknown officers—Colonel Guillermo Alfredo Benavides and Lieutenant Yushi Mendoza. The violence and brutality of the assassinations, however, helped create the moral preconditions for the far-reaching changes in military structure and civil-military relations contained in the Chapultepec Accord.

Demilitarizing El Salvador: The Heart of Chapultepec

In the early stages of the peace negotiations, the FMLN insisted on radical changes in the structure of the military: either the FMLN fighters would be integrated into the FAES, or it and the FMLN would be abolished altogether. The guerrillas' abandonment of this demand in 1991 in favor of the inclusion of their members in the new National Civilian Police (PNC) removed one of the main obstacles to a settlement.[1] Once the FMLN made this critical concession, the door was opened for a number of substantive agreements regarding the military. Although the basic structure and organization of the Armed Forces survived intact, it suffered many important modifications.

Among the major changes called for in the Peace Accords were:

- Constitutional amendments strictly limiting the role of the military to the defense of the country's borders.
- Removal of public security from the realm of military control.
- Submission of the human rights records of the Officer Corps to civilian review by a commission — the Ad Hoc Commission —with the right to recommend disciplinary action against individual officers.
- Creation of the international Truth Commission to investigate major crimes and recommend remedial action.
- Reduction of the size of the military by one-half and the complete demobilization of rapid-response battalions.
- Development of a new doctrine for the preparation of military officers and creation of a new civil-military academic commission to oversee the military academy.
- Closing of the military intelligence unit and the creation of a new intelligence-gathering institution under civilian control.

How could the institution that dominated Salvadoran society for a half-century have ended up the big loser in a signed agreement between the Salvadoran government and the FMLN? Obviously, the first part of the answer is that the military lost its monopoly of power when the FMLN was able to expel it from large areas of the Salvadoran countryside and fight it to a stalemate on a national level. The FMLN then used the negotiations to drive a wedge between the military and its civilian allies by emphasizing demilitarization over demands that could have led the country's civilian elite to oppose the agreement. At the same time, the U.S. government quickly tired of its protégé when it became clear that a military solution to the war was not possible. From the U.S. perspective, agreements decreasing the power of the military made economic sense and held out the possibility of a more stable transition to the free trade era.

The erosion of the traditional alliance between the military and the country's civilian elites constituted a key factor in the "sacrifice" of the military to the peace process.[2] Economic changes brought on by the war had changed the view of some of the economic elite concerning the importance of the sort of repressive labor environment—especially in the countryside—that made a strong military a necessity. Huge amounts of U.S. military aid had made the military less dependent on the economic elites and had actually established the military as an important competing economic power. Finally, the terrible human rights record of the military created a situation in which there was political-diplomatic capital to be made by projecting the image of disciplining the military and limiting its role in society.

The final part of the puzzle concerns just how much the Peace Accords have resulted in real changes in the military and civilian-military relations—how much military prerogatives were really "sacrificed." Clearly, signing agreements under television lights and the auspices of the UN was one thing and actually carrying them out in the Salvadoran context was quite something else. As with other parts of the Peace Accords, implementation of the agreements regarding the Armed Forces was a slow, difficult process. Nonetheless, the Armed Forces that emerged from the war showed important differences from the institution that had dominated Salvadoran life for more than a half-century.

Structure and Organization

The two main figures within the military are the Minister of Defense and the Chief of Staff of the Salvadoran Armed Forces, the former selected by the president and the latter chosen by the military hierarchy itself. Defense Minister René Emilio Ponce and nearly all the other members of the High Command were among those 102 active-duty officers charged by the Ad Hoc Commission with major violations of human rights. These same officers also figured prominently in the report of the Truth Commission (See Justice, Human Rights, and Public Security).

When Ponce finally stepped down as part of a general command rotation on July 1, 1993, national and international forces spoke out in favor of the naming of a civilian Defense Minister, but the military made it clear that it would not accept such a move. Those in favor of a civilian in the post were also hampered by the lack of civilian knowledge of military affairs.

With the departure of Ponce and Juan Orlando Zepeda, Cristiani named Colonel Humberto Corado Figueroa as Minister of Defense. Corado was from the younger group of officers who had gained combat experience under the class of Ponce and Zepeda, *"los hijos de la Tandona"* and are said to have been even more hard-line than their predecessors.[3] The Salvadoran Nongovernmental Human Rights Commission charged that Corado had been responsible for human rights violations during the war.[4] Despite such allegations, Corado reportedly has taken some serious steps to expand human rights education within the FAES as part of an overall effort to reform the image of the military with regard to human rights.[5]

The Armed Forces includes three services: Army, Air Force, and Navy. Institutional rivalries among the three service branches hampered military efforts throughout the war. The FAES, in August 1994, formalized the existence of three separate administrative units each with its own high command. After having numbered at most 11,000 before the war, the FAES claimed to have 62,000 active-duty officers and soldiers at the war's end but most observers thought the actual total was closer to 55,000.[6] By late 1992, the Armed Forces had completed a reduction to just under 31,000 active-duty personnel. The cuts mandated by the Peace Accords did not, however, result in a shrinkage of the Officer Corps, with approximately 2250 members. During the war, the FAES also maintained a large structure of irregular civil defense and village patrol units. These were all formally disbanded as a result of the Peace Accords.[7]

Until 1992, the FAES also provided public security at the national level through the National Guard, the Treasury Police, and the National Police (PN)—three corps created between 1850 and 1937 and notorious for human rights violations. The first two were disbanded in early 1992 and the National Police disappeared in early 1995. Responsibility for public security passed to the newly created Civilian National Police (See Justice, Human Rights, and Public Security).

Crime, always a problem in El Salvador, exploded as a national phenomenon in the immediate postwar period. Almost immediately, rightwing politicians began to decry the "security vacuum" that they claimed was caused by the withdrawal of the security forces. They insisted that the government either re-establish the old repressive forces or call out the FAES to control criminal activity. President Cristiani obliged them in mid-1993 by calling out the Army to patrol the main highways and to protect the coffee harvest.

Although the Calderón Sol administration did increase the budgetary commitment to the PNC and fully deploy it in place of the PN, it continued to look to the military to play a public security role. In the face of the crime wave wreaking havoc in Salvadoran society, this dangerous view had a certain public appeal. In addition to being a demonstrably inadequate and inefficient anticrime strategy, the restoration of the public security functions of the military directly contradicted the spirit and the letter of the Peace Accords.

At the height of the war, about 30 percent of the government's budget was reserved for defense and public security but these functions were actually absorbing closer to 45 percent of total operational expenses of the government.[8] Apart from these funds, the military also had access to large amounts of military, police, and intelligence aid flowing directly from the United States (See U.S.-El Salvador Relations).

Two financial issues emerged for the Salvadoran military in the postwar period: the size of its budget and its financial autonomy. The Salvadoran government did not make substantial cuts in the budgetary assignment to the Armed Forces immediately after the war, citing the high costs of demobilizing troops and the time needed to reorganize.[9] U.S. military aid did decline precipitously, however, leaving the military in control of substantially less resources.

On the issue of financial autonomy, the military has traditionally managed its budget with absolutely no oversight by civilian authority. Despite pressure for civilian review of the budget, the military was able to retain this critically important feature of its relation to the government. The Legislative Assembly never formally discusses any aspect of the military budget except the total.

During the war, the military coordinated a huge intelligence-gathering operation through its National Intelligence Department (DNI). Dossiers were maintained on thousands of individuals and groups. The Peace Accords closed down the DNI and created the State Intelligence Agency under the direct control of the president. The military, however, declined to pass on the files of the DNI to the civilian agency and merely transferred them to the new intelligence unit which continued to gather intelligence on behalf of the armed forces. ONUSAL, however, was allowed to review the files in question.

The system of military education is crucial to any armed force. The vast majority of Salvadoran officers and all senior commanders have passed through the Gerardo Barrios Military Academy since the academy was opened in 1930.[10] Critics of the Salvadoran military often trace difficulties in civilian-military relations to a military education that has produced arrogant officers that are distrustful and disdainful of civilian politics and disrespectful of human rights. The deadly attack on the Jesuits was launched from the Barrios Academy.

Shortly after the end of the war, the FAES announced that the Barrios Academy would move from its tainted site near the Central American University (UCA) to the spacious grounds previously occupied by the Police Training Academy in Ciudad Merliot. The site had often been mentioned as an ideal place for the new National Public Security Academy for training agents of the PNC. The military declined to offer the grounds for that use, and the government declined to pressure them on the issue.

Recognizing the importance of formulating a new military doctrine for the postwar period, the FMLN insisted that the Chapultepec Accord establish a joint civilian-military commission to oversee the military academy. The new commission began functioning in late 1992 and reports a generally cooperative attitude from the FAES participants. It will be years, however, before this effort at civilian input on military education can be fully evaluated. All training outside of the academy remains under the exclusive control of the FAES.

The Peace Accords also terminated the policy of forcibly recruiting young men for military service. That policy had resulted in the conscription of thousands of young men from poor families during the war. In most cases, this conscription was achieved by sweeps through rural and poor urban areas in which young men who had not completed their "obligatory military service" were essentially abducted and taken to military garrisons for the beginning of their basic training.

A Military Service Law was passed by the Legislative Assembly in 1993. The law gave the military the right to establish recruiting centers in every town in El Salvador to assure adequate numbers of recruits.[11] Given the reduced size of the military, and the difficult economic conditions in the Salvadoran countryside, the FAES appeared to have no major problems meeting peacetime recruitment needs.

The *Tanda* System of Military Promotions

One of the structural characteristics of the Salvadoran military that most annoyed the U.S. military advisors responsible for training the Salvadoran military during the war was the *tanda* system which continues to govern promotions of FAES officers. As suggested above, the *tanda* system begins at the Gerardo Barrios Military Academy, which graduates classes of junior lieutenants.[12] Each class, or *tanda*, then jointly rises in grade until reaching the rank of colonel. Bound by loyalty to their *tanda*, the officers mutually assist one another in what is, according to a U.S. military report, "a West Point Protection System gone berserk."[13]

The system was established by Col. Oscar Osorio who occupied the presidency from 1948 to 1956. Osorio designed the system to reward patience in young officers and thereby limit the intergenerational conflict that had rendered the military structure highly unstable. The *tanda* system has partially resolved this problem but has created many others.

This system of advancement and solidarity means that officers rise in rank regardless of merit or competence. Loyalty to one's class is absolute, even exceeding commitment to the military as an institution, making it almost impossible to combat corruption or abuses of power. Despite repeated U.S. attempts to "professionalize" the Salvadoran armed forces, and all of the changes initiated by the Peace Accords, the *tanda* system continues to dictate mobility and duty assignments within the military structure.

In October 1988 the 35th class, which graduated in 1966, rose to the top positions within the Armed Forces. Known as the *tandona*, or big class, it had 45 members, approximately double the normal number, and was known for its hard-line officers and extreme solidarity. Along with Generals Ponce and Zepeda, members of the *tandona* include Col. Mauricio Staben, a battalion commander against whom charges of running a kidnapping racket for ransom were dropped "for lack of evidence" after members of the *tandona* rallied in his defense, and Gen. Mauricio Vargas (retired), who served as a member of the Salvadoran government's team in the negotiations with the FMLN.

The *tandona* maintained an iron grip on military control from 1989 to 1993, causing at least two later *tandas* to be passed over in the process. Col. Benavides, one of the officers charged in the Jesuit case, was a *tandona* member and at least 20 other members of the 45-member class were named by the Ad Hoc Commission as major violators of human rights. The group's top leadership, however, was able to maintain itself in command positions until the normal command rotation in July 1993 when they stepped down as heroes in an orgy of adulation. Ironically, the younger officers who believed the *tandona* was blocking their promotions became advocates for the government's full compliance with the recommendations of the Ad Hoc Commission.

The Military and Death Squad Activity

With names like the Secret Anticommunist Army, White Warriors Union, and the Revolutionary Anticommunist Extermination Action, well-organized and heavily financed death squads have terrorized the Salvadoran popular movement since the 1970s. The continuing existence of these death squads represents one of the greatest remaining threats to the Salvadoran peace process (See Justice, Human Rights, and Public Security).

Salvadorans of all political persuasions firmly believe that the country's security apparatus was behind the formation of the death squads. Nonetheless, the FAES has consistently denied the existence of death squads while also maintaining that no connections exist between the Armed Forces and any illegal armed groups. A chorus of voices questions that denial.

Throughout the 1980s, journalists and human rights groups presented evidence of the military-death squad connection.[14] In its 1988 report, *El Salvador: Death Squads—A Government Strategy*, Amnesty International concluded that the so-called death squads "are simply used to shield the government from accountability for torture, disappearances, and extrajudicial disappearances committed in their name....Squads are made up of regular army and police agents under orders of superiors."

In November 1983, with the popular movement decimated by death squad violence and the 1984 elections just around the corner, U.S. Ambassador Thomas Pickering connected several military and public security officials with the death squads and expressed his intent to pressure the Salvadoran government to act against these elements. The following month the Reagan administration sent Vice President Bush and Oliver North to San Salvador to warn the Salvadoran military that gross human rights violations would no longer be tolerated and to stress the importance of cleaning up death squad activity prior to the presidential elections scheduled for the following year. The U.S. indignation was highly cynical given the administration's tendency to look the other way during the worst of the death squad killing and the evidence of the connections between U.S. military assistance and intelligence operations with the earliest death squad structures.[15]

In late 1989 a deserter from the D-2 intelligence division of the Salvadoran Army's First Brigade, César Vielman Joya Martínez, created a stir when he acknowledged that he had participated in death squad murders organized by the intelligence division. Joya Martínez, who claimed that he was in charge of executions while others handled the "heavy interrogation" or torture, also charged that U.S. advisers were aware of the activities of his "special corps." In fact, one U.S. military adviser shared an office with him. He said U.S. advisers gave his clandestine unit instruction in "special planning" for urban counterinsurgency war and that they received special compensation from the U.S. military. Col. Elena Fuentes, commander of the First Brigade, admitted that Joya Martínez was a former member of the Brigade but dismissed him as a thief and liar.[16]

After the war ended, the connection between the military and the death squads could be more precisely elaborated. In March 1993, the Truth Commission drew the following conclusion:

"The Salvadoran state, through the actions of members of the Armed Forces and/or civilian officials, is responsible for having participated in, promoted and tolerated the functioning of the death squads that illegally attacked members of the civilian population." [17]

The Truth Commission also acknowledged the financial and logistical role of civilians in the squads, but declined to make any of those names public. The report did not recommend any concrete actions against the death squads other than a complete investigation with the assistance of international police operatives.

Previously classified CIA documents released in November 1993 greatly strengthened the prevailing vision of the death squads as a shadowy group of military and police officers working in close connection with wealthy civilians. These documents mentioned several prominent civilians by name, including then-candidate Armando Calderón Sol. The documents repeatedly refer to the role of D'Aubuisson and private *escuadroneros* like Héctor Regalado, perhaps overstating their importance. The CIA makes scant mention of the assassination squads of the Army's SII and security forces, which the FMLN feared much more than D'Aubuisson and the private death squads.

The resurgence of death squad activity in late-1993 led to a United Nations call for yet another commission, the Joint Working Group for the Investigation of Illegal Armed Groups (See Justice, Human Rights, and Public Security). This commission conducted a much more in-depth evaluation which unearthed information which could probably serve as the basis for criminal prosecutions. The Joint Group Report concluded that death squads could not function without the knowledge and participation of military and police officials, and it also suggested that the traditional death squad structures had long since diversified into organized crime which made their elimination even more urgent. In the postwar period, criminal networks expanded their involvement in drug-trafficking, money-laundering, kidnapping-extortion, and stolen vehicles. [18]

There can be little doubt that during the war the death squads were an institutional strategy of the Salvadoran state and military establishment—with critical support from Salvadoran civilians and U.S. military and intelligence operatives—to physically eliminate the country's political opposition. Although postwar manifestations of the death squads may be less an institutional expression of military strategy, there is still considerable military participation and the squads could certainly not exist if the military was intent upon eliminating them.

Corruption and Wealth Within the Officer Corps

Corruption within the officer corps is also part of the Salvadoran military tradition. Upon graduating from the military academy and achieving the rank of officer, members of the military receive their first taste of the economic privileges that accompany this promotion. Graduating officers obtain the right to import a car duty-free, a payoff that most young officers sell to wealthier members of the society. According to one retired officer, "Their goals are largely materialistic." The military represents a path to the middle class for poor young men.[19]

Once officers rise to command positions they control a lucrative system of patronage and graft. During the war, one source of extra funds was the common practice of renting out troops as security guards to plantation and factory owners, charging $200 to $300 per man per month. Colonels also grew rich siphoning off money from their base's payroll and food budgets. One of the most inventive ways of making the army a business was to fill one's command with ghost soldiers or *plazas ficticias*. One major told the *New York Times*, "Just about every brigade lists at least one 50-man company that isn't there. Each of those 50 pay slots brings [in] 500 *colones* [equivalent to $100] a month."[20]

During the war, high casualty levels carried unexpected benefits to military commanders. As Joel Millman, writing in 1989 in the *New York Times*, pointed out: "Every time a soldier deserts, or dies in action, the commander can add to his list of ghost soldiers, earning himself yet another salary." Another wellspring of graft was the practice of mandatory deductions or *descuentos obligatorios*. Soldiers are charged for food, boot polish, toothpaste, and uniform accessories, and lower officers collect the profits as a type of commission. Soldiers of the Third Brigade even paid to build a wall around their own base. The end of the war has narrowed the opportunities for this graft and forced many in the military to seek new sources of illicit income. The 1994 report of the Joint Group for the Investigation of Illegal Armed Groups described the involvement of active-duty members of the Armed Forces in drug-related and other organized crime activities.[21] The report did not publicly name those officers involved in such activities.

Following the Guatemala model, the Salvadoran army in the 1980s became an economic power in its own right. High-level officers complemented corruption income with the benefits of a booming military-business complex. Salvadoran firms commonly place colonels on their boards of directors, and many officers run their own agribusiness operations—with the luxury of never paying any taxes. Although the military never reached any sort of economic parity with civilian elites, economic competition from the military did become a concern for some businesspeople.

The major cash reserve of the military as an institution is the Social Provision Institute of the Armed Forces (IPSFA), a social-security fund into which each recruit pays $150 through obligatory deductions before leaving the army. Since 1989 the fund has grown from $2 million to more than $100 million.[22] IPSFA has become a major investor and the largest source of liquid capital in the country. Just before the war's end, IPSFA bought a $2 million oceanside resort and invested in a 500-lot housing development. The institute also invaded Salvadoran capital markets through its involvement in mortgage lending and other credit activities.

As part of the debate about the cost of demobilizing soldiers, IPSFA presented data suggesting that its financial situation was too fragile to bear the financial burden that major reductions in military personnel would cause. Fraud and mismanagement may have left the system overextended, but these claims of fragility may also have been concocted to limit cuts in the military and coax more resources out of the U.S. government. Some younger officers clearly wonder whether or not there will be anything left in the huge fund when it is time for them to take advantage of it.[23] Whether or not IPSFA is solvent, there is no question that the war greatly increased the personal wealth of top-ranking military officers and made the military an important institutional presence in the Salvadoran economy.[24]

Civic Action and National Reconstruction

From 1983 onward, "civic action" — humanitarian or social-development actions carried out by military personnel to achieve military or political goals — stood at the center of the government's counterinsurgency efforts. After it became clear that security problems had made civilian actions related to government programs impossible in large sectors of rural El Salvador, a series of military civic action campaigns were planned to pursue the "hearts and minds" component of low-intensity conflict strategy. The largest of these campaigns, dubbed "United to Reconstruct" (UPR), functioned from 1986 to 1987.

These campaigns resulted in the flow of some resources to rural areas but overall were considered dismal failures. An AID-funded evaluation and an independent study by four U.S. colonels criticized UPR for its poor planning and orientation toward building the power of local field commanders rather than the Salvadoran government.[25]

Civic actions also provided important information to military intelligence units during the war.

In limiting the role of the FAES to national defense, the Peace Accords clearly defined defense as the assurance of the country's sovereignty and protection of its territorial integrity. Security, on the other hand, encompassed a range of other social, political, and economic functions to be carried out by the state and other sectors of society.[26] The Constitutional Reforms ratified in 1992 enshrined as law this limited view of the military's role.

Despite this apparent constitutional prohibition on civic action, the FAES was intent on expanding its civic action role in peacetime. The government reconstruction planning team included FAES representatives—the DNI and the Armed Forces Center for Professional Rehabilitation (CERPROFA)—from the moment of its formation in 1990. The inclusion of the soon-to-be-disbanded intelligence unit is indicative of the nature of military interest in civic action. The rehabilitation professionals were not accompanied by engineers or educational experts.

The military initiated new civic action initiatives almost immediately after the signing of the Peace Accords.[27] Besides robbing civilian institutions of valuable experience, the extreme budgetary autonomy exercised by the FAES makes review of project planning and civilian audits of the use of project funds virtually impossible. Nowhere does the FAES claim that its civic action projects involve project beneficiaries in any meaningful way nor do anything to build local democracy in El Salvador. FAES civic action is, therefore, objectionable on more than just constitutional grounds. An outright prohibition, however, would have required an aggressive posture from a Salvadoran government with close military ties.

In late 1991, officials of AID had reached a consensus with Pentagon brass that U.S. aid would flow exclusively through civilian channels, with the FAES playing only a "support" role. This consensus, however, did not hold up as the money for the National Reconstruction Plan (PRN) began to flow. AID continued to emphasize the importance of using civilian channels and insisted that the military had nothing to do with the largest of the civilian channels, its Municipalities in Action (MIA) plan. Nevertheless, despite the initial opposition of the U.S. Military Group (MILGROUP), the Pentagon eventually gave a green light to expanded civic action for the FAES.

Collaboration between the U.S. Army Corps of Engineers and FAES civic action programs increased leading up to "Strong Roads" (*Fuertes Caminos*), a joint U.S.-Salvadoran civic action program which involved over 400 U.S. military personnel. In announcing the program to the U.S. Senate in April 1993, General George Joulwan of the U.S. Southern Command presented the exercises as a way of supporting "the appropriate role of the military in a democratic society."[28]

Whether or not the FAES was directly participating in projects of the MIA program became a secondary concern with the arrival of the first U.S. *Fuertes Caminos* contingent on August 11, 1993. The United States had put a huge stamp of approval on FAES efforts to consolidate its action in an area explicitly closed to it by the Peace Accords. After a break for the elections in early 1994, a second contingent of U.S. military personnel arrived in El Salvador for maneuvers later that year.[29]

Reconstruction and Veterans' Programs

The Peace Accords explicitly state that the National Reconstruction Plan must achieve the reintegration of the excombatants of both sides into civilian society. The experience of neighboring Nicaragua, where disgruntled excombatants of both sides took up arms and significantly disrupted the peace process, made this a particularly pressing concern.[30]

In the case of the FAES, discussions following the signing of the Peace Accords resulted in an agreement that only those members of the Armed Forces demobilized as a result of the Peace Accords would be eligible for reintegration benefits such as land, credit, and training. Those soldiers who had served during the worst years of the war but left the Armed Forces prior to the end of the war would not receive such benefits. Similarly, the thousands of Salvadorans who formed part of the civil defense units and village patrols were to be demobilized without any transitional benefits.

This huge number of individuals had no strong advocate during the negotiations. The FMLN surely was not going to support the demands of people who they saw as the perpetrators of many of the worst excesses of the war. In addition, both the government and the FAES sought to minimize the tremendous financial and organizational burden of distributing veterans' benefits.

Although the excombatants of the FMLN also faced serious reintegration problems, their higher level of organization left them in a better position to claim postwar benefits.[31] Ex-soldiers of the FAES received their benefits very much at the whim of their commanding officers who shared information about programs only as it suited them. This situation was so bad in Usulután that the director of the European Union reintegration program there was compelled to create the Salvadoran Veterans Foundation, an EU-funded service organization designed to inform FAES veterans of benefit programs and organize them to participate.[32]

The decision not to give adequate attention to the needs of veterans had a variety of negative consequences in the immediate postwar period. All credible analyses of the postwar crime wave make reference to the impact of the large number of excombatants—often still armed and trained in weapons use—who faced very limited economic options after the war ended. Some percentage of these veterans—from both the FAES and the FMLN—turned to criminal activity as preferable to life as a marginal farmer or an underemployed, unskilled worker.[33]

Apart from augmenting an already serious crime wave, discontent among veterans of the Armed Forces emerged as a highly explosive factor that threatened the stability of the entire peace process.[34] By late 1993, veterans supposedly covered by the Peace Accords and civil defense members excluded from the provisions of the agreement had organized into the Association of Demobilized Members of the Salvadoran Armed Forces (ADEFAES). The organization demanded the fulfillment of severance commitments to some members and the inclusion of others in the lists of beneficiaries.

Angered by what it saw as a lack of concern for its members' needs and unjust benefit packages for high-level officers, in 1994 ADEFAES carried out militant actions that included occupations of the Legislative Assembly in which deputies were taken hostage. The government made a series of promises to resolve those crises but failed to make good on their commitments to provide severance checks and open up new programs.

In January 1995, ADEFAES mobilized thousands of members to occupy the Legislative Assembly, IPSFA, and the Treasury Ministry. The group also took control of land and housing and blocked the Pan American highway and other main highways every day for a week. The government, to its credit, acted with restraint in the face of these highly coordinated actions carried out with military precision.[35]

The availability of ONUSAL Chief of Mission Enrique Ter Horst as a mediator made possible negotiations between the government and ADEFAES that ended the standoff, but not until the country had lived through several days of extreme tension and fear of pending confrontation.[36] The government agreed to speed delivery of benefits to some ADEFAES members and add others to the list of beneficiaries of training and other existing programs.

President Calderón Sol publicly warned of the existence of a "dark hand" behind the actions of ADEFAES and barely concealed his contention that the FMLN was guilty of such manipulation.[37] An ADEFAES member quoted in *Primera Plana* insisted that, "We aren't manipulated by anyone...only by hunger and need." [38] Others expressed doubts that a group of uneducated ex-soldiers accustomed to following orders could have planned and carried out such sophisticated actions without some sort of external leadership.[39] Regardless of who led ADEFAES or for what purposes, the discharged members of the Armed Forces made it clear that they expected to receive their share of the benefits of postwar reconstruction in El Salvador. Their demands present another long-term challenge to the Salvadoran government from an unexpected place—the very men who acted as the guardians of the state during the armed conflict.

Military and the Future of Democracy in El Salvador

For sixty years, the military was the unquestioned center of political power in El Salvador. In an uneasy alliance with the country's economic oligarchy, it dominated society so completely that even in the moments of democratic opening the country relied on one sector of the military to carry the banner of democracy against other, more conservative, sectors.[40] Since the military was never entirely separated from the levers of political power, the ascendancy of moderate or reformist officers defined a political opening.

The formal restoration of civilian rule in 1982 and the new constitution of 1983 did nothing to fundamentally reverse this trend. The political-military struggle of the FMLN did, however, succeed in breaking the seemingly invincible monopoly of power of the Armed Forces, and made possible a reconsideration of its role in society. The Peace Accords, signed in 1992, reflected a social consensus concerning the military and struck a powerful blow against militarism. History is likely to remember this blow as the central achievement of the FMLN. The unprecedented changes in civil-military relations represented by the Peace Accords were so profound that some experienced analysts have suggested that consolidating demilitarization may be the most achievable of the "unfinished tasks" of democratizing El Salvador.[41]

Although this may be true, it is not quite true to say that the Salvadoran civilian elites "sacrificed" the military to achieve peace. Retired military commanders still sit at the head of many key state and parastatal institutions, and the military still retains complete control over an important percentage of the public budget. More than one hundred officers were "purged," but none will be found selling pencils in San Salvador's central market. Many of those forced to leave the military prematurely left as wealthy men with the connections and power to greatly expand that wealth. The FAES also retains its intelligence apparatus, the heart of its repressive capability.

The Peace Accords strictly limit the functions of the military, but before the accompanying constitutional amendment could be ratified, FAES leaders were busy staking claims to areas of function clearly outside of the new constitutional mandate. National reconstruction and public security are the most important of these areas.

The 1994 incident in which members of the military fired, with deadly results, on a demonstration of bus operators in San Miguel suggested that the critical issue of the role of the military was far from resolved. Many observers saw the militant actions of demobilized members of the armed forces as a thinly disguised effort to reassert the traditional role of the military in a much more profound and troubling way.[42]

The report of the Joint Group can be added to the mounds of evidence suggesting other dangerous areas of continuity with past military practice, namely death squads and organized crime. The Peace Accords shook the very foundation of the institutional impunity enjoyed by members of the Armed Forces but did not shatter it. Acting against this particular exercise of the traditional prerogatives of the military remains the most pressing task for civil society, and no one expects much help from the military in that effort.

The question of the future of the military is often reduced to whether or not "they will stay in their barracks." The number of military coups in El Salvador over the past century make that a valid question, but the sense that the actions of the military will determine the course of future civil-military relations may itself be a result of decades of military control of society. One must also question whether or not Salvadoran civilians will act to keep the military in its barracks.[43]

Will civilian leaders and academics take the admittedly dangerous step of studying military affairs enough to develop the expertise to debate issues of military policy with the FAES and foreign governments? Will they develop a coherent policy toward the military in a democratic context? Will such a policy serve as a tool in the effort to gradually submit the armed institution to real civilian control? And, finally, will traditionally polarized sectors of Salvadoran society take advantage of this historic opportunity to resolve peacefully the lingering structural problems that led to the civil war and that will, sooner or later, create another moment of social upheaval and chaos which will invite the repressive intervention of the military?

Even more than the inclinations of a new generation of military leaders, the resolution of these questions will determine the "place" that Armando Calderón Sol assured the military in his inaugural address. If El Salvador is to advance toward democracy, the answers must come from outside the battered walls of the complex that houses the military High Command. History suggests that if civilians cannot answer these questions in the affirmative, the military will one day have the answers for them.

Part 3

Justice, Human Rights, and Public Security

© ES' Nueva Imagen

Military defendants stand trial for Jesuit murders, September 1991.

System of Justice

For Salvadorans, the unforgettable images of mutilated corpses at the side of rural paths and urban avenues dominate the social memory of the late 1970s and early 1980s. Places like *El Playón* along the coastal highway and *La Puerta del Diablo* (the Devil's Door) on the outskirts of San Salvador became infamous as preferred spots for the death squads to leave their victims. Thousands of cases of torture, abductions, and assassinations were denounced, first by a few brave Salvadorans—many of whom paid for their courage with their lives[1]— and then by international human rights groups.

By the early 1990s human rights groups were reporting between 40,000 and 50,000 deaths from political violence during the war.[2] Socorro Jurídico, a Catholic human rights group started by Monseñor Romero, recorded 25,000 deaths from political violence in the two years following Romero's killing in March 1980.[3] In 1992 the UN Truth Commission collected 22,000 denunciations of human rights abuses that occurred during the war, 85 percent of which were attributed to government agents, the death squads, or paramilitary groups associated with the death squads. The military alone accounted for 60 percent of all reported violations.

A key element in the repression was the impunity enjoyed by those committing the abuses. They could commit any atrocity, secure in the knowledge that they had nothing to fear from the country's justice system. Regarding the administration of justice in El Salvador, the Truth Commission stated:

> If the judicial power had functioned satisfactorily, not only would it have clarified, in a timely fashion, the acts that this Commission has had to investigate, but it also would have applied the appropriate sanctions. In that sense, the inability of the judicial branch to apply the law to acts of violence committed under the direct or indirect protection of public authority forms

an integral part of the reality in which these acts took place, and is inseparable from them.[4]

From this perspective, the decision of thousands of Salvadorans to take up arms against this system can be seen as a decision to "take justice into their own hands" and punish the crimes that the legal system refused to recognize.[5]

The bulk of human rights abuses were carried out either directly by members of the military-public security structures or by privately-funded "death squads" with close ties to those structures. New forms of popular organization, increased international attention to El Salvador in the mid-1980s, and the adoption of a "low-intensity conflict" strategy by the Duarte administration led to a gradual decline in the numbers of violations, but the repressive structures remained fully intact and untouchable by the justice system.[6] Even as the 1980s drew to a close, no military or police officers had yet been tried and convicted for human rights abuses against civilians.[7] The few prosecutions of enlisted men were principally in cases involving crimes against U.S. citizens.[8] Two of the officers involved in the 1989 Jesuit murders were the *only* officers convicted for human rights violations during the war years. This case can hardly be considered a definitive blow against military impunity: ranking officers who ordered the killings, covered up afterwards, and limited the investigation were never brought to trial.[9]

At the insistence of the FMLN and Salvadoran civil society, the Chapultepec Accord targeted impunity as one of the primary obstacles to the achievement of democracy and outlined a series of steps designed both to deal with past abuses and create judicial and public security systems that would leave all Salvadorans subject to and protected by the rule of law.

The accords included these steps:

- Establishment of an Ad Hoc Commission to investigate the human rights records of military officers and recommend the purging or transfer of those involved in human rights abuses.
- Naming of a Truth Commission to investigate some of the most serious cases of human rights violations by governmental and non-governmental actors.
- Creation of a transitional international human rights observation team under the United Nations (ONUSAL), and a Salvadoran Ombudsman for Human Rights (PDH).
- Construction of a new public security system based on a Civilian National Police force independent of military control.
- Implementation of a series of judicial reforms designed to depoliticize and professionalize the legal system.

The Salvadoran government carried out these measures only partially and after tremendous pressure by national and international forces. The spectacular crime wave that dominated public attention in the postwar period and the deterioration of the human rights situation as killings reminiscent of earlier death squad actions reappeared in late 1993 evidenced the extent to which the goals of ending impunity and improving conditions of public security remained unachieved tasks.

Investigating Past Abuses: The Ad Hoc Commission and the Truth Commission

The Peace Accords reflected a reluctant social consensus that the investigation of the massive violations of the human rights of Salvadorans during the war was a precondition to national reconciliation and the consolidation of peace.[10] For this purpose, the accords mandated the creation of two separate commissions: the Ad Hoc Commission and the Truth Commission.

The Ad Hoc Commission was composed of three distinguished Salvadorans—Abraham Rodríguez, Eduardo Molina, and Reynaldo Galindo Pohl—appointed to investigate the human rights records of all military officers including the High Command. The Truth Commission, on the other hand, was made up of three international dignitaries—former Colombian President Belisario Betancourt, former Venezuelan Foreign Minister Reinaldo Figueredo, and U.S. lawyer and president of the Inter-American Human Rights Institute Thomas Buergenthal. Like the members of the Ad Hoc Commission, the members of the Truth Commission were selected by the UN General Secretary with the consent of the government and the FMLN.

Many doubted that a group of Salvadorans would be able to resist military pressure and present a thorough review, but the Ad Hoc Commission did precisely that, presenting their report to President Cristiani in September 1992. They recommended the transfer or removal of 102 officers including several members of the Armed Forces High Command such as Defense Minister General René Emilio Ponce and his Vice-Minister, Juan Orlando Zepeda. President Cristiani insisted on the confidentiality of the list of officers named in the report, delayed action on the recommendations as much as possible, and reneged on at least two agreements made with the United Nations, but he eventually took action against all 102 officers.[11]

General Ponce and other members of the High Command did not step down until July 1, 1993, after the publication of the Truth Commission report. When they finally left, they did so as heroes with no mention of their past human rights abuses.[12] Despite its limitations, this civilian review of the Salvadoran Armed Forces was unprecedented in the country's history and of great importance to the effort to de-militarize Salvadoran society. The Truth Commission released its report to the public. The report, entitled *From Madness to Hope: Twelve Years of War in El Salvador*, created a major sensation and dominated public discussion in El Salvador for several months. The commission made the historic decision to name those individuals who it could connect to some of the heinous crimes committed against the Salvadoran people during the war.

Among the dozens of civilians and military people named by the commission was Major Roberto D'Aubuisson, singled out as the chief architect of the plan to assassinate Monseñor Oscar Romero in 1980. Then-Defense Minister René Emilio Ponce and Vice-Minister Juan Orlando Zepeda were named with other members of the military High Command for their role in ordering and then covering up their responsibility in the 1989 murders at the Central American University. Joaquín Villalobos and other leaders of the ERP were held responsible for their part in the FMLN's killing of many mayors between 1985 and 1988.[13] Although the commission investigated incidents involving the FMLN, the vast majority of individuals mentioned were connected with the Salvadoran Armed Forces. The report recommended the removal of all named individuals from their military or government posts but stopped short of recommending their prosecution by the country's justice system.

The lack of recommendations involving specific legal remedies resulted from the commission's belief that partiality, corruption, and inefficiency rendered El Salvador's judicial system incapable of prosecuting high government and military officials. Instead, the report offered serious criticisms of the judicial system and recommended its complete overhaul, beginning with the resignation of Chief Justice Mauricio Gutiérrez Castro and the rest of the Justices of the Supreme Court.[14] Finally, the Truth Commission discussed in detail the operations of the death squads and their connections to wealthy civilians who offered financing and sometimes participated in the planning and execution of their activities. It recommended urgent action to prevent the resurgence of these death squads, but declined to make public the names of the civilians with death squad ties.[15]

Reaction to the unprecedented report was swift and harsh. The Supreme Court rejected the report out of hand and made no secret of its refusal to comply with the recommendation that all the Supreme Court justices resign. The military immediately rejected the report as blatantly partial and rumors of a military coup circulated widely in

San Salvador. ARENA also condemned the report as biased in its emphasis on abuses committed by the military and, within a week of the release of the report, pushed through the Legislative Assembly an overly broad amnesty law that made virtually no exceptions, even for crimes *not* subject to amnesty under international law.[16] At least part of the truth about human rights violations had been spoken; but, in the end, the great historical weight of impunity prevailed.

President Cristiani kept his promise to promote only limited compliance with the Truth Commission's recommendations despite considerable pressure from the international community. Apart from the self-interested criticisms of those implicated in the report and their allies, more objective observers have pointed out important structural weaknesses in the report and the investigative work behind it.[17] Nevertheless, the decision of respected international figures to investigate some of the most heinous crimes committed against the Salvadoran people during the civil war and to take the unprecedented step of assigning blame for those cases and naming the names of the perpetrators represented an important break with an oppressive past of taboos and obligatory silence in which the truth on such matters could not see the light of day.[18]

Human Rights Protection: ONUSAL and the Salvadoran Human Rights Ombudsman

The Salvadoran peace process also took into account the need for ongoing human rights protection and established a number of mechanisms intended to insure such protection. In the San José agreement signed in July 1990, the two sides agreed to the establishment of a United Nations Observers Mission in El Salvador (ONUSAL) to verify respect for human rights and overall compliance with any agreements reached between the negotiating parties. The Constitutional Reforms of April 1991 also called for the creation of a new institution called the Office of the Human Rights Ombudsman of El Salvador (PDH). This was to be an official institution with sufficient resources, independence and authority to insure human rights protection at a national level.

ONUSAL initiated its human rights observation work in July 1991, well before the signing of the final peace agreement. Although ONUSAL was criticized by the extreme right, the Salvadoran popular movement viewed its installation as an important victory.[19]

Although it took time to get its massive operation underway, the tremendous resources available to ONUSAL and the freedom-of-movement it was accorded as a representative of the United Nations quickly put it in the forefront of human rights verification in El Salvador. From the beginning, leaders of the nongovernmental human rights organizations wondered how the presence of this new major actor would affect the capacity and credibility of their organizations.[20] By the beginning of 1992 ONUSAL was involved in activities as varied as providing human rights education to enlisted men in the Salvadoran army, following up on specific complaints of denial of due process in the Salvadoran courts, and investigating and intervening in individual cases of human rights violations.

In its early stages, most of the criticism of ONUSAL involved government charges of UN favoritism toward the FMLN, but, over time, the popular sector, particularly those involved in the protection of human rights, became more critical of ONUSAL's perceived inability to connect human rights violations to a system of impunity and suggest concrete steps to bring about an efficient administration of justice.

By May 1994, the Human Rights Institute of the Central American University (IDHUCA) was suggesting that the UN's 10th Human Rights Report suffered from the need to present El Salvador as a successful case of UN intervention. As a result, systematic analysis was sacrificed in favor of "short-term visions, diplomatic rhetoric, and public relations." This orientation prevented the "presentation of concrete alternatives to overcome the obstacles to ending the impunity still prevalent in the country." [21] Such criticism represented something of a refrain from parts of the nongovernmental human rights sector.

Part of the problem resided in the expectations for ONUSAL, especially in terms of human rights monitoring. During the war, human rights monitoring was done by small, nongovernmental groups with almost no resources. Because the government viewed them as enemies, these groups worked under constant harassment and without access to any information other than the testimonies of victims and family members.

When ONUSAL arrived on the scene with dozens and then hundreds of staff, apparently unlimited resources, diplomatic weight, and unprecedented access to information, Salvadoran human rights activists expected the mission to have an immediate and dramatic impact.

Intensification of criticism from both the left and the right suggested that ONUSAL was able to achieve some measure of independence in its human rights monitoring work. Furthermore, even the mission's most vociferous critics acknowledged important improvements in the country's human rights situation as a result of ONUSAL's presence. Key unanswered questions about ONUSAL include whether or not the massive resources devoted to the mission were optimally used to better the country's human rights situation, and whether or not the mission did enough to build the capacity of Salvadoran institutions to protect human rights with or without the presence of ONUSAL.

The PDH was a new entity created by the accords. From its inauguration in 1992, it was hampered by a lack of resources and support from the government, and by a lack of leadership from Carlos Molina Fonseca, its first director. Supposedly independent, its budgetary dependence on the government seriously limited its capacity to become a leading force in the protection of human rights. In response to the report of the Truth Commission, the PDH announced a decision to implement those minor recommendations pertaining to its work, but it took no leadership role in encouraging government implementation of the commission's major recommendations. Similarly, the ombudsman was silent on the crucial issue of the constitutionality of the amnesty law.[22]

ONUSAL, in its last year, began working closely with the PDH to help develop its capacity to take over more of the monitoring and protection role played by the UN for much of the early postwar period, but it is too soon to assess the concrete results of this cooperation. Similarly, the United Nations Development Program (UNDP) provided significant financing and technical assistance to the PDH in an effort to build its institutional capacity.

In the wake of the 1994 elections, the PDH still seemed unable to overcome the institutional problems and lack of credibility that plagued it from the start. When the PDH did make clear recommendations, the government paid little attention to them. With ONUSAL in place, there was less need for decisive action by the ombudsman, but the demands on the PDH must change dramatically with the departure of ONUSAL.

Given the history of human rights protection in El Salvador, the creation of a legitimate official human rights monitoring entity was an undeniably important step. The early history of the PDH, however, brought into question the institution's capacity to lead in the indispensable effort to guarantee human rights by challenging the impunity still enjoyed by other elements of the government.

Following a long debate, Victoria Velásquez de Aviles, head of the PDH's Office for the Rights of Children, was named El Salvador's second Human Rights Ombudsman in early 1995. At least in the first weeks of her tenure as head of the PDH, Velásquez appeared to be taking a more proactive stance than her predecessor. Under her leadership, the PDH published paid announcements in newspapers denouncing human rights violations by the PNC and was generally more willing to offer criticisms of the government on human rights issues.[23]

ONUSAL's 11th Human Rights report in mid-1994 highlighted the resilience of impunity in El Salvador and the challenges still facing the new ombudswoman when she took office. In that report, the UN presented a study of 75 of the most significant cases of human rights abuse reported to ONUSAL in the two years after the signing of the Peace Accords. The police had conducted investigations in only 27 of the 75 cases, and only nine suspects were in custody in relation to those cases. Most striking was ONUSAL's conclusion that "no one has been tried or sentenced for having committed any of the 75 most serious cases of violations of the right to life reported to ONUSAL."[24] As ONUSAL prepared to conclude its mission in April 1995, even its critics viewed its departure with anxiety. Given the weaknesses of the PDH, El Salvador will continue to rely on the efforts of nongovernmental groups—whatever their limitations—for leadership in the area of human rights protection.

Redefining Public Security: Civilian National Police

Arguably the most important new institution created by the peace process was the Civilian National Police (PNC). All analyses of the trampling of human rights in El Salvador before and during the war were replete with references to the repressive role of the nation's three "security forces," and the close relationship between the National Police (PN), the Treasury Police (PH), the National Guard (GN), and the death squads. Previously classified documents released by the Clinton Administration in November 1993 confirm that U.S. intelligence had information about the operations of death squads within the security forces in the early 1980s.[25] In an attempt to prevent such abuses in the future, the Peace Accords eliminated those three organizations, replacing them with a new, professionalized, depoliticized police force under civilian control—the PNC. The creation of the PNC also followed an international trend toward the separation of public security functions from purely military ones as a way of increasing efficiency and controlling corruption.

Not surprisingly, a range of manipulations accompanied the demobilization of the GN and the PH. They were not actually eliminated but were incorporated into the FAES as the Border Police and the Military Police, respectively. The PN was to be kept in place as a transitional force until PNC deployment allowed it to disappear (June 1994, according to the accord, January 1995 in reality).

Nor was the birth of the new police without its complications. The creation of the new academy to train the PNC was delayed by funding shortfalls and by the refusal of the FAES to turn over the facility previously projected as the site of the Academy. Despite the obstacles, the National Academy of Public Security (ANSP) opened in September 1992—symbolically in the former quarters of one of the recently demobilized elite military battalions—and began training the unique mix of civilians, former combatants of the FMLN, and ex-members of the National Police making up the PNC.[26] During the first several months of deployment in 1993, the PNC took over from the PN in one rural department after another to the enthusiastic reception of many local citizens.[27] In many areas, the PNC scored some impressive early successes against criminal elements running rampant in the postwar period. As late as September 1993, international observers described the deployment of the PNC as a "successful experience to date."[28]

By early 1994, however, perceptions about the PNC had begun to change dramatically. More conservative forces in government had stopped opposing the PNC and delaying its deployment in favor of carrying out a plan to influence the character of the new police. By February 1994, on the eve of the general elections, while noting that the PNC "continues to perform effectively and to enjoy broad popular support and high popular expectations" the Washington Office on Latin America noted several disturbing trends in the PNC, which appeared to be moving it away from its original mission.[29] They included:

- Lack of commitment of top PNC leadership to the vision of the institution contained in the Peace Accords.[30]
- Wholesale shifting of the Anti-Narcotics (UEA) and Special Investigations (CIDH) units into the PNC without adequate evaluation or transitional training.
- Diminished cooperation between the Police and Human Rights Divisions of ONUSAL and the PNC.
- Persistent difficulties in recruiting civilian and ex-FMLN components of PNC personnel and evidence of a coordinated plan to place former National Police and other demobilized members of the military and security forces in the PNC.
- Increasing reports of human rights abuses attributed to the PNC.
- Continuing lack of adequate resources to support PNC operations.

By all appearances, the government was attempting to increase the influence of the military and the old security forces in the new PNC. In addition, the slow pace of demobilization of the PN led to fears that ARENA might seek to justify keeping the PN in place alongside the PNC.

Concrete steps were taken in 1994 to address such concerns, including the removal of the PNC's director of operations, but the problems of the PNC persisted. Complaints of human rights abuses against the new police continued to mount.[31] When, at the urging of

ONUSAL, PNC leadership sought to remove seventy drug enforcement agents who had entered the institution from the PN without receiving proper screening or training, the entire drug enforcement unit went on strike. Half of the four hundred drug enforcement agents left the PNC as part of the agreement ending the strike. Finally, the PNC showed little capacity to overcome the serious weaknesses of the PN in the area of criminal investigation.[32]

The events of June 1994, Calderón Sol's first month in office, greatly accelerated the demobilization of the PN. At the height of the public outcry over the increase in crime, a group of armed men, some dressed in PN uniforms, held up an armored car in downtown San Salvador before hundreds of onlookers. Three security guards were killed. That night, the TV news showed a videotape that indicated the participation of the former head of the PN investigation unit, Lt. José Rafael Coreas Orellana.[33]

The following day a visibly perturbed Calderón Sol announced the immediate demobilization of the PN intelligence unit and promised to close down the PN by the end of the year. In January 1995 the last PN units formally handed over their command to the PNC.

Despite the demise of the PN, the trends highlighted above raised concern about the PNC, an institution that, as a civilian force committed to protection of human rights, was seen as a "first line of defense against impunity." In addition to the PNC's internal problems, the tremendous postwar surge in criminal activity appeared to be overwhelming the capacity of the new police to guarantee public security. This perceived public security vacuum fed the dangerous call for the military to assume a more active role in resolving the crime problem and maintaining public order.[34] In early 1995, President Calderón Sol mobilized seven thousand members of the Armed Forces to reinforce the PNC in high-crime areas throughout the country (See Military).

Judicial Reform: A Supreme Challenge

To the extent that an impartial and efficient administration of justice are critical to the construction of a democratic society, the Salvadoran judicial system has posed a formidable challenge to those who would democratize the country.

Very simply, the system traditionally worked for those with money and power and worked against those without. While wealthy Salvadorans could pay or threaten their way out of any legal tangle, defendants with less influence routinely served long prison terms without ever seeing their cases come to trial.

Several critical problems confronted the efforts to reform the system in the postwar period. These included:

- Almost complete centralization of judicial power within the Supreme Court.
- Control of the dominant parties in the legislative and executive branches over the selection of Supreme Court justices.
- Widespread partiality and corruption on the part of lower court judges.
- Lack of due process guarantees throughout the system.
- Excessive reliance on extrajudicial confessions rather than professional investigation as a basis for legal action.

Under the old system, the leading party in the Legislative Assembly could dictate the make-up of the Supreme Court simply by mustering a majority vote in the Assembly. At the war's end, this system had given El Salvador the Supreme Court led by Mauricio Gutiérrez Castro. The Truth Commission saw that court as such an obstacle to efforts to reform the judicial system that it recommended that the entire court immediately resign without waiting for its term to expire.

Given the unquestioned power of the Supreme Court to hire, evaluate, and fire lower court judges and other judicial functionaries, the politicization of the entire system was thus assured. The National Judicial Council (CNJ), which was allegedly established to assure the professional character of the courts, was, itself, appointed and controlled by the Supreme Court.

Constitutional reforms agreed to in April 1991 sought to break the political control over the system.[35] The Supreme Court was to be elected by a two-thirds majority of the Legislative Assembly from lists of candidates provided by the CNJ. As a means of assuring the independence of the CNJ, the Assembly, and not the Supreme Court, would choose CNJ members—again, by a two-thirds vote.

The first Supreme Court election under the new system occurred in mid-1994. The CNJ provided the Assembly with lists of highly qualified professional jurists, but political bickering took over as soon as the debate opened. Dogged insistence by ARENA and the opposition on "their" candidates left the country without a Supreme Court for a full month as the deputies searched for the compromise required by the constitutional reforms. In the end, the Assembly arrived at a Court that was, by all accounts, much more professional and representative than its predecessor.[36]

Perhaps suffering a bit from the euphoria of having completed an arduous month of political horse-trading, FMLN Deputy Orlando Quinteros called the election of the new court a "pillar of the birth of a new democratic Republic, participatory and with social justice," and predicted that the new court would "respond to the expectations for a new and transparent administration of justice in the country."[37]

In practice, the efforts to decentralize judicial power away from the Supreme Court had less impact. The CNJ gained more power over the appointment of lower court judges, but the Supreme Court was still running the show. A more independent and professional Supreme Court and a more independent CNJ, however, should gradually result in less corruption and more professionalism at all levels of the system.[38] Within six months of taking office, the new Supreme Court had begun removing lower court judges for corruption and dereliction of duty, and had initiated a complete review of all judges.

Due process reform was not an explicit part of the constitutional reforms, and progress on basic legal changes has been slow and uneven. Even before the end of the war, an AID-sponsored judicial reform project proposed a number of due process reforms that for years languished in the Assembly awaiting consideration. The Truth Commission recommended, in 1993, action on those reforms and a number of others, such as the elimination of the broad use of extrajudicial confessions in judicial proceedings. According to AID, the Assembly was to have considered these reforms for passage by mid-1995.[39] Meanwhile, Salvadoran prisons remained overcrowded with prisoners who had not stood trial but had served more time than the maximum sentence for the crime for which they were jailed.[40]

In reviewing the judicial system almost two years after the constitutional reforms of 1991, the Truth Commission lauded those reforms but recognized them as insufficient. The commission's report recommended that Salvadoran society build on the momentum of the reforms to proceed to a complete overhaul of the judicial system. Two years after the Truth Commission report, a new and better Supreme Court was in place and working gradually to address the need to professionalize the system at all levels. The CNJ was showing new signs of vitality and the Judicial Training School, long a national embarrassment, had a new director and was cooperating with the efforts to raise professional standards.

At its base, however, in the routine judicial proceedings where most Salvadorans experienced the corruption and inefficiency of the judicial system on a daily basis, the system showed great resistance to change. Too often, the relative influence of accuser and accused still determined whether or not a case was investigated, and the powerless still preferred to stay out of the system rather than risk losing a case. In that critically important sense, the reform of the judicial system remained a dangerously unfinished task.

Death Squads and Organized Crime: Permanent Public Insecurity

In the postwar period, all public opinion polls highlighted the massive public concern with the crime wave that touched all social sectors.[41] Apart from increasingly violent common crime, the crime wave also included a resurgence of violent crimes with apparent political motivations carried out in the familiar style of the notorious death squads (See Military). These two trends provided clear evidence of the inadequacy of the measures taken to ensure protection of human rights and to improve public security.

Death squad-style killings never completely stopped after the war, but they failed to gain international attention—at least until three top former commanders of the FMLN were killed in late 1993. The nature of the killings suggested that death squads in El Salvador remained highly organized and that their networks of financial and military support survived at least partially intact.

Under intense international pressure, President Cristiani agreed to the formation of a four-member Joint Working Group to investigate the death squads.[42] After six months of investigation, the Joint Working Group published a document confirming that the death squads still existed and had forged new relations with organized crime. The report suggested the involvement of active-duty military and police personnel but failed to produce groundbreaking or definitive evidence.[43] The group report declined to publicize names but instead revealed the names of suspected death squad collaborators in a confidential annex delivered to government officials.[44] The Joint Working Group, like the Truth Commission, left the burden of acting against the death squads to the government.

The report only intensified the unprecedented public pressure on the new government to act against organized crime. Presidential runner-up Rubén Zamora remained "skeptical" about Calderón Sol's will to move aggressively against criminals and highlighted the importance of international pressure on the administration. Ironically, rightwing commentator and ARENA critic Kirio Waldo Salgado agreed from the opposite end of the political spectrum.[45] In any case, given the historical connections between the ARENA and the death squads, Calderón Sol is unlikely to move aggressively against groups that limit their actions to attacks on leftwing political targets.

The resurgence of the illegal armed groups must be seen in the context of the postwar explosion of organized crime activity. Crime is not a new phenomenon in El Salvador but the scope of the problem increased dramatically when thousands of members of the FAES, the FMLN, and the police forces were demobilized without adequate programs to reintegrate them into civilian life (See Reconstruction and Veterans' Programs).[46] It became commonplace to hear Salvadorans say they felt more secure during the war when they knew where the violence was coming from and had some idea how to avoid it.

The Salvadoran government attempted to trace the crime problem to the withdrawal of public security forces from many areas as the National Guard and Treasury Police were demobilized. Early ARENA proposals to solve the crime problem involved a new lease on life for the old National Police and the gradual return of the military to public security functions.[47] While the ARENA party eventually accepted the demise of the PN, prominent members continued to emphasize the importance of calling the military out of its barracks to fight crime.

The withdrawal of both armies and the security forces did create a vacuum of authority after the war, especially in the countryside, and organized crime moved quickly to take advantage of this opening. In some cases, the work of criminals was made easier by their connection with the army and the security forces. Never was that connection more clearly expressed than in the June 1994 armored car robbery when an officer of the PN was videotaped leading the assault.

The public outcry in response to such a bold attack hastened the demobilization of the PN and appeared to strengthen the hand of those who would pursue an anti-crime strategy based more on strengthening the PNC and breaking the connection between public officials and organized crime. Even as former members of the Armed Forces held Legislative Assembly members as virtual hostages to assure the disbursement of military severance pay, little mention was made of the importance of effective reintegration programs for the ex-combatants of both sides or the effect of increased levels of poverty in the crime wave.

Street gangs or *maras*, strongly influenced by gangs formed among Salvadoran youth in Los Angeles and other U.S. cities, constituted another important element of the crime problem.[48] Gang members are responsible for much of the increase in common street crime in San Salvador. These turf-based groups existed during the war but became much more significant in the postwar period. Their connections with gangs in the United States have quickly involved them in international crimes, such as stolen car rings and the black market in assault weapons. As the *maras* became more widespread and their methods more violent, they illustrated the degree to which violence as a way of life had become ingrained in Salvadoran youth during the war.

The full deployment of a well-trained civilian police force should, over time, provide a partial solution to the crime problem. The criminal upsurge also has structural causes related to the economic inequalities of Salvadoran society and the culture of violence that became deeply rooted during the war. A real solution to the lack of adequate public security will require deep structural changes that go beyond the deployment of a new police force.

In the opinion of one Salvadoran legal expert, the Peace Accords "came up short" in the legal area, perhaps because of a lack of appreciation by the negotiators of the importance of legal transformation to the overall democratic project.[49] Subsequent events appear to bear out such a view.

The persistence of both the death squads and organized crime related to the military and police forces illustrate the degree to which such elements continue to act with impunity. The Joint Working Group report failed to recommend specific action against individuals, but it unquestionably confirmed the strengthening of the ties between the structures primarily responsible for the increase in organized crime and the resurgence of illegal armed groups with political motivations. Such ties always existed, but they took on new forms without the cover provided by the armed conflict.[50]

The investigators provided government officials with the names of individuals involved in such structures. Although the PNC did form a small, specialized unit to fight organized crime, there were no improvements in overall PNC investigative capacity. The relevant Salvadoran institutions were slow to act upon the other Joint Working Group recommendations regarding legal reforms and new judicial practices to fight organized crime.

Human Rights and Salvadoran Democracy

Speaking before the United Nations General Assembly in late 1993, President Cristiani made the following triumphal observation:

> ...the change has been carried out in an irreversible way ...(either) the conflict exhausted the resources of violent conflict in the country, (or) the end of the war and the force of the democratic process has generated the conditions for the emergence of a culture of tolerance, of understanding and reconciliation; in a word, a culture of peace.[51]

The vast majority of Salvadorans would welcome such a culture. But most would agree that the actual situation is closer to the situation described by ONUSAL in their September 1993 human rights report:

The generally positive trends brought about in the area of human rights are not yet...irreversible. Such trends can endure only if the institutions established as a result of the peace function effectively, if State institutions observe the law scrupulously, if the judiciary has the authority and autonomy to carry out investigations and mete out appropriate punishment, if the [Ombudsman's office] is strengthened and its constitutional functions respected by State agencies...[52]

The unevenness of its democracy and the potential reversibility of its institutional reforms are among the key characteristics of El Salvador's unstable political system. The quality of the administration of justice and respect for the human rights of all Salvadorans will continue to be an important barometer of the degree to which durable changes have occurred in El Salvador. As of early 1995, the barometer was giving uncertain readings. One of the major tests for the second ARENA administration will be whether or not it takes decisive action against a system of impunity from which the Salvadoran military and many of its own party stalwarts continue to benefit.

Part 4

Economy

© Jim Harney

Overview of the Economy

The economic injustices of El Salvador's centuries-old agroexport economic model were a central cause of the country's civil war. Whether the featured export was cacao, indigo, or coffee, the Salvadoran economy showed a consistent capacity to produce tremendous riches. The injustice lay in the economy's failure to distribute those riches in a way that guaranteed a decent life for the majority of Salvadorans.

Critics of the Peace Accords suggested that the agreement did not give sufficient attention to the structural problems of the country's economic system. Defenders of the accords, on the other hand, argued that an insistence on changing economic structures through the Peace Accords would have rendered a negotiated solution impossible, and that the great achievement of Chapultepec was a democratic opening that would make possible gradual economic change.

In July 1994, the President of the Salvadoran Central Reserve Bank held a news conference to announce triumphantly that the Salvadoran economy was the most stable and dynamic in Central America. Government statistics suggested that the new prosperity was already diminishing poverty levels.

Few could dispute that, in statistical terms, the economy which limped into the 1990s in the most precarious of conditions looked much better after five years of structural adjustment (See Structural Adjustment). During the 1994 elections, however, the opposition suggested that this economic growth was not sustainable in even the medium term and questioned whether the expansion was improving the desperate living conditions of poor Salvadorans.

Renewed Economic Growth

The claim of success cited above was based primarily on the sharp increases in economic activity after the Cristiani administration assumed power in 1989. In 1990, after the guerrilla offensive of 1989 and with the war still in full swing, the economy showed a shaky growth rate of 1 percent. By 1992 that rate had jumped to almost 5 percent and continued above 5 percent between 1993 and 1994 (Figure 4a).[1] This growth had been achieved in the same period that the country's major export, coffee, had experienced a drastic decline in value. In the period 1989-94, inflation had been brought below 10 percent, the exchange rate of the national currency, the colón, had been fairly stable, and the country's hard-currency reserves had increased dramatically.

Figure 4a
Change in El Salvador's GDP, 1983-1993

Percentage change from previous year

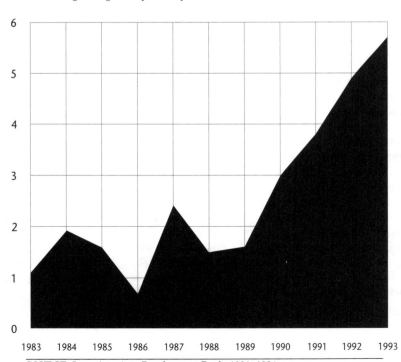

SOURCE: Inter-American Development Bank, 1991, 1994.

The bulk of the new activity occurred in three sectors: construction, trade, and services. These are important economic areas, but their growth does not imply a growth in El Salvador's productive capacity. The construction boom, for example, is rooted in postwar real estate speculation and an increased demand for luxury housing. Neither this expansion nor the growth in demand for consumer goods

---

Structural Adjustment

In the face of the debt crisis that swept the developing world in the early 1980s, international lending institutions like the International Monetary Fund (IMF) and the World Bank began to arrive at a set of prescriptions to bring about what they saw as necessary structural change in the economies of Africa, Asia, and Latin America.

Few denied that the economies of poor countries like El Salvador needed profound structural changes. The question is whether or not the prescriptions of the World Bank and the IMF are more likely to solve structural economic problems in the long run or make them worse.

Structural adjustment programs typically featured measures to "liberalize" local economies by removing the state as much as possible from economic activity and broadening the role of markets as the primary means for the allocation of goods and services. Specific recommendations included the lowering of tariff barriers, the floating of currency exchange rates and interest rates to market levels, the elimination of state subsidies, and the sale of state-owned assets and corporations to private investors. Alongside these policy changes, structural adjustment recommended legal and institutional reforms of the state in preparation for its new, streamlined role.

Experiences in Latin America and elsewhere have shown that rapid implementation of structural adjustment policies has had undeniable negative consequences, especially on the segment of the population already living in poverty.[1] People have lost jobs in privatized industries, prices of previously subsidized goods and services have increased, and the dropping of tariff barriers has put thousands of small and medium-sized businesses as well as much of the agricultural sector under new competitive pressures. Proponents of structural adjustment acknowledge these and other negative effects but justify them as necessary short-term dislocations which are more than made up for by long-term improvements in economic health.

---

1. In 1993, a coalition of U.S.-based NGOs initiated the *50 Years Is Enough* campaign to draw attention to the need to alter the programs of the World Bank and the IMF. As part of that campaign, Oxfam America published an excellent report on the impact of structural adjustment on its partners around the world. *The Impact of Structural Adjustment on Community Life: Undoing Development* (Boston: Oxfam America, 1995).

from the U.S. is likely to serve as the basis for sustained economic growth. Agricultural production showed very weak growth compared to other sectors; manufacturing, the other core production sector, grew very little outside of the area of textiles.[2]

Growth and the Persistence of Poverty

At the beginning of his term in office, Alfredo Cristiani surprised many critics of the ARENA party by highlighting the continuing existence of extreme poverty as a critical national problem and committing his administration to the struggle to eradicate that poverty (Figure 4b). By doing so, Cristiani gave credence to the view that the success or failure of an economy like El Salvador's (or any other, for that matter) cannot be judged solely by the stability of macroeconomic indicators. The record of El Salvador's economic performance of the 1960s and 1970s gives ample evidence that strong statistical performance can mask a gathering social crisis.

Even in the best of circumstances, the implementation of World Bank-style structural adjustment policies worsens the social conditions of a society's poorest sectors.[3] The removal of subsidies directly impacts the lives of the poor who depend on them. Privatization costs jobs and, at least in the short run, puts more people in a situation of poverty. The opening of new external markets seldom compensates those who have lost jobs or small businesses to the pressure of inter-

Figure 4b
Poverty Indicators

Life expectancy at birth (years)	
Female	68
Male	63
Infant mortality per 1,000 live births	51
Percent of children with inadequate nutrition	23%
Physicians per 10,000 people	7.5
Hospital beds per 1,000 people	1.03
Access to safe drinking water (% of population)	47%
Access to sanitation services (% of population)	58%
Percent of government expenditure allocated to health	8%

SOURCE: *Mexico and Central American Handbook*, 1995 (Bath: Trade and Travel Publications, 1994); *Central America Report*, March 31, 1995; United Nations, *UN Statistical Yearbook, 1992-1993*; U.S. Agency for International Development, *May 1994 Report*.

national economic competition. Pressure to reduce government budget deficits compromises already inadequate social programs, while the "modernization" of tax systems often makes them more regressive. El Salvador's "model" structural adjustment was certainly not immune to these consequences. Even after a war in which the power of the country's oligarchy was seriously challenged, El Salvador remains one of the most unequal societies in Latin America. The Economic Commission for Latin America (CEPAL) reported that, whereas 68 percent of El Salvador's inhabitants lived in poverty in 1980, 71 percent suffered that fate in 1990.[4] In addition, CEPAL found that, in 1990, the wealthiest fifth of Salvadoran society received 66 percent of the national income while the poorest fifth received close to 4 percent. The distribution of wealth is more difficult to determine, but when a significant percentage of the population is reduced to a situation of subsistence, wealth is even more concentrated than income.[5]

Discussions of the impact of structural adjustment on poverty in El Salvador have become mired in a numbers game with the government insisting that its statistics point to a lessening of poverty during the Cristiani years, and the opposition insisting that the figures say otherwise.[6] The economists at *Proceso* shed some light on how the government arrived at its optimistic poverty statistics. While preparing the 1992 report, the Ministry of Planning (MIPLAN) altered its way of calculating income by including family remittances in total family income. This obviously caused an abrupt increase in income levels. At the same time, MIPLAN updated the cost estimates of the "basic needs basket," which should have raised the poverty income level but they did not immediately incorporate figures on the cost of living into a new calculation of poverty-level income. As a result, reported income jumped through the inclusion of remittances while the poverty line stayed the same. Not surprisingly, many Salvadorans statistically were no longer living in poverty.[7]

An AID-funded land-tenure study published in 1992 found that even after the major land reform program conducted in the 1980s and major out-migration from rural areas because of the war and economic hardship, there remain 330,000 landless or land-poor adults living in the Salvadoran countryside (54 percent of the agricultural labor force and about the same absolute number as at the beginning of the war).[8] Furthermore, many farmers who are not land-poor still live in conditions of poverty.[9]

Apart from the jumble of statistics, the signs of increasing poverty are all over El Salvador. While the end of the war and the demobilization of members of the opposing forces aggravated the crime situation, increased delinquency became a crime wave because of the desperate economic situation in which demobilizing combatants found themselves. Another sign of poverty is the multiplication of poor children on the streets of San Salvador combining work with begging alongside the new Wendy's and Pizza Hut franchises blossoming on Los Heroes Boulevard. Despite the city government's efforts to stop their proliferation, *champas*, the makeshift houses of poor Salvadorans, continue to fill every nook and cranny of the Salvadoran capital.[10]

Economic Stabilization in El Salvador

Any discussion of the Salvadoran economy in the 1990s begins with the country's structural adjustment program. During the 1980s the Duarte administration in El Salvador halfheartedly implemented austerity programs and other economic reforms but never wholeheartedly embraced structural adjustment enough to satisfy the big lenders that it was serious about real change. A full implementation of structural adjustment would have implied a dismantling of many of the reforms—like the nationalization of banking and foreign trade—that stood at the center of the Christian Democratic project. More importantly, its negative effects on the population could have threatened the political stability of the counterinsurgency effort. By its massive funding of the Duarte government, the United States made it clear that political considerations gave El Salvador a temporary reprieve from deep structural adjustment.

The rise of ARENA meant the end of that reprieve. ARENA promised in its 1989 campaign that it would leave the big-government, populist policies of the PDC in the past and carry out a full structural adjustment of the Salvadoran economy, even in the midst of the armed conflict. FUSADES, the private sector think tank, had worked for five years on its plan for a revitalized economy and that plan became the economic action plan of the new government. Mirna Liévano de Marqués, a FUSADES economist who had been instrumental in the drafting of the plan, became Cristiani's Minister of Planning. The "Government's Economic Plan: 1989-94" suggested a willingness to face the popular opposition that was sure to greet structural adjustment policies in El Salvador.

The rewards for taking the path of structural adjustment came quickly for ARENA. In August 1990, only fifteen months after Cristiani assumed power, the government reached a contingency agreement with the IMF establishing the quantitative outline of the structural adjustment program. The agreement defined how much credit the government could receive on a quarterly basis and how much the country's money supply could be allowed to grow. While placing limits on the assumption of new debt, it also set goals for the growth of international reserves and interest payments on existing debt. The agreement puts the IMF in the position of supervising the implementation of economic policy in El Salvador.

Two additional agreements followed this one, covering the remaining years of the Cristiani administration. El Salvador did not even take advantage of the direct financial benefits of the IMF agreement, but the agreement had the much more significant effect of sending the "all clear" signal to other financial institutions.

The signing of the agreement with the IMF opened the floodgates to a bonanza of international financing, primarily from the World Bank and the Inter-American Development Bank (IDB). By the end of 1992, the Salvadoran government had signed loan agreements with the World Bank, the IDB, and the IMF totaling over a billion dollars, and had negotiated an agreement with the United States for the forgiveness of nearly another half-billion in credits.

The ARENA government did not get all of this support because they simply wrote a good structural adjustment plan. The Cristiani government quickly took concrete, and sometimes costly, steps to rapidly implement many reforms, even in the context of a continuing armed conflict. Among other reforms, subsidies were cut, tariffs lowered (though by no means eliminated), export taxes eliminated, and a privatization program initiated.

Social compensation programs designed to alleviate some of the costs of structural adjustment have also been an important part of the Salvadoran economic reform. Noting the high social cost of adjustment, the World Bank in the mid-1980s began to encourage countries to launch externally funded social programs alongside adjustment reforms. By the time violent riots greeted the implementation of structural adjustment reforms in Venezuela in 1989 and the Dominican Republic in 1990, social compensation programs were a central feature of World Bank reform policy.

In El Salvador, the Social Investment Fund (FIS) was created on Halloween Day, 1990. Salvadorans still debate whether the FIS was a trick or a treat. The fund is essentially a public-works employment program that provides people short-term employment building classrooms, latrines, health clinics and other small-scale infrastructure projects throughout El Salvador, in areas where such infrastructure is in undeniably short supply. The FIS began with only $3.5 million in initial funding, but by 1994 was moving as much as $75 million annually with funds provided by the United Nations Children's Fund, the IDB, and the governments of Germany and Japan, among other donors.

While all observers admit that the FIS administers its funds in a highly efficient manner, critics are quick to point to the fund's shortcomings. First, the intended beneficiaries participate little in FIS projects, which often are implemented by contractors who barely consult the local population, let alone encourage its participation. Furthermore, while the FIS does not have access to enough funds to even begin to solve the social problems of the nation, the government uses each project for political purposes. During the 1994 campaign, PDC Vice-Presidential candidate Atilio Viéytez voiced a popular refrain when, in a televised debate, he said "The FIS is like an ambulance that goes around and picks up the victims of ARENA's economic plan and takes them to the hospital."

Although the World Bank and the IMF conditioned economic support on the implementation of structural adjustment in El Salvador, those institutions did not "impose" reforms on the ARENA government. The main structural adjustment reforms were entirely consistent with the free market ideology espoused by ARENA, and the party built its economic program around economic liberalization. ARENA made structural adjustment its own to such an extent that an evaluation of economic performance during the Cristiani period becomes an evaluation of structural adjustment and the compensatory programs which accompanied it.

The ARENA reform program has benefitted from the end of the war and has been buoyed by the repatriation of Salvadoran capital in

Figure 4c

El Salvador's Principal Exports and Imports, 1993

In millions of U.S. $

Exports

Coffee	227.8
Garments	34.5
Medicine	33.5
Sugar	31.1
Paper and cardboard packaging	29.4

Imports

Raw materials and intermediate goods	825.4
Capital goods	564.9
Consumer goods	522.0
Building materials	140.6
Fuel	123.0

SOURCE: Economist Intelligence Unit, *EIU Country Report: El Salvador*, 1995.

foreign banks, high levels of foreign aid, and especially by the massive remittances of dollars by Salvadorans living in the United States. Any evaluation of the Salvadoran experience with structural adjustment must take these factors into account.

International Trade Imbalances

As a small, populous country with limited natural resources, El Salvador depends on international trade for many critical economic inputs. Economists argue about how much the country should emphasize the international market, but there is no dispute about the importance of being able to import a wide range of goods. The country's sunny economic picture clouds somewhat upon examination of its trade situation (Figure 4c).

Prior to the war, El Salvador's exports were dominated by agricultural products which were marketed to the United States and Europe. Coffee became the "golden grain" of this economy in the middle of the nineteenth century and has maintained that position for over a century. Beginning in the 1950s, the search for new export possibilities led to increased cattle raising and wider cultivation of cotton and sugar cane. These exports, combined with a small but dynamic manufacturing sector, gave El Salvador impressive economic growth rates and a relatively even balance of trade with the rest of the world during the 1960s and 1970s. As late as 1980, El Salvador ran a small international trade surplus. A number of factors caused a sharp decline in export income during the 1980s. The increasingly active guerrilla movement targeted the agroexporters and created a situation of insecurity that limited production and made investment imprudent, thus decreasing the production of all the country's major exports. Wild fluctuations in the markets for coffee, cotton, and sugar cane made matters worse. The dollar value of exports declined from $1 billion to $500 million during the 1980s. Even based on an extremely conservative 50 percent inflation rate during the 1980s, the real value of exports decreased by two-thirds.

Even as export income plunged, Salvadorans developed a hearty appetite for imported goods of all types.[11] When coffee prices collapsed in 1989, the 1980 trade surplus had become a half-billion dollar trade deficit.[12]

All the economic growth of the early 1990s showed no signs of reversing this situation. Instead, the trade deficit quickly worsened. Despite the talk about "export-led" growth, imports have continued to grow much faster than exports. Ironically, given the prominence of trade and services in El Salvador's consumption-led economic growth, the country may be experiencing a temporary "import-led" growth surge. By 1993 the trade deficit had doubled from the 1989 level, surpassing $1 billion in 1993 and again in 1994, when the deficit was $1.2 billion (Figure 4d).

Exports of finished textile products did, however, grow quite dramatically during the early 1990s. This *maquila* production involves Salvadoran workers turning imported materials into garments for foreign markets. The government offers substantial tax breaks and other incentives to the mostly foreign capital involved in *maquila* production, and wages are low and rates of profit extremely high.[13] The instability of the war prevented major investments in this area before 1992, but the rate of growth has been substantial since that date.

Since *maquila* production utilizes mostly imported raw materials and provides minimal tax benefits for El Salvador, the level of the sector's exports overstates its value to the Salvadoran economy. Nevertheless, the Salvadoran government has put *maquilas*, and the attraction of foreign capital in general, at the center of its new economic agenda.

Continuing Government Budget Deficits

Structural adjustment insists that governments undergoing the "cure" cut spending to reduce the drain on the economy caused by budget deficits. Surprisingly, though, budget deficits actually worsened mildly in the immediate postwar period, reaching 4.2 percent of GDP in 1992.

The Salvadoran planning minister traced the deficit increase to the high costs of postwar reconstruction programs and the disappointingly slow pace of privatization of state-controlled industries and services (See National Reconstruction).[14] She might have added the level-funding of the Salvadoran Armed Forces even after the war's end (See Military), massive tax evasion by wealthy and middle class Salvadorans, and the preposterous costs of programs like the privatization of the banking system.[15]

Under pressure from international lenders, the government, over the objections of the opposition, rushed a new value-added tax (IVA) through the Legislative Assembly in 1992 to replace the outmoded stamp tax. Much of the IVA is passed onto final consumers at the point of sale. As a result, even though some basic consumer goods are exempted, it has a much more regressive incidence than the country's income tax. Within six months of its initiation, the controversial IVA was accounting for nearly one-half of government tax income.

While lauding the success of the IVA, the government has done little to fight evasion of the income tax. Income tax revision is part of all structural adjustment packages but is always undermined by gov-

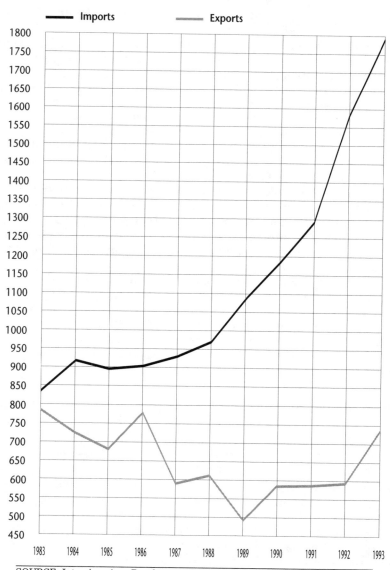

Figure 4d

Change in El Salvador's Exports and Imports, 1983-1993

In millions of U.S. $

SOURCE: Inter-American Development Bank, 1991, 1994.

ernments representing wealthy potential taxpayers. Governments often prefer taxes like the IVA, which have less impact on economic elites.

In El Salvador, total tax collections amount to just over 9 percent of GDP (over half of that in the relatively regressive IVA, less than one-quarter from income taxes), one of the lowest proportions in the world (along with neighboring Guatemala). Many estimates place income tax evasion at over 50 percent. The government runs TV commercials highlighting the patriotism of paying one's taxes, and occasionally threatens to aggressively prosecute the guilty, but such campaigns traditionally bear little fruit.[16]

Buoyed by the IVA, government income increased in 1993 and the budget deficit fell to under 2 percent of GDP. Even with the huge inflow of international donations and accelerated economic growth, budget deficits persist. From the perspective of structural adjustment, these deficits need to be controlled, but moderate fiscal deficits may actually stimulate the economy if they represent investment in the country's human capital stock.

While the fiscal deficit has stayed within manageable limits, no economy the size of El Salvador's can absorb huge trade deficits for very long without runaway inflation or other serious economic problems. Inflationary pressures partially resulting from such imbalances ruined the Sandinistas in Nicaragua. What has allowed the Salvadoran government to avoid this fate?

Three major sources of hard currency allowed El Salvador to compensate for the commercial and fiscal imbalances of the past few years: hard currency transfers from other governments in the form of both loans and donations; remittances of Salvadorans living abroad; and, more recently, the repatriation of capital that had left the country during the war years. In that sense, the impressive growth may stand on very shaky legs.

Dependence on Family Remittances

Coffee exports maintained the trade balance of the Salvadoran economy for more than a century. At times, the coffee export tax provided half of all government income. In the 1980s, however, when the war brought a steep decline in coffee income, El Salvador found another export to bring in the needed foreign exchange—its people. During the 1980s, as many as a million Salvadorans left their country for a combination of political and economic reasons. The costs of migration were tremendous, both in terms of the loss of human resources and the human cost of the destruction of the extended family unit.

Those Salvadorans that were lucky enough to arrive in the United States did not forget about their family members. Many new arrivals found work and began sending part of their pay back to El Salvador. The amount of these remittances increased throughout the 1980s, first surpassing the value of coffee exports, and then reaching levels in excess of the value of all export sales. Soon after assuming office in 1989, ARENA promoted the legalization of *casas de cambio*, exchange houses which encouraged remittances by giving Salvadorans a way to legally change dollars at near the black market rate. These new houses had the double benefit of quickly bringing dollars into the formal financial system where they could be used to finance import purchases.

By 1994 family remittances had reached $965 million and had become a critical stabilizing factor in the Salvadoran economy. Their importance is reflected in the seriousness with which the Salvadoran government treats any uncertainty in the immigration status of its nationals residing in the United States (See U.S.-El Salvador Relations). The rate-of-growth of family remittances will surely slow as El Salvador enters the next century, even if Salvadorans do not face a radical change in their immigration status in the United States. Unless mass deportations occur, however, remittances are likely to remain high for the foreseeable future.

Dependence on Foreign Aid

Foreign aid has been critical to the economic stability of the Salvadoran government ever since the beginning of the war. During the 1980s, the United States was the primary source of direct transfers, providing over $4.5 billion in formal aid and an estimated $500 million in covert money.[17] At its height, U.S. aid constituted as much as one-half of the public budget (See U.S.-El Salvador Relations). Even before the end of the war, U.S. aid began to taper off, and this trend is expected to continue as AID seeks to "downsize" its operation globally. Other sources, like the IMF, the World Bank, the European Union, and, especially, the IDB have stepped forward to make up for the decline in U.S. assistance in the short term. Estimates put the total aid received during 1992-93 at $800 million.[18] These funds have supported the social compensation and institutional modernization components of the structural adjustment program, and the various aspects of the country's National Reconstruction Plan (PRN) (See National Reconstruction).

The bulk of the new funds have come to El Salvador in the form of loans. The loans are long-term credits at preferential rates, but they will have to be paid back at some point. Because of all the economic aid received by El Salvador during the war and the debt restructuring that occurred alongside the structural adjustment agreements, the country's debt situation is not as serious as many of its Latin American neighbors.

In 1993 El Salvador's debt service totalled 31 percent of its export earnings, compared to 16 percent for Guatemala and 35 percent for Honduras.[19] For 1994 the country devoted 22 percent of its budget to debt service, just below the 26 percent devoted to all social spending (Figure 4e).[20]

Observers expect that levels of external aid to El Salvador will begin, in the mid-1990s, to decline until the presumed end of the country's reconstruction program in 1997. At that point, aid levels will most likely plummet.

Capital Repatriation and Lack of Investment Growth

During the early years of the war and throughout the period of Christian Democrat dominance of national politics, wealthy Salvadorans moved billions of dollars out of their country rather than reinvest it in El Salvador. This capital flight was partly caused by the insecurity prevailing in the rural areas where the guerrillas had successfully challenged the profitability of the oligarchy's investments as well as their previously unquestioned political authority.

The oligarchy's distaste for bank nationalization, state control of foreign trade, and other economic policies of the PDC also fed this massive capital outflow.[21] Hundreds of millions of dollars left the country in this way between 1980-85, much of it ending up in Miami-based banks.[22]

Attitudes changed after the election of the ARENA government in 1989 and capital began to trickle back into the country. President Cristiani moved quickly to show that he planned to turn ARENA's pro-business rhetoric into concrete changes. Not only did the new gov-

Figure 4e
External and Domestic Debt

External debt	$2.2 billion
Debt service actually paid	264 million
Outstanding external debt as % of GDP	26%
Debt Service as % of exports	31%

SOURCE: Inter-American Development Bank, *1994 Report*; U.S. Agency for International Development, *May 1994 Report*.

ernment move quickly to put foreign trade and the banks back into the hands of the oligarchy but it also changed tax laws and other regulations to benefit investors.

By 1991, all signs pointed to an end to the armed conflict. With steadily declining interest rates in the United States also playing no small part, what had been a trickle of "repatriated" capital quickened to a steady stream of $86 million in 1992 and $164 million in 1993.[23]

The return of this money helped stabilize the fiscal and trade imbalances outlined above, but it surely cannot be relied upon as a long-term source of balance of payments relief. Furthermore, while it has quickened the pace of certain highly visible economic activities in San Salvador—most notably construction, financial services, and retail trade—capital repatriation has not fueled the expected boom in productive investment, such as new factories or agricultural facilities. After reaching a peak of 25 percent of GDP in the late 1970s, investment declined drastically during the war to a low of just over 10 percent in 1985. Investment growth began again in 1990, but only very slowly, reaching 16 percent by 1994. Government investment has grown more quickly than that of the private sector.[24]

Wealthy Salvadorans have preferred short-term commercial investments and speculation in real estate and financial instruments over investments in the future of their beloved *patria*. In that sense, self-interest has overshadowed any sense of allegiance to the ARENA government. In its "El Salvador Strategy 94-99: Social Solutions and Economic Reforms", FUSADES signals the weakness of an economic recovery driven primarily by consumption and makes the increase of total (public and private) investment from 16 percent to 22 percent of GDP a priority goal for the Calderón Sol administration.

Agriculture: Seeds of Recovery?

Although the civil war dealt El Salvador's agrarian economy a severe blow, agriculture continues to be a critically important economic sector. It still accounts for nearly 10 percent of the national product (Figure 4f) and half of all export income, and directly employs more than a third of the work force (Figure 4g). Agriculture is a dual economy, sharply divided between the export and local food production, and structural adjustment policies favoring export production have exacerbated this duality.

Despite the recovery of coffee prices, which will most likely lead to a temporary recovery in export income, El Salvador's traditional export sector is struggling to regain its pre-war vitality. Total value added in the traditional exports actually decreased by a quarter between 1979 and 1993. Production of basic grains, on the other hand, increased by more than a third during the same period. But the relative weight of the export sector meant that total agricultural production had decreased by about 1 percent since the commencement of the war. Such stagnation clearly placed in question the role of agriculture as the foundation of the Salvadoran economy.

Agroexports: Province of the Oligarchy

Coffee, shrimp, sugar, and cotton are, in that order, the leading agroexports. Coffee has been the undisputed king of the export sector for more than a hundred years. By the 1920s coffee accounted for 95 percent of the country's exports.[25] The plummeting coffee prices of the Great Depression era sparked a rural rebellion among Salvadoran campesinos, which was suppressed by the infamous *matanza* of 1932 when the army and vigilante bands killed thousands of suspected rebels and sympathizers. The terror of 1932 quieted widespread rural unrest for a half century.

Figure 4f
GDP in El Salvador by Economic Sector, 1993

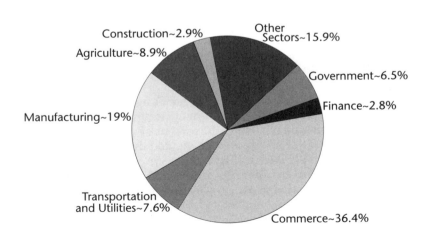

Construction~2.9%
Other Sectors~15.9%
Agriculture~8.9%
Government~6.5%
Finance~2.8%
Manufacturing~19%
Commerce~36.4%
Transportation and Utilities~7.6%

SOURCE: Economist Intelligence Unit, *EIU Country Report: El Salvador*, 1995.

Prior to 1980 El Salvador was the largest and most efficient coffee producer in Central America, and the fourth largest in Latin America following Brazil, Colombia, and Mexico. But the disruption caused by the war and disagreements between coffee growers and the government led to a steep decline in coffee production during the 1980s.

Although the country's oligarchy is present in all economic sectors, it is most firmly based in the coffee estates that cover the rich volcanic uplands. The coffee oligarchy fought successfully against the enactment of Phase II of the 1980 agrarian-reform program, thereby excluding most coffee estates from the land-redistribution program and preserving the economic base of the most reactionary elements of the oligarchy.

After the 1989 elections, ARENA immediately set out to reverse what it saw as the anti-coffee policies of the Duarte government. Control over international trade in coffee, which had been nationalized under the PDC, was returned to the coffee traders of the oligarchy. The Salvadoran Coffee Research Institute was also privatized with the help of a $10 million grant from AID.

Figure 4g
Employment in El Salvador by Economic Sector, 1992

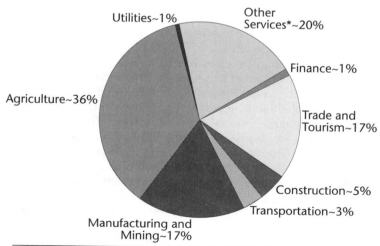

*Community, Social, and Personal Services
SOURCE: United Nations, *UN Statistical Yearbook, 1992-1993.*

Growers gave ARENA a vote of confidence by attempting to increase production during the 1989-90 harvest despite the FMLN offensive. The weather cooperated and the harvest increased by 50 percent over the previous year, but coffee prices took a drastic dive. The price drop, primarily the result of the collapse of price and production agreements sponsored by the International Coffee Organization, plunged the industry into a deep crisis.

The market shift did not drive many of the coffee barons into poverty, but it did affect the thousands of poor rural laborers who depended on coffee income for survival. Wages stagnated and employment declined drastically as, in many cases, prices fell below the costs of production. Whereas, as late as the mid-1980s, government income depended on the coffee export tax, in 1993 the political influence of the coffee growers led the government to offer coffee producers a cash payment of $15 per hundredweight of coffee exported.[26]

Coffee prices recovered in the mid-1990s through a combination of the organization of a sort of coffee-producers cartel and bad weather in Brazil that radically reduced that country's production. Although the price increases were temporary, experts do not expect that market to return to the low point of the early 1990s.[27]

The once-thriving cotton industry has all but disappeared. Cotton, stored in huge "mountains" in rural areas, was an ideal target for guerrilla sabotage.[28] The industry's heavy reliance on expensive chemical and mechanical inputs made it particularly vulnerable when world market prices sagged. Cotton production recovered slightly after the war, but this production was more oriented to the domestic production of cottonseed oil than world export markets. Not only is El Salvador no longer exporting much cotton, the country has had to resort to importing the vegetable oil that formerly was produced locally from cottonseed.

Sugar and shrimp production are the only traditional export crops that have maintained or increased production levels, although together they still account for less than 10 percent of agricultural exports. Sugar production is important for its role in the domestic economy, meeting the large internal demand and providing a major source of rural seasonal employment. There is a tobacco industry in El Salvador, but the British-owned Salvadoran Tobacco Company sends raw Salvadoran tobacco to Guatemala for processing, explaining why almost 50 percent of the tobacco used in cigarette manufacturing is imported from Guatemala.

Much is being made of the need to diversify agricultural production in El Salvador. There is, however, little to show for the nontraditional agroexport projects administered by FUSADES and backed by AID and the IDB. Besides shrimp, melons are the only significant new nontraditional agroexport. Cantaloupe and cucumber production are also being promoted but with discouraging results. Most of the small local demand for fruits and vegetables is met by imports from Guatemala. El Salvador is, as a result, a net importer of fruits and vegetables.

Less Food and More Import Dependence

ARENA made much of the increase in basic grain production in the early 1990s, yet this increase was as much the result of favorable weather conditions and the end of the war as it was a triumph of the government agrarian policy. The decision of the government to let grain prices rise in the domestic market, however, did allow for a rise in producer income, thus offering some incentive for increased production.[29]

The increased production, however, was not sufficient to meet increased food demand in El Salvador. Between 1992 and 1993 commercial imports (as opposed to food aid) of corn and rice increased by 8 percent and 97 percent, respectively. These figures would have been much higher were it not for the continuing PL480 food aid program from the United States. Salvadoran officials recently announced their intention to discontinue the country's participation in the PL480 program. It is doubtful, however, that they will follow through on such a plan as to do so would surely worsen the country's food production deficit.

Projections from the Salvadoran Ministry of Agriculture and Cattle-Raising for the 1994-95 growing season suggested that production of corn, beans and rice would each fall at least 40 percent below projected demand. These projections of "effective demand" do not, of course, take into account that Salvadorans living in extreme poverty do not have sufficient income to demand even a minimum diet of basic grains.

While the Salvadoran people have had increasing difficulty buying enough food to meet the minimum nutritional requirements, another population has been quite well-fed—poultry. During the 1980s the poultry industry rapidly expanded to meet the demands of the middle and upper classes. It also exports large quantities of eggs and broiler chickens to other Central American countries. During the 1980s corn consumption by humans actually declined while corn consumption by animals doubled.[30] Not only does the poultry industry benefit from corn imports under the U.S. food-aid and credit programs, it is also bolstered by imports of wheat and breeder chicks.

From Agrarian Reform to the Land Transfer Program

The 1980 Land Reform Law was a key element of the "hearts and minds" strategy for defeating the guerrillas. It was thought that the land redistribution program would simultaneously create a popular base for a centrist government, undermine the power of a reactionary oligarchy, and open the way for increased agricultural production. By the early 1990s, the program's failures and the hostile attacks of the ARENA government had brought the agrarian reform to a standstill. In the postwar period the momentum of land distribution in El Salvador shifted to the Land Transfer Program flowing from the Chapultepec Accord.

On many counts, the 1980 agrarian reform program failed. Over the decade the oligarchy maintained its dominant economic position while increasing its political power. In solely economic terms, the program has had mixed results, at best. Agrarian reform cooperatives producing export crops performed a shade better than private-sector producers during the 1980s, while performance on basic grains cooperatives did considerably worse than their private-sector competi-

Three Phases of Agrarian Reform

In 1980 the Duarte-led junta instituted a land reform in three distinct redistribution programs (Phases I, II, and III). Phase I provided for the transformation of estates of more than 1235 acres into cooperatives. Compensation for land expropriated under Phase I was provided to a majority of the former owners in the form of interest-bearing government bonds.

Phase II, which was seriously undercut by legislative amendments and never implemented, was to have affected holdings between 247 and 1235 acres—which would have included the richest and most productive estates—equivalent to about 24 percent of the country's primary cropland. Political pressure led to an increase in the lower limit to 618 acres. This was clarified in the 1983 constitution, which established a limit of 605 acres that an individual could own, with the state allowed to expropriate without compensation any excess. However, landowners were given a three-year period to dispose of this land by themselves. A separate constitutional article sought to prevent sale of such land to blood relatives but was not aggressively enforced. As a result, it is unclear how many of the 640 properties that were originally eligible under the revised version of Phase II could actually be expropriated. Nevertheless, on December 3, 1987, the Assembly passed laws to implement Phase II, providing for the evaluation and negotiation of properties, determination of the price and form of payment to the former owners, and selection of the beneficiaries.

tors.[31] Even these mixed results were only obtained at the cost of a giant credit commitment from the government which issued interest-bearing bonds as a means of payment for the agrarian reform land. Only 3 percent of the mortgage credit extended to the cooperatives was ever paid back, and the record on production and investment credits is not strikingly better.[32] Some cooperatives did become efficient producers, but these probably number no more than one-third of the total.[33]

In a political sense, the reform sector proved to be an important source of support for the Christian Democrats and gave credibility to the reformist image of the government, particularly through the critical 1981-1986 period of the U.S. counterinsurgency project.

Once in power, ARENA moved quickly to undermine Phase II compliance in favor of the Phase III individual recipients of agrarian-reform land (see Three Phases of Agrarian Reform). The centerpiece of the ARENA offensive was Decree No. 747, a law passed in 1991. The new law, which was bitterly opposed by the cooperative federations, set up a system to eventually collect at least part of the long overdue cooperative mortgages. More importantly, Decree 747 established powerful incentives for the division of cooperatives into parcels

---

Phase III was a "Land to the Tiller" program that included all rental lands under 17 acres. Peasants who worked those lands were empowered to apply for title. Altogether, 40-45 percent of the country's agricultural lands were to have been redistributed. By the cut-off date of June 30, 1984, 63,640 persons had filed claims, representing more than 300,000 family members. Phase III affected many small landowners who rented out part of their land, and the legislation was strongly resented by them. Many landowners filed protests, and many contested claims became bogged down in legal processes, which were usually decided in favor of the landowner. Moreover, owners resistant to Phase III engaged in extra-legal activities, including violence and forced eviction of potential beneficiaries.

The reform fell far short of its original redistribution goals. Less than 20 percent of the country's agricultural lands were affected. Within this reform sector, Phase I cooperatives control about 73 percent and Phase III parcel owners control 24 percent, with the balance in the hands of beneficiaries of other land reform programs. Total beneficiaries of the reform as of 1992 were 85,227 campesinos, of whom 36,697 were cooperative members—falling far short of the 300,000 beneficiaries initially promised by AID.

SOURCE: "Parcelación o Colectivación: Dilema de la Reforma Agraria en El Salvador," *Realidad Económico-Social*, September-October 1988; all figures except the reference to the AID goal come from *XI Evaluación del Proceso de Reforma Agraria* (PERA) quoted in Seligson, op. cit., pp. 3-8, 3-9.

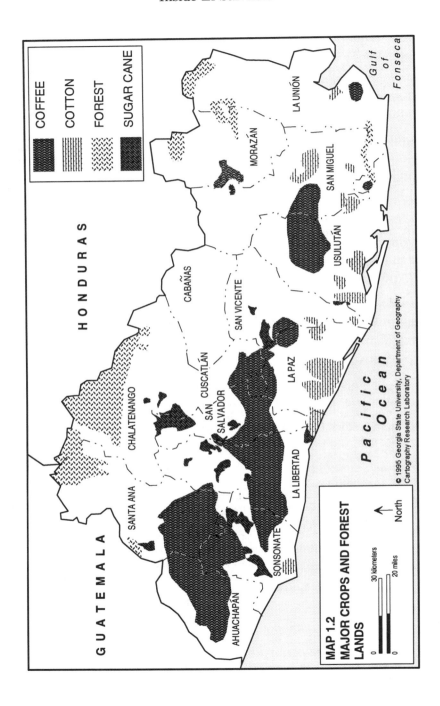

MAP 1.2
MAJOR CROPS AND FOREST LANDS

COFFEE
COTTON
FOREST
SUGAR CANE

© 1995 Georgia State University, Department of Geography
Cartography Research Laboratory

under the guise of offering "new options" for cooperative land tenure. Many cooperatives opted for subdivision under the new decree prior to the 1994 elections.[34]

The impact of subdivision on the cooperatives will not be seen for several years, but cooperative leaders fear that the process will eventually lead to the transfer of cooperative lands back into the hands of the private sector. Legislative Assembly member and author of the original agrarian reform law Jorge Villacorta showed no uncertainty about the impact of the ARENA policy. "I have no doubt that in a few years most peasants would sell or have their lands put up for sale by banks holding their property as collateral. Then we're back to the days when a few families owned most of the land—the same agrarian inequities that brought us to war in the first place." [35]

The various cooperative federations slowly came to the conclusion that the only defense against subdivision was organizational and technical improvements which would transform the cooperatives into viable economic units.[36] They were moving decidedly in this direction by the mid-1990s and showing signs of overcoming the limitations placed on them by the conditions of their war-time birth. By all accounts, however, ARENA halted the momentum toward further land distribution under the agrarian reform law, thus putting the cooperative movement on the defensive.

While the force of the 1981 land reform had ebbed by the war's end, poor campesinos continued to demand access to land. The redistribution of land in the country's conflictive zones formed part of the FMLN's absolute "bottom line" in the peace negotiations. Civilian supporters had repopulated and otherwise occupied large amounts of privately owned and state lands in the latter stages of the war. The Peace Accords contained an important provision recognizing the rights of the people occupying the land and the demobilized combatants of both armies to land. This land was to come from three possible sources:

- Undistributed lands in the hands of the Salvadoran Institute for Agrarian Transformation (ISTA).
- Market-rate purchases from the owners of occupied lands.
- Purchases of other privately owned lands in cases where the owners of occupied lands declined to sell and no state land was available.

Since the land was to be purchased in all cases, financing was critical. The Salvadoran government offered some funds, but the bulk of the money came from AID and the European Union (EU), which together provided in excess of $90 million for that purpose. The financing passed through the Land Bank, an institution created by the Salvadoran government to purchase land and resell it to landless farmers.

The Land Transfer Program (PTT) was fraught with difficulties from the start. Neither the FMLN nor the government is free of blame for the problems, but most analysts place the greater responsibility for the delays in land distribution on the government side. While the FMLN did shift people between pieces of contested land in ways that undermined the process and was not always forthcoming with the necessary information, the willful incompetence of the Land Bank and the political manipulations of the government were of much more consequence. As in the case of so many of the postwar programs, the government retained almost complete control over the complicated programs in which it had little political interest. At the beginning of the land transfer process many owners signaled an interest in selling but this openness evaporated when the PTT became mired in red tape. Landlord attitudes were also affected by the vociferous opposition of a minority of owners opposed to the redistribution of land to "ex-terrorists" who were unlikely to ever pay a cent for it.[37]

The PTT was closely linked with National Reconstruction Secretariat (SRN) reconstruction programs. The SRN repeatedly blamed the delays in the PTT for the lack of dynamism in its own programs. One of the key problems facing the entire postwar economic reactivation of the former zones of conflict is that many campesinos are unconvinced that the whole package of land purchase conditions and credit, training, and technical assistance programs offers them a chance to be viable farmers. One measure of the inadequate design and implementation of the PTT and the programs of the SRN is that, in some cases, poor, landless Salvadorans have simply declined to actively participate in the program.[38]

After much wrangling over the number of potential beneficiaries, the UN General Secretary reported in August 1994 that land would be transferred to a total of 40,648 people, including former combatants of both sides and civilian occupants of contested land. By that time, only 30 percent of the beneficiaries had received land, and the process had all but ground to a halt.[39] Frustration with the inefficiency of the Land Bank had caused some landowners to withdraw their offers to sell land, and a small number had even sold land to unrelated third-parties in total violation of the Peace Accords.[40]

Another more complicated issue involves the towns occupied by repopulating communities. Some of these were included in the PTT as lands of agricultural use, but others were clearly towns before the war and, as such, were not included in the inventory of PTT land. Since the repopulating communities made a huge investment in housing and other infrastructure on these sites, the new occupants were reluctant to leave them even if the old owners refused to sell.

The government agreed in early 1995 to extend the PTT by six months but still showed little capacity to facilitate the more difficult transfers. With emotions running high on all sides, land once again threatened to become a source of violent social conflict in El Salvador.

Even if all potential PTT beneficiaries receive land, the program is not an answer to the Salvadoran land problem. The 1993 AID land tenure study makes the somewhat questionable claim that the PTT might be able to resolve the land problems of 15-20 percent of the landless and land-poor population in the Salvadoran countryside. The high level of rural landlessness ensures that, despite twelve years of civil war, El Salvador will enter the 21st century still confronting new expressions of the land problem that has disrupted national life since the arrival of the Spanish.

National Reconstruction

Agreement on the need for the implementation of a massive National Reconstruction Plan (PRN) formed one of the key economic components of the Chapultepec Accord. In early 1992, the government devised a plan calling on the international community to provide over $1.5 billion to support the restoration of war-damaged infrastructure, the reintegration of demobilized combatants from each of the opposing armies in the conflict, and the economic reactivation of the 115 municipalities considered zones of high conflict during the war. Furthermore, the PRN was explicitly mandated to promote the postwar reconciliation of the Salvadoran nation. When the FMLN joined the government in its call for support, the international community responded favorably, pledging over $800 million at a World Bank Consultative Group meeting held in March 1992 in Washington.

AID offered a $300 million package combining existing programs and new funding as its support for the PRN. Although many donors recognized the need for some sort of mechanism that shared power over the use of reconstruction funds between the government and the FMLN, AID's decision to channel its support through the government's National Reconstruction Secretariat (SRN) undermined the search for consensus.

The government-controlled program for the reconstruction of the areas where the FMLN had exerted the most influence during the war was fraught with contradictions from the beginning. One problem concerned the role of the nongovernmental organizations (NGOs) that had been active in the reconstruction target zones during the war. While the FMLN and a portion of the beneficiary population saw these NGOs as the only legitimate vehicles of economic reactivation, the government saw them as politicized vestiges of FMLN domination whose influence needed to be minimized. These NGOs had to struggle for even limited participation in the PRN while other NGOs more friendly to the government—those aligned with the conservative Salesian fathers, for example—were given massive projects to manage.[41]

At the root of the conflict was a difference in vision over the strategic orientation of the PRN. The government insisted that the plan had to be consistent with its general economic plan (i.e. structural adjustment). As a result, the government saw the PRN as an opportunity to repair the destroyed infrastructure in the ex-conflictive zones and fund a series of anti-poverty programs and training programs to accompany the Land Transfer Program. Such a plan would essentially clear the way for the market system to work its magic and restore economic activity in those areas.

An unspoken, but no less important, goal was to manage the PRN so as to minimize the political benefits accruing to the FMLN through program implementation. ARENA accomplished this by combining a sophisticated mix of decisions about organizational channeling and geographic focusing of project activity with a well-funded public relations campaign to put its stamp on every PRN project, no matter how small.

The FMLN and, especially, some of the NGOs active in the reconstruction target zones, spoke of another type of PRN. This plan would design an integral package that would go beyond infrastructure repair and poverty alleviation to promote the creation of a viable rural economy out of the ashes of the war. Implicit here was the notion that the market alone would not open the space for the populations of the ex-conflictive zones to become active agents capable of determining their own economic destinies.

Political considerations surely influenced the FMLN position, but so did the new party's historical connections to the supposed beneficiaries of the PRN. Critics of the SRN were not, however, able to advance a coherent alternative to the government approach. Even though the SRN was notably stingy with the opposition NGOs, considerable funds did reach them through nongovernmental channels. While many impressive projects were developed, the NGOs found the transition from war to peace to be a difficult one. For a variety of reasons, this alternative effort at constructing a new economy has been unable to become an effective counterweight capable of altering the course of the PRN. With the government in almost uncontested control of the PRN purse strings, the alternative vision had little chance to define itself through the process of program design and evaluation.

By the end of the Cristiani administration, the PRN was a partial success, at best. It had prevented the mass rearming of the demobilized as occurred in Nicaragua, but had failed to reintegrate them into the economy in any meaningful way.[42] Projects were underway to repair bridges and roads and restore electrical and water services, but signs of economic reactivation were much harder to locate. Delays in the Land Transfer Program had undermined any vestige of coherence in SRN programs, but the government was not without responsibility for these delays.

The Calderón Sol administration signaled its intent to promote continuity on the issue of reconstruction by reappointing the controversial and vehemently anti-FMLN Norma de Dowe as head of the SRN.[43] The FMLN, by this point, was too embroiled in its own post-election conflicts to devote the necessary attention to the issue. As the various reintegration and reactivation programs limped toward their conclusion, the government announced that it was $137 million short of the minimum funding it would need to complete even its limited reconstruction plan.[44]

AID questioned some of the claims of the Salvadoran government but admitted that the PRN faced a financial crisis. With the El Salvador budget under increasing attack in Washington, officials doubted that AID would be able to fulfill even its initial pledge to the SRN.[45]

The demands of the former combatants of the Armed Forces further complicated an already difficult situation. These veterans, grouped in the Association of Demobilized Members of the Salvadoran Armed Forces (ADEFAES), carried out a series of militant actions in January 1995 designed to secure the fulfillment of existing commitments for land and severance pay. They also insisted on inclusion in reconstruction programs of former civil defense members and others not even mentioned in the Peace Accords.

Free Trade and Regional Integration

Perhaps the dominant international economic trend of the 1990s has been the globalization of the world economy in a way that exposes all national economies to more competitive pressures. To maximize the benefits of globalization, the United States has sought to unite the Americas in a hemispheric trade bloc under its hegemony. All observers agree that, to integrate itself into an increasingly global market, Central America will need to achieve some form of economic integration among the small economies of the region.

Almost since the moment of Central American independence in 1821, regional relations have been dominated by a powerful tension between integration and competition. Regional wars have been fought over the dream of Central American unity, and periods of more emphasis of unity have consistently alternated with moments of intensified national competition.

The late-1950s marked the beginning of an integrationist impulse under the intellectual leadership of CEPAL. By the early 1960s, bilateral treaties had blossomed into the Central America Common Market (CACM), and by the end of that decade regional economic integration reached perhaps its highest point of development.[46] Although the CACM never functioned as anything more than a sort of customs union that dropped regional tariff barriers and established a uniform structure to govern third-country trade, the rapid growth of the Salvadoran manufacturing sector during the decade is often traced to the new markets opened to it by regional integration.[47]

In 1969, the outbreak of the Soccer War between El Salvador and Honduras dealt the CACM a heavy blow. The border between the two countries was temporarily closed and thousands of Salvadorans who had been farming in Honduras were forcibly returned to their country. The integrationist flame survived the 1970s, though it flickered on several occasions. The 1979 victory of the Sandinista Front in Nicaragua, however, and the subsequent appearance of the region on center stage in the East-West conflict firmly pushed the pendulum back in the direction of regional conflict.

During the 1980s, tariff barriers were restored, and restrictions were placed on the flow of people and goods across borders. At the same time, individual Central American countries pursued radically different internal macroeconomic policies. At the political level, the intent to economically isolate Nicaragua led to a distinctly anti-integrationist climate throughout the region, and, for much of the 1980s, the outbreak of full-scale regional war was a real possibility.

Seeing the economic ruin inherent in regional competition, the Central American presidents included the notion of a return to economic integration in their 1987 Esquipulas Agreement. From that point forward, the regular Presidential Summits have become the mechanism for the advance of a new process of regional integration. This trend accelerated in the late 1980s, especially in 1988 when Nicaragua was forced to adopt a structural adjustment program not radically different from that being discussed or implemented in the other countries of the region. Integration did not, however, gain full momentum until the electoral defeat of the Sandinistas in February 1990.

While treating the question of economic integration in each of their meetings, the Central American presidents first agreed, in 1991, on an Action Plan for Central America. By February 1993, a special meeting was held in San Salvador to establish the System of Central American Integration, which was followed in October 1993 by the formal signing of a Protocol to the Central American Economic Integration Treaty. The Protocol called for the formation of a customs union not unlike the common market of the 1960s with the substantial difference that the new union would not be based on protective tariffs to promote import substitution. Behind the facade of these broad international agreements stood a menage of bilateral and sub-regional accords as well as more specific operational agreements.

Given that each of the Central American countries is implementing a structural adjustment program under the tutelage of the World Bank and the IMF, regional integration naturally showed a strong neoliberal tendency. The CACM of the 1960s was a regionalized effort to create a broader internal market and hasten the replacement of imports with goods produced in Central America while integration of the 1990s promoted a coordinated "opening" of the regional economy. The new regional economy was designed to present one large, uniform market for the exports of the developed world rather than six small, differentiated ones. Such an integration suggests nothing less than regionalizing structural adjustment in the service of free trade, under the assumption that a hemisphere without trade barriers will offer the best way for the Latin American economies to produce their way out of their social problems.

Despite the rapid-fire signing ceremonies in prestigious conference centers, the integration process faces a range of short- and long-term problems. Even the earliest of the agreements to coordinate customs policies and ease the flow of goods and people across borders were plagued by very slow and uneven implementation. Administrative problems have been compounded by outright opposition from some customs officials who have become accustomed to the lucrative corruption possibilities that would be severely limited by free trade across Central American borders.[48] Even by mid-1994, only those regional agreements dealing with short-term emergencies, such as the shortages of electrical energy or basic grains were being efficiently put into place.

At a more general level, throughout Central America the move toward integration was viewed by the public with a lack of interest that bordered on apathy. The nationalism so universally fostered during the war, not regionalism, dominated popular culture. The region's political parties showed themselves to be much too embroiled in the internal disputes of their nations to develop a regional view of economic progress. This was even true in El Salvador, which has traditionally been a hotbed of support for Central American unity. Furthermore, as a small country with a large industrious population,

El Salvador's potential manufacturing strength could serve it well in an integrated Central American market, making it one of the countries with the most to gain from integration. Out of self-interest more than apathy, Costa Rica has expressed little enthusiasm for integration with its neighbors.[49] The organized social movements of the various countries were pure spectators with no tangible role in integration. This was especially true in El Salvador, where the social movements struggled to remain relevant in the implementation of the Peace Accords and the elections of 1994. After the signing of the treaty protocol on integration, the Civilian Initiative for Central American Integration released a statement saying that "the current process, like that of the 1960s, has not effectively expressed the aspirations of the majority of the population. It has also failed to assure that it will benefit that population because it has not facilitated the participation of civil society in the dynamic of integration."[50] Given the neoliberal orientation of integration, the isolation of the social movements can be no surprise.

Perhaps the most vexing problem for integration, however, concerns the relationship between a new Central American common market and hemispheric free trade. The October 1993 Integration Protocol was signed even as the U.S. Congress debated the North American Free Trade Agreement (NAFTA). The Central American presidents quite consciously sought to take steps to put their economic house in order so that they might be extended the same privileges given to Mexico under NAFTA. Under the prevailing wisdom about the need to export their way out of poverty, linking up to NAFTA was seen as the only game in town. The risks of linkage for a small economy like El Salvador were seen as minimal compared to the risks of being left out in the cold, without access to the giant markets of the North.

The annual meeting of the Caribbean Basin Initiative occurred literally days after the approval of NAFTA by the U.S. Congress. In that context, the Central American presidents approached President Clinton about the possibility of the inclusion of their countries in the new initiative. All they could get was a commitment to "a serious study" about how such integration could occur in a gradual and realistic way.[51] It was soon clear that Central America was being offered free trade, but not the version being extended to Mexico and Canada through NAFTA. According to economist Luís Galicia of the Association for the Advancement of the Social Scientists, the chances of Central American inclusion in NAFTA are almost nil. "In Latin America the tendency is to integrate with the northern bloc, but this will be very difficult. Only a country with a strong economy like Chile has managed to do so after a two-year wait. This means it will be difficult for Central America."[52]

The dispute over the El Salvador's textile exports to the United States indicate the limits of the sort of free trade offered to countries like El Salvador. Because of the rapid expansion of *maquila* production in El Salvador, textile exports to the United States increased rapidly in the early 1990s. In a complaint filed in Geneva under the General Agreement on Trade and Tariffs (GATT), the U.S. government sought to establish a quota on Salvadoran cotton and synthetic shirts because those products were "disorganizing its [the United States'] market."

The Textile Oversight Organization found in favor of El Salvador, thereby denying the validity of the U.S. request. Of course the GATT cannot obligate the United States to refrain from placing a quota on Salvadoran shirts (a quota was in place at the time of the GATT finding): it only makes recommendations in such cases. The United States can abide by the GATT finding, eliminate the quota, and then simply remove the shirts from the list of products which can enter the United States under preferential terms under the General System of Preferences. In this case, the United States is protesting the results of one of structural adjustment's most cherished economic activities—*maquilas*. Central America may be integrating its economies to promote free trade only to find that trade might not be as free as it expected.

In their summit meeting held August 20, 1994, in Costa Rica, the Central American presidents for the first time showed a glimmer of realization that all-out integration into the emerging, U.S.-dominated free-trade bloc might not be the only goal worth pursuing. In the Declaration of Guácimo signed at that meeting, the presidents agreed on the need to review the form in which commercial agreements were constructed so as to achieve not only competitiveness, but also more social well-being. They recognized the absolute necessity of being part of economic blocs, but allowed themselves to wonder whether or not such integration was possible given that most of the economies of the region have lived a "lost decade" of cruel and costly armed conflicts.[53]

The declaration did not present specific measures to restructure regional integration or make structural adjustment compatible with social welfare, but it at least placed those questions on the regional agenda. The presence of critics of structural adjustment like President Reina of Honduras apparently opened the space for a discussion of integration as it is posed by Costa Rica-based political scientist Franz Hinckelammert: "Will integration be an agreement of the chickens to protect themselves from the fox; or an agreement of chickens designed by the fox so that he might eat a chicken each day?"[54]

New Popular Economy

Much discussion of the legacy of the war centers on the social and economic experiences of the people living in refugee camps, displaced communities, and the resettled communities of the former conflictive zones. One analyst coined the term "new popular economy" to refer to these experiences, which involved highly cooperative, sometimes collective, forms of social and economic organization.[55]

After the end of the war, the FMLN hoped that these organizational experiences, combined with the resources forthcoming from the Peace Accords would serve as the basis for the formation of dynamic local and regional economic systems. In time, these alternative efforts would be able to form links with other sectors such as the agrarian reform cooperative sector and organized urban consumers and producers to create an alternative economy that could challenge the hegemony of structural adjustment from the grassroots.

This optimistic view encountered a series of problems at the war's end. The first problem concerned the organization of the new popular economy. Although the people in the former conflictive zones—the presumed beneficiaries of the PRN—were highly organized, they were not organized to rapidly expand production in economic terms. They were organized for survival in war, not production in peace. The vast organizational experience accumulated during the war did not prove to be automatically or easily transferable to the postwar productive challenges.

To make matters worse, chaos reigned for the first eighteen months after the war's end as people moved all over the country to qualify for reconstruction programs and to locate themselves on the best possible land. For example, groups of campesinos moved from Chalatenango to southern San Vicente to take advantage of plentiful and productive land, then moved back when they encountered the coastal heat, mosquitoes and isolation. Each arrival and departure meant more productive dislocation and organizational problems.

The question of incentives—closely related to organization—also presented a challenge after the end of the war. During the war, the "common enemy" provided a powerful incentive for personal sacrifice that was constantly enforced by the close-knit, collective structure of community life. At the same time, since months of production could be destroyed in a five-minute army incursion, the incentive for productive agricultural work was not strong. At the community level, people worked hard based on moral incentives but the connection between productive work and material improvement—for either the community or the individual—was weakened.

The end of the war removed the incentive of the common enemy and relieved the necessity of close-knit collective structures. The old incentives were gone, but what was to replace them? Communities struggled to find a new combination of moral and material incentives that would encourage a new community or family ethic of productive work. After years of sacrifice, however, people wanted material improvements rather than more sacrifice and did not necessarily see the connection between the two. All efforts to increase production in the new popular economy confronted a serious problem of work incentives.[56]

The resources made available by the PRN and by international NGOs did not help smooth the transition in all cases. Despite the persistence of poverty, the primary problem of the new popular economy was not resources but the way in which resources were used and the economy's capacity to use or absorb external resources.

Land, the key resource acquired through the peace process, caused constant problems. Agricultural communities without clear title to land are seldom productive places, and rural El Salvador proved to be no exception. Three years after the signing of the Peace Accords, half of the recognized beneficiaries of the Land Transfer were still waiting for their land.

In many cases, the international organizations that had subsidized the new popular economy in wartime extended their commitments by approving relatively large development projects designed to jump-start postwar development. To their credit, international agencies in 1992 and 1993 provided as much as $25 million in reconstruction projects channeled through NGOs rather than the government reconstruction program. While many of these projects were adequately conceived on paper, conditions in the former zones of conflict seldom conformed to traditional development assumptions. Apart from the local organizational and incentive problems outlined above, the Salvadoran NGOs receiving project funds often had little experience with such projects and, hence, limited capacity to carry them out.[57] In retrospect, the international NGOs acknowledge that they may have underestimated the complexity of the transition from the survival economy of the war, to a subsistence economy of reconstruction, to an expanding economy with real development possibilities.[58]

Similarly, the many coordination problems of the government reconstruction program became, in essence, more obstacles in the path of the new popular economy (See National Reconstruction). For example, government programs that paid former combatants to attend postwar training courses met immediate economic needs but seriously aggravated the incentive problems outlined above. Agricultural credits that arrived after the planting season were useless from a production perspective. The government never intended to use reconstruction money to subsidize the efforts of the program beneficiaries to become a viable productive sector, so it should surprise no one that they did not do so.[59]

By January 1995 communities had stabilized considerably. Based on that stability, people began to seek an alternative productive organization that would allow them to take advantage of the land and other resources to which they had access. In doing so, they constructed housing, cultivated increasing amounts of land, and restored local social and productive infrastructure. They also took the time to evaluate their first postwar economic experiences, and plotted new courses of action, when necessary.[60] Although the new popular economy remained a diverse experiment, a few general tendencies began to emerge. Credit systems, often administered through informal means at the local or regional level, replaced donations as the motor force of the economy. The economy increasingly became a mixture of individual and cooperative forms of property with most production carried out by family units cooperating in the purchase of outputs or the marketing of production. While production of staple crops such as corn and beans continued to form the base of the economy, efforts at productive diversification increased dramatically. Finally, the wartime emphasis on individual communities organized for their own survival gave way to a more regional orientation in which interdependent communities seek the most efficient way to fit into emerging regional economies.

In the face of the difficult realities facing the new popular economy, much of the baggage of the great expectations of others was removed from the shoulders of the men and women trying to build new lives in El Salvador's former zones of conflict. By the mid-1990s few external observers identified the new popular economy as the beacon of an alternative, "bottom-up" vision of economic life for the entire country.

There is reason to expect that, given time and ongoing national and international support, the economic experiments underway in El Salvador's former conflictive zones will develop sufficiently to survive and facilitate the dignified productive integration of some percentage of those campesinos most affected by the conflict. In the political and economic context of El Salvador in the mid-1990s, that would be no small victory.

Uncertain Economic Prospects

Notwithstanding the optimistic pronouncements of government officials, the economic news from El Salvador is not all rosy. Important macroeconomic indicators have taken a more stable path and economic activity has increased dramatically, but these changes are based on factors like foreign aid, family remittances, and the reversal of the capital flight of the 1980s, which may turn out to be transitory factors. Economic growth has been centered in trade, services, and construction, each one a shaky pillar for a lasting recovery. The anticipated postwar investment boom has not materialized, giving this consumption and import-led expansion an even more contingent character.

Contingent or not, the economic improvement has had a positive impact on the lives of some Salvadorans, and this improvement was one of many factors that benefited the ARENA party at the polls in 1994. Structural adjustment has, nonetheless, aggravated the already critical condition of the country's poorest sectors, but probably not as much as it might have in the absence of foreign aid to antipoverty programs and reconstruction programs and the stream of money orders from relatives in the United States.

Despite the antistatist orientation of structural adjustment, deficit spending by government has been another important stimulating factor. In the absence of increased tax income, government deficits have been financed by external borrowing. The country's debt burden remains mild, relative to that of some of its Latin American neighbors, but debt service is bound to become more of an issue as the grace periods on the current massive round of borrowing begin to expire.

From the first days of the Calderón Sol administration, economic policy reflected an awareness that the policies of the Cristiani years would not succeed in the long run. Rumors of a plan to deepen structural adjustment by more radically opening the nation's economy appeared in the latter part of 1994 but were quickly denied by the government. In January 1995, the Calderón Sol administration unveiled a plan that confirmed its sense of the limits of structural adjustment as implemented to that point. Based on the notion that Salvadoran capital had not answered the call to revitalize agriculture and industry, the new plan looked to foreign capital as the salvation of the national economy.

By proposing a rapid withdrawal of restrictive tariffs on imported goods and a fixed exchange rate between the dollar and the Salvadoran colón, the plan's creators hoped to make El Salvador a new platform for foreign productive investment. The president of Honduras suggested that El Salvador wanted to make itself the "Hong Kong of Central America."[61]

Privatization of the largest state-owned enterprises (phone, water, electricity) and an increase of the IVA to 15 percent constituted the other two pillars of the new plan. Symbolically, the plan was first publicized by Enrique Hinds, a Salvadoran working at the time as a World Bank consultant. Hinds was quickly named El Salvador's Treasury Minister.

The plan had something for almost everyone to oppose. Workers took to the streets to oppose privatization, which they insisted would cost jobs and benefit only the purchasers of the government resources. Producers, from small farmers and industrialists, feared that a rapid decrease in tariffs would unfairly expose them to foreign competition. Nearly all sectors opposed the economic burden represented by a further increase in the IVA, and even the Central American presidents rebuffed Calderón Sol's plan on the grounds that it would endanger the entire process of regional integration by proposing a tariff-reduction schedule that the other Central American countries could not accept.[62] Only those sectors heavily involved in commerce and trade spoke in favor of the plan.[63]

The fierce opposition to the plan caused major changes by the time Calderón Sol presented it on national radio and TV in early February 1995.[64] While the government insisted on the necessity of a higher IVA, the Central Bank delayed the implementation of the fixed exchange rate and the pace of tariff reduction was slowed somewhat.[65] Notwithstanding these concessions to Salvadoran business, the Calderón Sol administration had put the country and the entire Central American region on notice that it was ready to replace a strategy of export promotion that had shown only sluggish results with a strategy of foreign-investment promotion based on a radical opening of the economy.[66]

Is There An Alternative?

Midway through the 1990s the neoliberal vision of structural adjustment continued to exert virtual hegemony over the economies of El Salvador and the rest of the Central American countries. In El Salvador, ARENA, the party of unbridled neoliberalism won a landslide electoral victory that will leave it in power at least through 1999. Even in those cases where a critical opposition was able to defeat parties tied to neoliberalism, implementing truly alternative policies proved to be difficult because of the pressure to maintain good relations with the IMF and the World Bank.[67] Access to multilateral financing became the single most important determinant of the success or failure of domestic economic policy.

In El Salvador, the electoral coalition led by the FMLN never offered any comprehensive alternative to the policy that had made Alfredo Cristiani a model neoliberal. Presidential candidate Rubén Zamora spoke of renegotiating elements of the country's relationship with the multilateral lenders, but his political coalition went to great lengths to assure the business community and the general public that there would be no break with the broad outlines of structural adjustment. The World Bank showed an almost arrogant confidence in the continuity of adjustment regardless of who won the elections.[68]

All signs pointed to a deepening of the country's structural adjustment experiment in the wake of ARENA's resounding victory. Although one key proposal, the fixed dollar-colón exchange rate, runs counter to certain tenets of structural adjustment, the economic reform plan presented by Calderón Sol in early 1995 represents just such an intensification of structural adjustment. The relative hegemony of neoliberal policy does not, however, mean that all opposition to it has evaporated. To the extent that neoliberal economic policy has worsened conditions of those citizens not in a position to shake the invisible hand of the market, it has been met by popular opposition. Such opposition has taken several forms and has often altered the forms taken by structural adjustment.

The inclusion of a social compensation component in structural adjustment programs also failed to halt opposition to them. The band-aid approaches of poverty-alleviation programs like the FIS were not sufficient to smooth the transition to a market economy. When citizens began to express their anger with economic reform by rejecting governments identified with such policies, the rhetoric of poverty alleviation and social compensation began to shift to social reform.

The aforementioned 1993 conference sponsored by the IDB and the UNDP in Washington was designed explicitly to bring home the point that economic reforms might never reduce poverty levels in Latin America unless they are combined with long-range investments in human capital. This lesson was well integrated into the 1994 election campaign of ARENA in which the party endlessly emphasized its commitment to increase spending in health and education through programs like Education with Community Participation (EDUCO) (See Schools and Students). ARENA's "Governmental Plan: 1994-99" emphasized social reform, and the concept was even elevated to the title of FUSADES' economic plan in 1994.[69] One-half of the three-year, $1 billion loan approved for El Salvador by the IDB in mid-1994 was destined to support social investments, while the other half was for modernization of the Salvadoran state. At the Central American summit in San Salvador in March 1995, President Calderón Sol committed his government to devote one half of its total budget to social spending by the end of the decade, nearly doubling the 1995 percentage.

In El Salvador, another type of opposition to structural adjustment arose directly from the experience of the war, and involved the attempt to erect local and regional economic alternatives driven directly by the needs of the country's rural and urban poor. Especially, but not exclusively, in the areas of the country where FMLN influence was greatest, circumstances forced residents to develop new forms of social and productive organization as a survival strategy.

The postwar effort to turn this survival strategy into the basis for a "new popular economy" has run straight into a neoliberal central government that sees only the need to reintegrate those who have been outside the market economy back into the mainstream. In addition, efforts to stimulate this economy have had to confront a complex transition at the community level from the war economy of survival to a viable peacetime economy with vastly different organizational demands.

The new popular economy involves only a very small sector of the Salvadoran population. Despite its reduced size and the myriad difficulties that face it, the movement for alternative forms of economic development continues to be an important source of opposition to the neoliberal steamroller in El Salvador. While it cannot be expected to pose a comprehensive national alternative to structural adjustment, it at least offers the possibility of some local and regional economic options for poor Salvadorans.

In El Salvador as in the rest of Latin America, the work of economists in academic research institutes has had some impact on the debate around economic reform policies. Institutions like CENITEC, FUNDE, and the economics faculties of the University of El Salvador and the Central American University have all advanced serious critiques of structural adjustment.[70] In general, these critiques recognize the need to modernize the state and develop a new vision of decentralized, participatory public service, but they tend to accord the state a broader social and economic role than is envisioned in the neoliberal model. Furthermore, the critics emphasize the importance of developing the country's export sector but insist that real "comparative advantages" can only emerge from a productive sector producing for a vibrant internal market. Finally, most critics applaud the renewed emphasis on investment in human capital, but call for cuts in unnecessary defense spending and increased income taxes on the wealthy to fund that investment rather than massive borrowing from international lenders.[71]

Perhaps the most trenchant critique of structural adjustment emphasizes that the war has done little to change an extreme division of the economic product into wages, profits, and taxes in El Salvador. By any measure, the owners of capital in El Salvador end up with an extraordinary amount of the national product in the form of profit and rent.[72] Without reforms that allow workers to demand and receive a larger share of the national pie, no growth will effectively combat poverty.[73] In addition, according to this argument, the "export and get rich" thrust of neoliberalism will always appear sensible simply because most people do not have enough disposable income to make production for the home market worthwhile.

In the first three years after the Peace Accords, few structural changes in the Salvadoran economy occurred to the benefit of the country's poor majority. With powerful international pressures pushing the country in the direction of further neoliberal reforms and the ARENA party firmly in control of the government, El Salvador is likely to continue on the path of World Bank-style structural adjustment for at least the rest of this century.

Since more privatization and reforms opening El Salvador to the international market are likely to negatively affect most Salvadorans who lack direct access to the benefits of economic growth, popular opposition to neoliberal policy is likely to grow. Whether or not popular opposition will be able to alter national economic policy will depend on the level of unity and the organizing capacity of the popular movement (See Social Organizations and the Popular Movement).

Such changes will also depend on the response of the government to popular initiatives. The ARENA government will be offered choices between a path of dialogue and inclusion in the formulation of economic policy, and the traditional path of exclusionary politics in which the ruling party and its allies determine the economic policy of the nation. Those choices will reveal the extent to which the democratic opening achieved by the Peace Accords was sufficient to bring about gradual structural changes in the Salvadoran economy.

Society and Social Policy

San Salvador's gigantic Central Market dominates the
national informal economy.

Schools and Students

The prestigious journal *Estudios Centroamericanos* undertook a comprehensive study of the Salvadoran educational system on the occasion of the tenth anniversary of the ambitious educational reform of 1968. That study found a system that, despite the infusion of unprecedented economic resources, remained grossly inequitable and highly inefficient.[1] Furthermore, the study noted that the goals of educating the nation's youth were on the verge of disappearing in the social and economic crisis that was about to plunge the country into civil war.

From a variety of perspectives, the educational system became a battleground in that war. Students and teachers of all levels stood in the forefront of the social movements that eventually became the revolutionary movement.[2] The military closed the National University (UES) at several points during the 1980s (most notably for the entire period 1980-84) and several military confrontations actually took place on the campus. In the conflictive rural areas of the country, the public educational system ceased to function and hundreds of schools were destroyed in the fighting.[3] Finally, the budget for public education was gutted as state monies flowed to the war effort.

If the educational system was in trouble in 1978, it emerged from the war in a desperate state. Everyone in the country, including the business sector, called on the government to devote resources to both rebuilding and reforming the educational system. The ARENA party made such reform a cornerstone of its 1994 electoral campaign.

Educational System

The structure of the Salvadoran public educational system is similar to that of other Latin American countries. Four levels of instruction are offered: *parvularia* (ages 4-6), *básica* (primary education, through ninth grade), *media* (grades 10-12), and *superior* (higher education).

A private educational system also provides education to students of all levels. The percentage of students attending private schools grew rapidly during the war, especially at the secondary and university level. By 1992, over two-thirds of university students were attending private universities.[4]

Although the importance of preschool education is universally acknowledged, *parvularia* is seen as something of a luxury in El Salvador. In 1990, these schools enrolled only 3.3 percent of public school students and little coverage existed outside of urban areas.

The overwhelming majority of the one million children who attend school—86 percent—are enrolled in primary schools. In 1992, the average primary school teacher had a class of 41 students.[5] Most teachers relied on pedagogical methods emphasizing verbal and written repetition. Textbooks, where available, were often so old as to be irrelevant and in terrible condition.

For a combination of reasons, 15 percent of Salvadoran children never attend school at all. For many, there is no functioning school near their home; others are kept away by the increasing cost of education. While tuition is not charged at public schools, registration fees are increasingly common and students are required to buy school supplies and uniforms. Faced with the burden of paying significant amounts of money to send children to inadequate schools, many parents keep their children home or send them to work, instead.

Those children that do attend school show astounding drop-out rates. Half of all entering students have dropped out by the sixth grade, two-thirds fail to finish the ninth grade, and only 18 percent of the students that enter first grade graduate from secondary school.[6] A 1989 study by CENITEC finds that two causes lead to a majority of primary school drop-outs: health and nutrition problems cause students to lose too much time to catch up, and economic problems cause parents to send the students to work.[7] Only one-quarter of Salvadorans over the age of 15 have completed sixth grade.

Rural areas had always been underserved by the educational system, but the complete withdrawal of educational services from entire areas of the country during the war exacerbated this problem. All indices of school attendance and achievement show significant gaps between rural and urban children. At the war's end, the index of rural illiteracy was more than double that of urban areas. Rural women working in the home showed an illiteracy rate of 58 percent.

At the secondary level, eleven separate tracks (one academic and ten vocational) lead to the *bachiller* certificate. All of the tracks include a common core of general education in Spanish language and literature, English, mathematics, sciences, social studies, and art.

Postsecondary education offers several options for the tiny minority of students that qualify. Less than a fifth of all students make it from first grade through high school, and no more than a fifth of secondary graduates finish college. The government administers nine technological institutes throughout the country that train teachers and technical specialists, as well as a national school of agriculture and one for physical education and sports. The military operates its own school (*Escuela Militár*), a school of nursing, and a school of higher education that is essentially a military university.

Striking changes have occurred in higher education. Until 1965 the country had only one university, the UES. The Central American University (UCA) was established in 1965—consciously as a political counterweight to the leftist influence of the UES—under the leadership of the Jesuit order. At that time a procedure was established for accreditation of private universities, and by 1980 four new universities were recognized by the Ministry of Education.

After the 1980 closing of the UES, numerous private universities sprang up almost overnight to fill the gap. By 1992 there were 36 private universities and several more were in the process of accreditation. The UCA sets the standards for academic excellence in El Salvador, and some of the other private universities, such as the Albert Einstein and the José Matias Delgado, are fine universities with excellent facilities. Many, however, are of dubious quality. There is no standardized set of course requirements for degree programs. Each university sets the curriculum and requirements for its various degree programs.

UCA and the National University

Although the UCA parted political company with the Salvadoran government over the teachers' strike in 1972, the quality of its academic programs continued to attract many students from the more privileged sectors of Salvadoran society. While the war was still in progress, noted theologian Jon Sobrino suggested that the majority of UCA students probably supported ARENA. The administration put in place a series of scholarship programs and sliding fee arrangements to increase access to poor Salvadorans, but most were excluded by the university's academic requirements. Despite the relatively conservative nature of its student body, the UCA came under increasing fire during the 1980s for the critical nature of its faculty publications—such as *Proceso*, *Carta a las Iglesias*, and *Estudios Centroamericanos*. The UCA publishing house continued to release texts by Jesuits and other writers that the government considered subversive. Perhaps most irritating to the extreme right was the consistent public support of UCA leaders like Ignacio Ellacuría for a negotiated solution to the armed conflict. Despite its political problems and the frequent attacks on its campus by the extreme right, the UCA continued to set the standard for academic excellence in El Salvador throughout the war. The 1989 attack in which members of the elite Atlacatl Battalion killed six Jesuits, their housekeeper, and her daughter on the UCA campus tore the academic and institutional heart out of the university.

In the aftermath of the killings, those who remained dedicated themselves to the rebuilding of the university. An unprecedented outpouring of local and international support—in both material and human resources—allowed for some degree of institutional stabilization in the early 1990s. By early 1995 the inauguration of new programs and facilities, including a heralded new program in public health, suggested that the UCA had regained much of its institutional stature within Salvadoran higher education. Many observe, however, that the UCA has not yet regained the prophetic voice it had in Salvadoran society before 1989, pointing out that finding that voice is not merely a matter of new buildings and administrative stability.

The attractive campus and modern facilities of the UCA stand in stark contrast to the deteriorated *Ciudad Universitaria* that houses the National University. Those buildings that were not damaged in one or another military incursion into the campus were destroyed by the 1986 earthquake. Lack of basic maintenance also took its toll during the long years when the government hoped to strangle the UES by limiting its budget. The similarities between the UES and the rural zones of conflict is no coincidence, as both were considered during wartime as enemy areas by the Salvadoran government and military. The UES may be the most thoroughly and frequently sacked university in the world.

Because of its modest fee structure, the UES is less economically exclusive than the UCA or any of the other private universities. It also maintains compensatory academic programs as a means of helping students meet academic entrance requirements. Despite these programs, the small percentage of Salvadoran students graduating from secondary school assures that only a tiny fraction of Salvadoran youth have access to an institution like the UES. The war totally disrupted the institutional life of the university, and its survival is one of the curiosities of the conflict. The grounds of the university were used as a base of operations by the FMLN during the November 1989 offensive, and the top floor of the Medical School still bears a reminder of that time—a gaping hole caused by a rocket fired from a plane during the armed assault on the campus. After the offensive the campus was sealed off and occupied by soldiers of the neighboring First Brigade. The occupying forces further damaged the facilities and removed anything of value. Most observers expected that the UES would be closed for years as it had been in 1980.

The university continued to function in a limited manner in buildings rented throughout San Salvador, and students and university authorities began a campaign to force the Armed Forces to reopen the campus. By June 1990 the campus was back in the hands of the university administration, and workers and students joined in the massive clean-up job. Such episodes indicate a tremendous institutional survival instinct, but they also greatly undermined the functioning of the UES as an educational institution.

The complexity of internal politics at the UES presents another barrier to institutional recovery. The war turned the UES into a battleground for the different ideological and political interests that coexisted within the FMLN. Whereas the administration of the UCA expressly prohibited politically oriented worker and student organizations within that university, each of the five parties of the FMLN organized actively and successfully within the UES. The organizational ferment assured that every wall of the university would be jammed with political graffiti and presented a great challenge to the intelligence organs of the state. This complexity also rendered the UES all but ungovernable for its internal authorities.

In this context of physical and institutional deterioration, the size of the student body dropped drastically, and the numbers of graduates declined even more dramatically. The disruption reached the point where it took an average of ten years to complete the five-year undergraduate program in economics, and the vast majority of students never completed their degrees at all.

Amidst the chaos, many dedicated individuals were able to maintain innovative programs like the training of popular educators and programs to measure the psychological impact of the war on Salvadoran children. Through the worst of the war years, the university continued to serve an important social function.

Dr. Fabio Castillo, a former rector of the UES and member of the short-lived reform government of the 1960s, returned from exile in Costa Rica to become rector of the UES in 1992. While fighting with the government for budget increases and a full recognition of the importance of the UES to the nation, Castillo also undertook an ambitious internal reform of the university. The reform aimed to simultaneously rebuild the university's physical infrastructure, modernize its curriculum, and streamline its administration.

Major infrastructural improvements like the new library built with funds from the Spanish government stand as monuments to Castillo's successes. At the same time, the reform plan has continued to face the same debilitating internal divisions that hampered university governance during the war. By early 1995, as Castillo campaigned for reelection against his vice-rector and several other candidates, the UES still struggled to assume its critical role as the sole provider of public higher education in postwar El Salvador.

As political progressives fought among themselves for control of the university, more conservative groups and individuals gained increasing influence within the UES. Such groups, which always existed but had little voice during the war, see the salvation of the UES in an abandonment of leftist recipes concerning the "social function of the university" in favor of improved relations with the government and the private sector. They see university reform in terms of tailoring university programs to the needs of the private sector in a changing economic environment. Adherents of such a market-driven view of the university achieved postwar changes in such important departments as economics and medicine. If those who promise a renovation of the university based on a continuing commitment to the poor majority of Salvadoran society are not able to speak with a single voice, the UES may enter the twenty-first century a very different type of educational institution.

Popular Education

The term *educación popular* is used in El Salvador to describe two overlapping, but quite different experiences. On the one hand, the alternative education system that grew up in the country's conflictive zones during the war is called the popular education system. On the other, popular education also refers to an alternative educational method used by educators in formal and informal educational contexts all over El Salvador. Both are important forces in the Salvadoran educational system.

The popular educational system emerged after the state withdrew educational services from large areas of the country. Although it existed before the repopulation movements of the late 1980s, the return of large numbers of refugees and displaced people to the conflictive zones led to a major expansion of that system.

During the war, popular education in places like eastern Chalatenango and northern Morazán relied on the efforts of large numbers of volunteer teachers, usually from the communities. These popular educators, often with no more than a third grade education themselves, taught local children with little in the way of teaching materials or school supplies. Educational quality was uneven and the war and other emergencies constantly interrupted class schedules. Nonetheless, the system represented a valiant effort to address the educational needs of thousands of rural children.

By the war's end, international support and the continued commitment of local teachers had allowed the popular education system to grow and achieve some level of institutionalization. By 1992, in the department of Chalatenango, 177 teachers were giving classes to 3100 primary school students. Of these teachers, 79 percent were under 25 years old, and 94 percent had a sixth grade education or less.[8] Because of funds received from the German Catholic Church through MISEREOR and from other international donors, popular teachers in Chalatenango were receiving a 200 colon ($23) monthly stipend. Other large systems existed in Cabañas and Morazán, and smaller coordinations were scattered throughout the former zones of conflict. After the signing of the Peace Accords, the government sought to reestablish its institutional presence throughout the country. The reentry of the Ministry of Education into zones previously served by popular schools meant a major challenge to the alternative system.

Popular teachers are painfully aware of the economic limitations of the popular education system and of their own need for further training. They want the Education Ministry to take economic responsibility for the schooling of all children, while insisting that those who have been doing the teaching be recognized as formal parts of whatever new system evolves. The ministry uses the lack of academic qualifications of the popular teachers as a pretext for not recognizing them, but it also needs the services of the popular schools since government resources do not exist to wholly replace the alternative system. Many educators fear that the national system will supplant the popular system only to revert to the traditional pattern of providing no resources for education in these areas of El Salvador.[9] While the relation of the popular schools to the national system remains in doubt, the popular teachers continue to accumulate experience and training and thousands of children continue to receive an education they would otherwise be without.

As explained above, popular education in El Salvador also refers to practitioners of an alternative educational methodology emphasizing democratic and participatory forms of teaching.[10] This method seeks to break down traditional distinctions between students and teachers, making the students more active participants in their own education. It also seeks to tailor education to the cultural experience of the student. Many social organizations adopted this approach in El Salvador, especially those connected to the cooperative movement, and it served as the basis for the formation of several organizations committed to eradicating illiteracy.[11]

Perhaps the most influential popular education group in El Salvador is Equipo de Maíz. Maíz originated in the early 1980s from a group of activists in the Christian base community movement who saw the need for more community education that could actively involve people in the topics under discussion. Members of the group went to Mexico to learn from the popular education experiences in that country. When they attempted a wholesale transfer of those methods to their work in El Salvador, they failed miserably because they were adopting methods developed by others for Mexican, rather than Salvadoran, campesinos. Nonetheless, the experience sparked a long process of trial and error that has resulted in a highly effective educational program. That Maíz was able to do this work in the context of wartime repression speaks to the group's single-minded focus on education for its own sake.[12]

Maíz publishes short pamphlets on key national issues that minimize the use of text in favor of entertaining cartoons. In addition, the group organizes an annual series of educational workshops that are held all over the country. Perhaps the most influential of these workshops is a semiannual series of music workshops in which participants learn church music in relation to a particular social theme. Over its ten years of operation, Maíz has succeeded in creating a community of popular educators with considerable influence at the national level. Unfortunately, experiences like that of Maíz have had much more influence in the area of informal education than in the pedagogical approach in the public schools, which continues to be criticized for its authoritarianism and lack of creativity.

Educational Reform

Everyone in El Salvador agrees that the educational system is in profound crisis and needs to be reformed. The 1994 elections saw little debate on educational policy, however, as all parties advocated more funds for education as part of a reinvigoration of the social services neglected during the war. The government, through clever use of the mass media, presented itself as the party that would guarantee education to all Salvadorans.

In the early 1990s, the ARENA government embarked on an ambitious educational reform generously supported by AID, the World Bank, the IDB, and other donors. The reform seeks to achieve three primary goals: improved administration of public education funds; broadened coverage to reach more students; and major improvements in the quality of education, especially primary education.

Key programmatic initiatives include the Program to Reform the Ministry of Education, Education with Community Participation (EDUCO), and Solidifying Salvadoran Primary Education (SABE). The reform of the ministry is designed to reduce bureaucratization by modernizing administrative controls and decentralizing educational decision-making to the local level. EDUCO provides funds for local education associations to hire teachers in underserved areas of the country.[13] SABE received $33 million through 1995 to do everything from reconstructing primary schools to reforming curricula.

While significant amounts of money flow into programs like SABE and EDUCO, these are still tiny programs relative to the problems they are designed to confront. EDUCO may look good on paper, but the program is known to suffer a huge dropout rate and promises no long-term solution to rural education problems. In the 1995 budget, education receives 15 percent of the national budget. This remains less than the 17 percent dedicated to education in 1990, the year following the November offensive of the FMLN, and far below the 23 percent appropriated for education in 1980. The 1995 budget amounts to less than $200 million for more than a million students. Without a truly massive budgetary increase, all efforts at administrative reform look more like political campaigning than real educational change.

Cristiani's Minister of Education, Cecilia Gallardo de Cano retained her position in the Calderón Sol administration. While she has made important improvements in the administration of the education budget, her main claim to fame is that she has been able to defuse the demands of ANDES 21 de Junio, the national teachers' union, and keep labor unrest at a minimum. ANDES opposes the ARENA reform saying that it is little more than a cover for the privatization of the public schools, and that the proposals for putting decision-making in the hands of parents' groups is designed to pit the parents against the teachers. ANDES president Jorge Villegas agrees that reform is necessary, but rejects ARENA's notion of reform as overly politicized and inadequate.[14]

Health and Welfare

With the war over, one of the key threats to the health of the Salvadoran people became a thing of the past. Most people, however, continued to live in a terribly unhealthy environment. Sewage runs openly alongside the homes of hundreds of thousands of people living in the marginal areas around San Salvador and the other main cities. Most rural children grow up playing in the same dirt occupied by pigs, chickens, and other animals. Even during the war, easily treatable diseases like measles, intestinal disorders, and upper respiratory ailments claimed more lives than the bombs and the bullets.

Each year, at the beginning of the rainy season, the incidence of intestinal diseases skyrockets as the rains wash the refuse of the dry season into the drinking water system. For relatively healthy Salvadorans, the *mal de mayo* is no more than a minor inconvenience, cured by any one of a number of products hawked through special *mal de mayo* advertisements on television. But these seasonal intestinal disorders present a quiet death sentence to untold numbers of children without access to safe drinking water or adequate health care.

The deadly disease of cholera was thought to have been eradicated throughout Latin America by the sanitary improvements of the late-20th century. The disease made an unexpected return to Peru in 1990, and, by August 1991, the first cases had been confirmed in El Salvador. By the time of the signing of the Peace Accords in January 1992, over two thousand cases had been officially confirmed and fourteen deaths reported. With the help of the French NGO, Medecins sans Frontiers (Doctors Without Borders), Rosales Hospital established a special cholera ward and several tents for actively symptomatic patients. By late 1992 the Ministry of Health reported that the epidemic was "under control," but as of January 1995, major outbreaks were still being reported and cholera continued to claim victims.

Salvadoran Health System

Article 65 of the Salvadoran Constitution makes the government responsible for overseeing national health policies and preserving and protecting the health of the population. That mandate remains an unfulfilled promise for many Salvadorans. Those with access to resources have always been able to pay for excellent private care in the cities, but the urban poor and those living in rural areas have suffered both preindustrial sanitary conditions and grossly inadequate health services.

As in the case of education, the wartime withdrawal of health services from as much as one-third of the national territory worsened an already critical situation for the inhabitants of those areas. Salvadoran officials point to improvements in social indicators like life expectancy and infant mortality during the period 1970-90 as evidence of the achievements of the state health service. Although such indicators do suggest real changes, in relative terms, El Salvador may be less healthy than in 1970. According to the Human Development Index developed by the UNDP to compare general living conditions across all countries, El Salvador is rated 112th among the 173 countries in the world for which the index is kept.[15] In Latin America, only Bolivia, Haiti, and Honduras place lower on that human development scale than El Salvador.

In the aftermath of the war, AID, the World Bank, the IDB, and other international organizations commissioned a group of experts to study the Salvadoran health system. The group, called ANSAL, concluded that the health system, despite its ability to make some important improvements in particular areas, needed drastic reforms to make it more equitable and efficient.[16] At the bottom line "under the current system, half of all children of future generations will suffer illnesses linked to poverty, which will limit their development."[17]

The institutions that provide health care in El Salvador are changing rapidly even as government leaders, international donors, and the country's civil society debate how to reform them. Most Salvadorans who receive health care are served by some public institution.[18] The largest of these institutions is the Ministry of Health, which provides primary health care through 360 clinics and health posts located around the country. Thirty regional hospitals and health centers provide a secondary level of care, and three large national hospitals—the Rosales, a huge general hospital; the Bloom for children; and the Maternity Hospital for women—provide the most sophisticated treatment available in the public system.

Rosales is the hospital of last resort for most Salvadorans; it is generally considered to be a medical nightmare.[19] Excess demand requires that two patients are assigned to each bed; medicines are only sporadically available; and sanitary conditions are nothing less than scandalous.[20] The first step in the treatment of a patient with any resources at all is to remove them from Rosales immediately.[21] Despite a Ministry of Health budget that devotes three-fourths of its resources to hospitals and health centers, Rosales suffers chronic budgetary crises. The 360 primary care centers receive only 25 percent of the budget so the solution is not to be found in simply channeling more money to the hospitals.[22]

The second large public health provider is the Salvadoran Social Security Institute (ISSS). The ISSS is a sort of single-payer system to which people gain access through their work. Between 12-15 percent of all Salvadorans get their care through this system. Since it is chronically underfunded, the services at the ISSS are extremely uneven, but poor Salvadorans consider it an achievement to gain access to the institute. Although ISSS patients receive some specialized services through the public hospitals and clinics, the reverse is true only in exceptional cases and there is little coordination between the two institutions.

Besides the Ministry of Health hospitals and clinics and the ISSS, at least seventeen public institutions provide some level of health services to their members and/or employees, thus creating a hopelessly complex web of competing and self-duplicating services. The largest of these are the Armed Forces, the phone company, and the electric company. The system, then, suffers from both excess centralization (top-heavy bureaucracies and concentration of resources on hospitals instead of primary care facilities) and fragmentation (over a dozen publicly supported health mini-systems).

The private health system also provides significant services to Salvadorans who can afford to pay for care. ANSAL calculates that the private system provides half of all out-patient consultations, and accounts for 10 percent of all in-patient registrations in the country. Approximately 2100 doctors work in that system, two-thirds of them practicing in San Salvador. That leaves approximately 700 doctors for the 3.5 million people living outside the capital (one doctor per 5000 people). The large private hospitals like La Policlínica and the Hospital Diagnóstico are known for providing excellent services, many of which are unavailable in the public hospitals at any price.[23]

Nongovernmental organizations (NGOs) also provide services to a half-million Salvadorans throughout the country in a highly decentralized manner. Much of this unusual service pattern resulted from wartime conditions when the public system ceased to function in much of the country. In those areas, church-related and secular

NGOs sought international funds to support a network of primary health services.

These services rested on the work of a small number of health professionals—mostly, though not all, expatriates—and a large number of health "promoters." These promoters were local residents who were given basic training in primary health-care techniques. In some cases, this NGO-supported system coordinated services with those doctors and other health workers collaborating directly with the FMLN. Although these "popular health systems" varied greatly from one area of the country to another, in many areas they became surprisingly sophisticated systems of local health care.[24]

The development of the alternative health care system was limited by several factors. First, the system operated, for the most part, in a theater of war, with very few material resources or trained health personnel. Second, the political complexity and security demands of the war situation meant that the NGOs supporting the provision of health services did not achieve high levels of coordination. Finally, the almost complete isolation of the system from the public health system considerably limited the services that it could provide.

The nongovernmental network continued to provide essential services in the postwar period, but it suffered from many of the same difficulties which hampered its wartime development. The war ended, but resources remained a critical problem and little was done to overcome the lack of coordination. One health professional reported on a visit to a rural community of one hundred families that was receiving simultaneous visits from five health "teams," none of which had prior knowledge of the other's plans.[25]

In addition, the health personnel of the alternative system were involved in a complicated process of integration with the Ministry of Health system. As in the case of relations between the popular education system and the government, the Ministry of Health openly questioned the qualifications of the health promoters who had, for years, been providing the vast majority of health services in the conflictive areas.

AIDS: A Crisis in the Making

Barring a major medical breakthrough, by the end of this century AIDS is likely to present the Salvadoran health system (as well as systems throughout Latin America) with another challenge for which it is even less prepared. Although the number of reported AIDS cases remains relatively low in El Salvador—according to the World Health Organization only 630 AIDS cases had been diagnosed in El Salvador through the end of 1994—that number represents less than the tip of the iceberg. Official statistics on AIDS will always be unreliable as long as an intense social stigma remains attached to the disease. Although the medical profession is rapidly gaining knowledge of the disease, many doctors remain unfamiliar with AIDS and are unlikely to diagnose it correctly.

There is debate about the early incidence of HIV infection among the country's gay and bisexual population, but there is no debate that it has become primarily a heterosexually transmitted disease. By early 1993 heterosexual transmission accounted for 60 percent of all known AIDS cases in Central America.[26] The pattern is unlikely to be markedly different in El Salvador.

As early as 1991, the public health education unit of the Ministry of Health launched a public campaign to increase awareness about AIDS. Working with limited resources, these campaigns placed public service announcements on the most popular radio and television stations and erected billboards throughout the country extolling the virtues—and the advisability—of fidelity. Such campaigns were important but clashed directly with deeply held sexual mores of a culture dominated by *machismo*. In addition, AIDS education had to combat the broad popular perception that the disease only affected homosexuals. Such mores and perceptions only assured a higher rate of transmission.

Only the most wealthy AIDS patients in El Salvador can hope to get anything like adequate medical treatment. Speaking about the region as a whole, *Central America Report* stated, "Families simply cannot afford the expensive tests and medicines required to diagnose and treat the opportunistic infections associated with AIDS, much less anti-retroviral drugs such as AZT."[27] By the mid-1990s, Salvadoran public health activists began to devise much more sophisticated educational campaigns and other strategies in response to the increasing incidence of AIDS. FUNDASIDA is an NGO formed in 1994 to carry out educational work and establish support networks for people with AIDS. It acknowledges, however, that important time has been lost in the nation's struggle against the epidemic.

A Healthier Road Ahead?

The October 26, 1994, issue of the magazine *Proceso* recounts the case of Trinidad Guadalupe Rivas, a seven-month old girl who entered the Bloom Children's Hospital for an operation to remove a benign brain tumor. Hours later, the child was in intensive care receiving treatment for severe electrical burns suffered on her leg during the operation. Stories of such medical malpractice are almost as common as the stories of people who die or become seriously ill for lack of simple treatments.[28]

The war in El Salvador pushed an already ailing system to the brink of collapse. The end of the armed conflict created the hope that health and sanitary conditions for the country's poor could finally become a national priority. For many working within the health system, that hope remains unrealized. Physicians at Rosales Hospital insist that the situation there actually worsened after the signing of the Peace Accords.[29] Labor conflicts at the hospital in the postwar period involved the traditional issues of pay and working conditions, but job actions in 1992 and 1993 also sought to force the hospital to demand more budgetary support from the government. In October 1994, the weekly newspaper *Primera Plana* published a series of articles on the pressing need for health care reform introduced by a front-page headline declaring "EMERGENCY: The Country's Health in Intensive Care."

In the 1994 campaign, the ARENA party ran on a platform of increased social spending. Candidate Calderón Sol insisted that the war and the subsequent needs of national reconstruction had limited the Cristiani government's ability to increase social spending. He pledged, however, that his government would honor expanded social spending commitments. Similar commitments were made in the structural adjustment negotiations with the World Bank, and in the negotiations which led to the mammoth IDB loan to El Salvador in 1994.

During the period 1990-94 (the first ARENA government), health spending increased very little as a percentage of the Salvadoran budget (from 8.86 to 9.20 percent). The first Calderón Sol budget increased health spending to 10.25 percent of total government spending, which still does not restore pre-war spending levels. The situation does not change markedly if health spending as a percentage of GDP is used as the key variable. In his study, "Reforms to the Health System: El Salvador 1994", physician and former legislative deputy Hector Silva suggests that health spending will have to rise to 7.5 percent of GDP by the end of the century if the country's health needs are to be met. In 1994 less than 2 percent of GDP was devoted to health. As with education, any successful health reform must begin with a massive budgetary infusion.

Until government income increases through true tax reform, social spending in El Salvador will remain highly sensitive to levels of international aid. Since foreign aid—especially that provided by AID—is likely to decline significantly in the medium term, there is reason to doubt the sustainability of even the moderate spending increases of the mid-1990s. In 1995, President Calderón Sol promised to increase social spending dramatically by the end of the decade. He did not, however, take firm action to increase tax collections so as to make increased social spending a real possibility.

In its analysis, ANSAL joined the call for the government to devote more resources to health but made it clear that money, alone, could not solve El Salvador's health problem. Concluding that the Ministry of Health is simply not suited to provide a wide range of health services, ANSAL recommends a health care reform based on an expansion of the ISSS to a point where it would serve almost 60 percent of all Salvadorans. Under such a plan, agricultural workers would gradually gain access to the Social Security plan. In addition to this reallocation of organizational responsibility, ANSAL calls for a new vision to govern public health services. This new vision would rest on four fundamental pillars:

- A preventive approach emphasizing health education and primary health care.
- Much improved access to health care, especially in rural and urban marginal areas.
- An integral system that permits efficient referrals of more complicated cases.
- Increased availability of safe drinking water and basic sanitation services.

Many questions arise about the viability of such a reform in El Salvador but the most vexing of the questions surely concerns the cost of such a program. Even with increased efficiency and improved preventive health measures and education, simply providing the existing level of ISSS services to four times as many people would imply a gigantic investment that would have to come primarily from the government. Once again, the argument returns to the need for the political will to increase public revenues and devote these revenues to the nation's health.

As of 1995, the government faced the pressing need to do something decisive about the health system but remained reserved about proposals like that of ANSAL. The Calderón Sol government's first Minister of Health, Eduardo Interiano, a stockholder in private hospitals like the Pediatric Hospital and Gynecological Center, is a former member of the national directorate of ARENA. Interiano favored a long-term reform process that would take 10-12 years, and would rely on the decentralization of the system and a shift to reliance on preventive care. In the early stages of reform, new investments by the government would not be the most important element of such a reform.[30]

Critics of the government understand Interiano's notion of decentralization as a watchword for the privatization of the health system. Melvin Guardado, a medical professor at the National University and former Chief of Surgery at Rosales, suggested that ARENA "wants to rid itself of the hospital [Rosales] and of thinking doctors. We believe that the government has the responsibility to give at least acceptable health services to the population."[31] Given that providing health services to poor people is not profitable, the privatization of an institution like Rosales Hospital would not involve its outright sale to a private company but would entail the progressive removal of its specialized services to other private and public facilities.

The NGOs working in health echo the idea that the government is interested in privatizing health services and insist on being directly included in health-reform debate from the very beginning.[32] More importantly, the NGOs acknowledge that they must improve coordination among themselves both as a way of offering better services and building their capacity to propose comprehensive national solutions to the country's health care problem.

Religion

Although the country is traditionally Roman Catholic, the constitution does not give Roman Catholicism any official standing as an established religion. In fact, the number of Protestants in the country, primarily of the fundamentalist denominations, has been growing rapidly, and the population is now estimated to be only about 75 percent Catholic. (As elsewhere in Central America, the common use in El Salvador of the term "evangelical" refers to all non-Catholic Christians, including pentecostals, fundamentalists, and mainline historical Protestants.)

Besides the one Catholic archdiocese (covering San Salvador, Cuscatlán, and La Libertad), there are seven dioceses (Santa Ana, San Vicente, Santiago de María, San Miguel, Sonsonate, Zacatecoluca and the newest diocese, Chalatenango) as well as a military ordinate. Archbishop Arturo Rivera y Damas, who had led Salvadoran Catholics since the murder of Monseñor Oscar Arnulfo Romero in 1980, died suddenly on November 26, 1994, at the age of 71. The Vatican appointed Fernando Sáenz Lecalle to replace Rivera y Damas in early 1995. Over two-thirds of the priests in El Salvador are natives, a higher percentage than in other Central American countries.

El Salvador was strongly affected by the development of the progressive "theology of liberation" tendency within the Catholic church from the 1950s on. This tendency within the church was expressed at the 1968 Medellín Conference of Latin American bishops, which called for a "preferential option for the poor." The institutional expression of this new tendency is the so-called "base community," groups of people who worship, study, and on occasion take action together. The study component often takes the form of consciousness-raising, with a progressive or even revolutionary emphasis.

The large number of base communities that formed in El Salvador were early targets of repression, with the assassination or disappearance of thousands of members between the mid-1970s and the end of the war. In the face of this repression, many base communities in the rural areas disintegrated, and the movement became concentrated in the poorer communities on the periphery of San Salvador.[33]

The persecution of Catholic clergy and laity began in the 1970s as a reaction to the increased identification of the church with the country's poor majority. In March 1977 Father Rutilio Grande, a Jesuit working in the conflictive parish of Aguilares, was murdered for his commitment to the poor. Grande's killing was only the most publicized act in an escalating spiral of violence against the base community movement. This violence claimed several other priests, such as Neto Barrera and Octavio Ortíz, and dozens of lay activists from the communities.[34] The young officers' coup of October 1979 occurred against the backdrop of this violence but did little to stem it.

On March 24, 1980, a death squad sniper took the life of the Archbishop of San Salvador as he said Mass in the chapel of the cancer hospital where he lived. The archbishop, whose political position had originally been moderate and passive, was transformed by his experience with the Salvadoran people to the point that he became the voice of the oppressed as repression grew.[35] His nationally broadcast weekly homilies, in which he denounced terror and pleaded for social justice, made him a hero to many Salvadorans but a target of the rightwing extremists. In his last Sunday homily, Monseñor Romero pleaded to the soldiers in the Salvadoran Army to stop the repression, even if it meant disobeying orders.

Archbishop Rivera y Damas was appointed to replace Romero and immediately attempted to chart a more moderate role for the church, both politically and spiritually. While Rivera was criticized for reining in the base community movement and lowering the profile of liberation theology within formal church teaching, he is also remembered for many important contributions to the peace process. According to Abraham Rodríguez, a prominent Christian Democrat at the time, "He was the first person in the country to speak about dialogue and a political settlement of the war. Our country is as indebted to him as it is to Archbishop Romero."[36]

Rivera y Damas worked tirelessly to bring the more conservative bishops of the Salvadoran Bishops' Conference around to his view of the need for dialogue. In July 1988 the archbishop launched a National Debate for Peace among nearly five dozen popular organizations which proved to be a major voice calling for a negotiated peace. Although Rivera y Damas was more moderate and careful, not to mention a great deal less charismatic, than Archbishop Romero, he did go to the pulpit before the 1994 election asking Catholics to "vote thinking of the future" and not to vote for a party with historical ties to the death squads and the killing of Monseñor Romero (an obvious reference to ARENA).

Following the death of Rivera y Damas, the Vatican lost little time in appointing a successor, naming Monseñor Fernando Sáenz Lecalle in April 1995. Born in Spain but naturalized as a Salvadoran in 1966, Lecalle was known for his ties to the ultra-conservative religious order of Opus Dei. The former military prelate and auxiliary bishop of Santa Ana, Lecalle has shown nothing but contempt for liberation theology and the Christian base communities.

Sáenz Lecalle's appointment represented a radical departure from the tradition of Rivera y Damas and Romero. Although most church activists feared that the Vatican would replace Rivera with one of the country's conservative bishops, few expected a choice as provocative as that of Lecalle.[37]

Rudolfo Cardenal, vice-rector of the UCA, called Sáenz Lecalle an unknown, but cautioned that his appointment was being applauded by the very same people that had killed Monseñor Romero. Monseñor Rosa Chávez, Rivera's auxiliary and the interim archbishop, attempted to respond in a conciliatory fashion, but insisted that "the Church's preferential option for the poor is non-negotiable." [38] Most observers predicted a time of sharp conflict within the archdiocese as Sáenz attempted to diminish the influence of the popular church.

Catholic Social Programs

The main social arm of the church is the Social Secretariat of the Archdiocese (SSA), which has been operating since 1981. The SSA is an agency of the archdiocese's Social Ministry Secretariat. It is responsible for the social assistance programs of the archdiocese but frequently administers programs in other areas of the country. The SSA receives international aid for health, agriculture, nutrition, and other humanitarian assistance programs for the displaced population and other disadvantaged Salvadorans. Much of the growth of the SSA during the 1980s was based on donations received through the Salvadoran ecumenical coordination for development, DIACONIA (See Nongovernmental Organizations). DIACONIA also served as a channel for international support of the social programs of the historical Protestant denominations, such as the Lutheran and Baptist churches. Shortly before the war, tensions within DIACONIA led Rivera y Damas to pull the SSA out of the ecumenical coordination. The funds available for the work of the SSA declined considerably and caused major program cutbacks.

Since the late 1980s the largest program of the SSA has been with the parish of Suchitoto. In that zone, parish workers carry out a large social service and agricultural support program in Suchitoto as well as the dozens of repopulated communities in the surrounding area. A number of international volunteer organizations like CONCERN, the Jesuit Refugee Service, and Christian Volunteer Missions work under the auspices of the social secretariat. The diocese of Chalatenango established its own social service organization on the model of the SSA.

Another important social institution is the national Caritas organization, which is administered by a board appointed by the National Bishops' Conference. Caritas distributes U.S. food aid from Catholic Relief Services as well as managing other assistance programs on a local level. FUNPROCOOP (Cooperative Development Foundation) is a Salvadoran nongovernmental organization closely linked to the SSA and the Catholic church. FUNPROCOOP, which receives mostly European funds, was created in 1968 by the archdiocese to encourage the development of rural cooperatives and to assist community development projects.

Church-State Relations

Despite its efforts to isolate the more radical elements of the base community movement, the institutional church was the object of state-sponsored repression throughout the war. Both the army and ARENA frequently charged that clerics and church organizations were linked to the FMLN, incensing the church hierarchy.[39]

Rightwing death squads constantly targeted Tutela Legal, the legal-aid office of the Catholic church which monitors human rights violations. The attacks on the Jesuits were also attacks against the Catholic Church. Rivera y Damas himself also received regular threats. In the wake of the 1989 Jesuit killings, Bishop Rivera reportedly demanded that the president post troops outside his residence. When the president agreed, Rivera is reported to have said, "Don't get me wrong. It's not that I trust the soldiers. It's just that, if I'm killed, I want it to be clear who did it."[40]

The right wing was not, however, without its allies within the church. In their efforts to associate the church with the FMLN, rightwing extremists were aided by a small conservative sector of bishops and clerics which included Bishop Lecalle. This group was particularly hostile to the base community movements in their areas, and one of them, Monsignor Fredy Delgado, even published a book called *The Popular Church Was Born in El Salvador*, which accuses church leaders of embracing Marxist theory.[41] After the signing of the Peace Accords, relations between the government and the Catholic Church improved somewhat, although Rivera's homilies consistently raised the ire of ARENA party officials and his name continued to appear on rightwing threat lists until his death.

Protestant Churches

Of all the protestant missions and churches founded in El Salvador, well over 50 percent have been opened in the past fifteen years. Since 1978 the annual rate of growth has ranged from 15 to 22 percent. Today over 20 percent of the Salvadorans are evangelicals. The country has over 3,300 evangelical churches operated by some 79 evangelical denominations and sects.[42]

Much of the Salvadoran Protestant experience has been conservative, even fundamentalist, in nature, but an important sector of churches do not fit that description. The historical Protestant churches—the Lutheran, Episcopalian, and Baptist—have often provided highly prophetic leadership and have made important contributions to both liberation theology and the base community movement.

The Assemblies of God is the largest evangelical denomination, followed by the Church of Apostles and Prophets, Church of God, and Central American Mission. Most evangelical churches are branches or associates of U.S. pentecostal and fundamentalist church organizations. The main exception to this is the country's second-largest church, the pentecostal Church of Apostles and Prophets, which is an indigenous institution. Three Guatemalan evangelical churches have also penetrated El Salvador, including Prince of Peace, Elim, and Shaddai.

Although the surge in evangelical growth is a recent phenomenon, Protestant missionaries began proselytizing in El Salvador nearly a century ago. Unlike other Central American countries, however, where missionaries began working first with English and Creole-speaking people living on the Atlantic coast, there has never been a strong English-speaking ministry in El Salvador. Protestant missionaries have been working with Spanish-speaking congregations in El Salvador since the 1890s. Early Protestant missionaries belonged to the Central American Mission, the California Yearly Meeting of Friends (Quakers, which had a base in Guatemala), the Seventh Day Adventist church, the American Baptist church, and independent pentecostal sects—all from the United States. It was not, however, until the 1950s that the evangelical missionaries began making a large impact. Of the evangelical churches now established in El Salvador, only 5 percent existed before 1950.[43]

The pace of evangelical growth has dramatically increased since 1978 with the Assemblies of God leading the way with its aggressive proselytizing and church-building campaigns. Other pentecostal churches—including Church of God, Church of Apostles and Prophets, and Prince of Peace—have also experienced sharp increases in members. Central American Mission, the largest nonpentecostal fundamentalist church, has not experienced the rapid growth enjoyed by the pentecostals.

In the last ten years, the number of evangelicals has almost tripled. Evangelical organizations like the Salvadoran Evangelical Fraternity (CONESAL) say that ambitious pastor training and evangelization campaigns explain this increase. But the spread of evangelical faith in El Salvador is also attributed to the internal political-economic crisis and the increased interest of U.S. evangelical organizations in the country. Beset by political violence and economic crisis, many Salvadorans have searched for refuge in a religious community that offers an escape from the political turmoil, emotional bonding, and hope for better days to come. In this, the evangelical churches have much in common with the Roman Catholic Church prior to Vatican II.

The Salvadoran evangelical movement did not rise independently from the crisis conditions but is largely a product of the increased U.S. evangelical presence. Televangelists such as Jimmy Swaggart and Pat Robertson have traveled to El Salvador to preach before massive crowds in the national stadium. They have been joined by an array of independent sects including Maranatha, Gospel Outreach/El Verbo, Chapel Hill Harvester, and Evangelistic Faith Mission.

Another factor in the evangelical boom is the presence of transnational, interdenominational evangelical organizations like Youth with a Mission and Campus Crusade for Christ. Evangelical humanitarian assistance agencies like World Relief, World Vision, 700 Club, Manna International, and Paralife International have contributed to this surge in evangelicalism. While they do not have a direct presence in the country, evangelical relief agencies such as World Concern and MAP International also bolster the evangelical movement by channeling relief supplies through conservative evangelical organizations like CESAD and Manna Bible Institute. Evangelical growth has also been fueled by the deepening dissatisfaction among middle- and upper-class Catholics over the influence within the Catholic church of Christian base communities and other advocates of liberation theology. Evangelical ministers say they are rapidly making inroads in the upper-class Escalón section of San Salvador.

Evangelical growth, however, is not simply a result of the deep pockets of U.S. churches, nor is it purely a middle and upper class phenomenon. Many of San Salvador's poorest slum neighborhoods seem to have a small pentecostal church on almost every block. The pentecostal preachers in such neighborhoods succeed because they respond to some deeply felt needs. The deep spiritualism may appeal to some, while the emphasis on sobriety and devotion to the traditional family strikes a responsive chord in others. According to one Salvadoran theologian, "the woman from the market in Santa Tecla does not take her basket into the pentecostal temple at the end of a long day because a North American church pays the pastor's salary. To believe such an absurdity misses the source of the power of the sects in our country."[44]

During the 1980s, most political observers believed that the rapid growth of the evangelicals added to the base of the conservative ARENA party. Asked to describe their politics, however, most evangelical representatives said that they were neutral—not aligned with either the right or the left. While proclaiming their political neutrality, the sermons of many evangelical pastors make repeated references to anticommunism, capitalist ethics, and their own pro-U.S. sympathies.

This all changed prior to the 1994 election when two parties with close ties to evangelicals registered and ran candidates (See Evangelical Parties). The Unity Movement (MU) gained enough support to place a deputy in the Legislative Assembly, and José Domingo Mendes, a lawyer with connections to the MU, was elected as the Chief Justice of the Supreme Court. MU and its leader, Jorge Martínez, appear to have a bright future in Salvadoran politics.

While the vast majority of Salvadoran evangelicals belong to pentecostal churches where conservative theology mixes easily with conservative politics, there does exist a significant sector of more liberal churches. During the war, the Lutheran church, the Episcopal church, and sectors of the Baptist church, for example, offered important support to displaced people and repatriating refugees and lent assistance to community organizing efforts that were often subject to harassment and violence by the military.

Lutheran Bishop Medardo Gómez was forced to flee El Salvador after receiving a series of death threats in November 1989. He later returned to the country escorted by a group of U.S. clerics and said: "I am not a criminal. I am not a terrorist. I am a pastor, and our work is to worry about the poor and is not inspired by any social ideology." Churches like the Resurrection Lutheran Church, the Emmanuel Baptist Church, and St. John's Episcopal Church all inspired Christian base community organizing similar to that which occurred in the Roman Catholic Church.

These and other evangelical churches, mostly mainline nonpentecostal ones, regard social assistance and community development activities as part of the practice of faith—not simply as a way to open the door for evangelism. They generally try to maintain their independence from AID and Salvadoran government programs. Because of the efforts of this small but influential sector of the evangelical community, ecumenism became an important social force in El Salvador, especially in comparison with the neighboring countries of Honduras and Guatemala.

Postwar Challenges

Feeling the threat of competition from the evangelicals, the Roman Catholic Church has taken a more aggressive posture in the postwar period. In an effort to regain the initiative and stem its losses, the Catholics launched a campaign called the "New Evangelization" designed to actively involve Catholic laypeople in spreading the teachings of the church. Many Catholic parishes have turned toward charismatic approaches that are often quite conservative as a means of attracting those believers that might otherwise be drawn to the evangelical churches.

One unfortunate outcome of this competition for the faithful has been a decline in the ecumenical ethic that was much stronger during the war. In many areas—such as the area around Nombre de Jesús, Chalatenango—relations between the churches have become increasingly hostile. Even in this context, many religious workers around the country report that, after years of emphasis on the social aspects of church teachings, people are now expressing more interest in pastoral programs designed to encourage lay people to take a more active role in the spiritual development of their communities.[45] Such work was highly consistent with what some church leaders and theologians saw as the key postwar role of the popular church—that of "keeping hope alive" in Salvadoran communities. Although events, such as the naming of the new Archbishop of San Salvador, challenged those who would see the church as a hopeful place in postwar El Salvador, Salvadoran church activists had long since proven their ability to answer difficult challenges.

Women in El Salvador

Not surprisingly, the war and the social and economic crisis that accompanied it had an enormous impact on Salvadoran women. Thousands of women were killed during the war—some as combatants, more as civilian victims of the conflict. Hundreds of thousands more were driven from their homes, captured and abused by the security forces, and suffered the loss of multiple family members. Many women participated directly in the war, but many more assumed the awesome responsibility of seeing to the survival of the basic building block of Salvadoran society, the extended family. The war greatly increased the percentage of families headed by women and forced an ever-increasing number of women to look to the economy's informal sector as a means to survival. In an economy where women already bore a disproportionate amount of the burden of poverty, the "feminization of poverty" became even more pronounced. Women organized throughout Salvadoran society during the war years, and the gains of that period would have been unthinkable without their participation. Much of the energy of women's organizations, however, was absorbed by the needs of the overall struggle to defeat the government, and relatively little attention was given to the particular needs and concerns of women.

In the postwar context, the reconstruction of Salvadoran society threatens to leave women in an even worse relative position than they were in before the war began. Facing this painful reality, women have been less willing to subordinate their needs and interests to the goals of other movements. New organizations have arisen and existing groups have demanded more autonomy to give voice to the demands of women for full and equal participation in the Salvadoran nation.

Social Condition of Salvadoran Women

In the unique situation of postwar El Salvador, women make up 53 percent of the country's population. In almost every social indicator for which separate statistics are kept for men and women, women fare worse than their male counterparts.

Whereas 27 percent of Salvadoran men are considered illiterate, 32 percent of women are unable to read. Female unemployment is almost one-third higher than male unemployment, and the statistics for underemployment show a similar trend. An unusually high 45 percent of the economically active population in El Salvador is women, and women are well-represented in the middle-class professions of lawyers (30 percent), doctors (33 percent), dentists (50 percent) and school teachers (50 percent). Despite the existence of this small, but important, contingent of middle-class women, fully 65 percent of economically active women work in the informal sector where long hours of work often barely yield a survival income. Four-fifths of the women in the informal sector are also heads of household.

In terms of schooling, the average educational attainment for women, nationwide, is the third grade. Males, on average, complete four years of schooling. Although many more women have gained access to university education in recent years, a man is still three times as likely to complete a university program as a woman (2.1 percent to 0.7 percent).[46]

The statistical situation arises from a cultural experience in which women are, at the same time, revered and reviled; where they are required to take tremendous responsibility for home and family, but are given little social or economic recognition for that sacrifice. The experience of the war fundamentally changed this situation for some women, but only added more economic responsibility to the burden of many more.

Violence Against Women

The work of women's organizations has brought to light other problems that were previously considered part of the "private" lives of Salvadoran women. Domestic violence is so widespread that, according to the office of the Attorney General, 8 out of 10 Salvadoran homes are the scene of some sort of family violence—physical, sexual, or psychological.[47] Surveys in Salvadoran schools show that over half of school-age children have witnessed the physical abuse of their mother by a man, and the World Health Organization reports that 57 percent of Salvadoran women suffer physical abuse at home.[48]

Lidia Tobar of the Human Rights Ombudsman's office reports that the five domestic violence complaints filed per day in her office are a "pale reflection of what is happening in the Salvadoran family."[49] Fear and shame combine with a clear pattern of police inaction to prevent the vast majority of battered women from coming forward.

In the midst of the 1994 election, sources close to the opposition candidate Rubén Zamora reported that ARENA candidate Armando Calderón Sol had beaten his wife so badly that she had to be hospitalized. ARENA tried to characterize the report as a politically motivated attack, but the scope of the domestic violence problem left room for doubt in many minds. Perhaps most disturbingly, polls showed that even people who harbored doubt about the incident did not change their presidential preferences and Calderón Sol was elected by a large margin.

Until the passage of the new Family Code in 1993, domestic violence was not even considered a crime under Salvadoran law. One activist considers the punishments for domestic violence "laughable." Provided that the battered can furnish two witnesses and incontrovertible proof of her injuries, the attacker may be sentenced to six months in jail. If he can post the Salvadoran equivalent of bail, he may be released without serving time. Needless to say, women's groups continue to press for further reforms to this law.

As of early 1995, only a single shelter for battered women existed in El Salvador, run by the National Coordination of Salvadoran Women (CONAMUS). According to CONAMUS, "the shelter is not a clandestine place, but we can't reveal the address, either...we have felt like we were under surveillance more than once. That means that we have to move the shelter every year or eighteen months."

The sexual violence of rape has also been the topic of more public discussion since the end of the war. Given the difficulty of prosecuting rape cases and the stigma attached to reporting such crimes, reliable statistics on rape are difficult to find. During 1993, 598 rapes were formally reported to the judicial authorities, but this was surely only the tip of the iceberg.[50]

Since the victim must present corroborating evidence from eye witnesses, a rape conviction is almost an impossibility. One woman was shocked when the investigating officer asked whether or not she was a virgin before the assault, but Salvadoran law actually prescribes a stiffer penalty for the rapist when his victim is a virgin.

The appearance of a serial rapist in San Salvador's Colonia Miramonte received significant publicity and horrified women throughout the city. Although the case generated much discussion of the problem and even resulted in the arrest of a suspect, no conviction resulted from the investigation.

Reproductive Health Issues

Childbearing, early and often, stands at the center of women's traditional role in El Salvador. At the time of the 1971 census, one-third of 14-year-old females had already experienced at least one pregnancy. El Salvador has only one maternity hospital to attend to the 262,000 births that occur in the country each year. Women with access to resources can always pay for prenatal and other birth-related health services in the private hospitals, but poor women are left to their own resources. Under such conditions, giving birth is one of the most dangerous things Salvadoran women do in their lifetimes.

Another even more dangerous step is the decision to terminate a pregnancy. According to the weekly newspaper *Primera Plana*, thousands of women die each year from failed illegal abortions.[51] Such abortions are the leading cause of death among women of childbearing age.[52] Another study found that one-third of the beds in the gynecological wards of public hospitals were occupied by women suffering from serious complications from badly performed abortions.[53] In a country where over 50 percent of women do not have access to contraceptives, and church opposition prohibits all public discussion of legalized abortion, women will continue to seek out illegal abortions as a means of dealing with unwanted pregnancies. "It would be better to avoid the problem," says one young single mother. "We need sex education and access to a variety of contraceptive methods, but religion and the family are opposed."

The government has aggressively supported family planning since the initiation of public family planning programs in 1968. Some women complain that they are under too much pressure in public hospitals to limit family size. A fine line exists between such pressure on women giving birth and the promotion of involuntary sterilization. In one study, one-half of the women using contraception report that sterilization was the method.[54]

In its "Salvadoran Women's Platform," the women's movement embraces the role of motherhood but insists that it be a "free and voluntary" choice (See Women's Organizing Takes A New Turn). The platform also calls for access to contraceptives as well as complete information about all methods, including their side-effects. Finally, the platform asked the political parties to support the call for "conditions allowing for the voluntary interruption of pregnancy without risk for the health and life of women." The parties—including the FMLN—had more difficulty with this section on reproductive rights than with any other aspect of the platform.

Women and the Salvadoran Economy

In economic terms, women face their increased economic burden even as national economic policies of structural adjustment place more pressure on the economic lives of the poor. With virtually no other option, thousands of urban women participate in the economy's informal sector. It is the energy and creativity of these women that accounts for the undeniable dynamism of that sector.

While increasing numbers of women have been forced into illicit occupations related to street crime, prostitution, and drugs, many more labor as street vendors and domestic servants. These activities have their own risks and frustrations, but have allowed women to somehow juggle the demands of family and economic responsibilities.

In downtown San Salvador, the area with by far the highest concentration of informal sector activity, street vendors—with women the vast majority—have been engaged in a struggle with municipal authorities for the right to make a living. Under pressure from local members of the Chamber of Commerce, the city government has moved aggressively to remove street vendors from many areas of the most lucrative downtown zone in the name of "beautifying" the city center.

The city wishes to move the vendors to a market area where it can register them, tax them, and charge them for their stall and utilities. Violent confrontations between police and vendors have occurred on several occasions, including a widely publicized incident during the ARENA party's final street rally prior to the 1994 elections.

For the vendors it is a question of economic survival. "I went into their market with 4000 pesos and left with one hundred," says Isabel Vides, a women who has taken her wares back into the streets and is ready to fight to stay there. "It is going to be a year of conflict," predicted one vendor as she looked forward to 1995.[55]

Maquilas, the factories where foreign entrepreneurs bring raw materials—mostly textiles in the case of El Salvador—to be assembled into finished goods, have been another important source of employment for Salvadoran women. Since 80 percent of the 40,000 people employed in Salvadoran *maquila* plants are women, the labor abuses of the *maquilas* are, overwhelmingly, abuses of women (See Labor and Unions).[56] For women, sexual harassment, physical intimidation, and psychological abuse are all part of the job in the *maquilas*, and they often receive less than the legal minimum wage for their trouble. Given the economic crisis gripping the country, however, young women continue to flock to these Salvadoran outposts of the new world order. As a result, women's organizations are among the first to shudder when they hear the talk about "one big free-trade zone."

In rural areas, women have looked to the Land Transfer Process (PTT) and the PRN to open up some possibility of economic advance. In the case of the PTT, who owns the land is a critical issue. "If the man is given the title to the land, what happens if we separate tomorrow?" asked Gloria Castañera, a former combatant of the FMLN and a member of the women's group, *Las Dignas*. "He keeps the land and I get the kids."

From this perspective, *Las Dignas* and other groups have fought to maximize the amount of land titled to women and jointly titled to couples. The issue is a real one. Of the 56,651 beneficiaries of the land reform program carried out by the Salvadoran government in the 1980s, only 6,713 were women. Many women are concerned that a similar problem is developing with the PTT. If the owner of a small piece of land in El Salvador must struggle with poverty, then the landless surely face destitution.

Since the end of the war the PRN has been carrying out a range of programs designed to reintegrate former combatants into civilian society and reactivate the areas of the country destroyed by the conflict. Many women among the presumed beneficiaries of the PRN feel that they have benefitted very little from the program. They find the programs poorly designed and do not see where the particular needs of women are addressed by the program. An AID-commissioned midterm evaluation of the PRN agreed with this assessment, and exhorted in-country staff to aggressively remedy this failure.[57]

In the postwar context, however, some new opportunities for women have arisen. When the first contingent of the newly created National Civilian Police (PNC) was sworn in on February 5, 1993, there were thirty-five women among the 527 new recruits. These were the first women to don police uniforms in the history of El Salvador. By November 1994, 361 women had entered the PNC representing 6 percent of the total.

The presence of women in the ranks of the PNC was one of the reasons that many women hoped that the new police force—which represented the removal of public security from military control—would more effectively deal with problems like domestic violence. Large numbers of women are excluded from employment in the PNC by educational and physical requirements, but many more are probably excluded by the social more that says police work is something that only men should do. One woman, a high-ranking officer in the force, observed that the most difficult part of the job was the long periods of separation from her family.

Those female former combatants of the FMLN who entered the PNC have long since become used to doing things generally reserved for men and are certainly accustomed to separation from their families. Sergeant Yanira Cristina Alberto, who spent ten years in the ranks of the FMLN, likes many things about her new job. "The work isn't as hard (as the war), there is less danger, and there is a salary, something that didn't exist in the mountains."[58]

The presence of women in the most important of the new institutions created by the Peace Accords is symbolic of the fact that, for some women, the war led to life changes that will never be reversed. Many poor women became effective leaders in their communities and assumed new roles at all levels of society. Six women were among those members of the FMLN elected to serve in the National Assembly in 1994. For the first time, women were among the justices named to the Supreme Court, seated in August 1994. These important gains, however, cannot obscure the fact that the vast majority of Salvadoran women continue to face formidable obstacles to social equality.

Nongovernmental Organizations

Nongovernmental organizations (NGOs) played a relatively minor role in Salvadoran society prior to the 1980s. In the highly polarized environment of the war, however, NGOs became central actors in the "other" war for the hearts and minds of the Salvadoran people. Dozens of newly formed organizations involved themselves in economic development, in the provision of basic services such as health and education, and in the humanitarian response to the national emergency brought on by the displacement of almost 20 percent of the country's population.

Not surprisingly, NGOs were as sharply divided as Salvadoran society itself. One group of NGOs became unmistakably associated with the counterinsurgency effort orchestrated by the Salvadoran government and AID, while another sought to root itself in a response to the needs of the social base of the FMLN and, therefore, developed a close relationship with the political project of the Frente. The latter group certainly maintained more independence from the government than the group associated with AID. Given the intensity of the conflict, survival for an NGO almost always meant an identification with one or another sector, and few could make a claim to any sort of neutrality in the conflict.

NGOs and the Private Sector

In search of the elusive goal of stable economic growth, AID undertook the structural reorganization of the Salvadoran economy in the 1980s. Given the Reagan administration's passion for unleashing the potential of the market, AID came to see the modernization, diversification, and reorganization of the private sector as critical to solving national economic problems. While much of AID's other work in El Salvador was carried out through government agencies and

U.S.-based NGOs, the agency saw to the creation of a network of Salvadoran foundations to carry out and manage its work with the private sector.[59] Certainly the most important of these was The Salvadoran Foundation for Economic and Social Development (FUSADES).[60]

AID funding established FUSADES in 1983, and within five years the foundation had spawned a swarm of private sector NGOs, each one responsible for a different aspect of the program of support to the private sector. Organizations like PRIDEX, FORTAS, and PROMIPE offered a range of training and support services to Salvadoran business and its various organizational expressions. Technical objectives predominated, but the program also sought to modernize the political vision of the private sector. The strengthening of the "moderate" sector of the ARENA party and the rise of Alfredo Cristiani spoke to the success of this effort (See ARENA: *Patria Sí, Comunismo No*).

By 1986, FUSADES was ready to create three new foundations—FEPADE, FIRPO, and HABITAT—that would play "a critical role in the development and implementation of a national social and economic strategy consistent with the objectives of FUSADES." [61] Through this and other actions, FUSADES attempted to establish a business-oriented nongovernmental presence in civil society that would legitimize its role in the development of national economic policy. To further extend the participation of private sector NGOs in civil society, FUSADES initiated a program to establish municipal foundations in many of the country's prime coffee-growing areas.[62] An entire network of NGOs was built at the local and national levels on the assumption that the private sector held the solutions to the country's social and economic problems. AID's financial support in this area amounted to three-fourths of all of the agency's support to NGOs. In the period 1982-94, FUSADES alone received $150 million.[63] This network had a considerable impact on the vision of Salvadoran business groups but accomplished relatively little in the social area. Given the nature of the war, these NGOs had very little influence in the conflictive areas or working experience with the people who lived there.

The entire AID program of support for the private sector received a serious blow in 1991 when a crew from "Sixty Minutes" produced a report on FUSADES' efforts to attract U.S. business investment to El Salvador. AID's support for efforts to move jobs from the United States to El Salvador drew fire from labor and other important constituencies, and the program became an issue in the 1992 campaign. The Clinton-appointed leadership of AID remained committed to support for NGOs but sought to alter the program's focus on the private sector.[64"]

Popular Sector NGOs

Even as AID was giving life to FUSADES and an overall strategy of nongovernmental support to the private sector, the devastation of the war constructed a very different nongovernmental sector. The "scorched-earth" tactics of the Salvadoran military had created a huge population of displaced people in the Salvadoran countryside.[65]

The government clearly identified the displaced with the enemy, and, far from providing them with adequate assistance, systematically violated their human rights.[66] Only a nongovernmental effort could hope to respond to the desperate situation of tens of thousands of Salvadorans.[67] Several refuges were established for displaced people in and around San Salvador—mostly under the auspices of the Catholic Church—and humanitarian aid was sought from a variety of international sources. In 1981, church-based NGOs cooperated with international donors on the establishment of DIACONIA, an unprecedented example of ecumenical cooperation for humanitarian assistance.[68] By 1986, DIACONIA handled $10 million in international assistance from dozens of international donors.

The initiation of the repopulation movement in the mid-1980s led to a broadening of the work of this growing network of NGOs serving the popular movement. While religious NGOs continued to play important roles, many secular NGOs were established as soon as the political opening of the Duarte period permitted.[69] As the popular movement expanded its organizing work to other sectors of Salvadoran society, new NGOs were established to serve the new organizations.

Although their mission was clearly defined as humanitarian assistance to civilian populations, these NGOs faced repression similar to that experienced by the popular organizations. They were unable to obtain any sort of legal recognition from the government and carried out their work under virtually clandestine conditions. The government claim of NGO connections to the FMLN was not completely baseless, but the humanitarian work of these NGOs was, nonetheless, protected by international conventions to which the Salvadoran government was a signatory.[70]

By 1986, when a major earthquake struck San Salvador, the popular NGOs had developed considerable capacity to undertake humanitarian projects, and they made important contributions to the emergency response to the earthquake. As more repopulated communities were established in the countryside, the NGOs expanded humanitarian operations and began more substantive work in the establishment of alternative systems of health and education.

Through the International Conference on Refugees in Central America (CIREFCA) the international community sought to encourage the beginnings of cooperation between the region's governments, United Nations agencies, and the NGOs involved in humanitarian assistance to refugees and displaced people. CIREFCA made available large amounts of aid contingent on the involvement of NGOs in project implementation. In that sense, the conference added greatly to the legitimacy of the NGOs and increased their scale of operations.[71]

Although the popular NGOs received funds from a wide variety of sources, for a decade they steadfastly avoided participation in what were seen as the counterinsurgency programs of AID. Much antipathy developed between the popular NGOs and those national and international organizations who did participate in government programs for the displaced under the auspices of the National Commission for the Restoration of Areas (CONARA). As the country moved toward peace, however, some of the NGOs began to show the same sort of flexible attitude toward AID that the agency was beginning to show toward them. The stage was certainly set for a new system of postwar relations.

NGOs in Postwar El Salvador

Each of the two major groups of Salvadoran NGOs—the private sector ones supported by AID and the popular NGOs—were important actors in the war through their identification with the opposing sides in the conflict. At the same time, the NGOs played an important role in the peace process.

The modernizing influence of the private sector NGOs helped moderate the views of many Salvadoran businessmen.[72] These attitude changes were essential to the government's ability to sign the Peace Accords. In the same way, the popular NGOs made possible the survival of the civilian population in the conflictive zones. The establishment of this population was an important part of the relative balance of power that brought both sides to the table in a serious way. Given the mutual recognition of the need for a massive national reconstruction effort in the wake of the Peace Accords, most observers expected that NGOs would become even more prominent in the postwar period.

For a variety of reasons, the NGOs have been slow to realize the potential created for them by the signing of the Peace Accords. While paying lip service to the importance of NGOs, the government crafted the National Reconstruction Plan essentially as a program of government action at the national and municipal level. Where NGOs were involved—within the programs of the National Reconstruction Secretariat—programming choices clearly favored U.S.-based NGOs and those with political ties to the ARENA government.[73] The situation improved somewhat after the 1994 elections, but the problem persisted well into the Calderón Sol administration.

The private sector NGOs were ill-suited to play a major social role because of their lack of experience in that area. Despite these limitations, the National Reconstruction Secretariat (SRN) sought, with little success, to give FUSADES and its associated NGOs a role in national reconstruction. The close association of these NGOs with the ARENA party assured them of continuing prominence in social and economic planning, but the declining availability of AID funds raised questions about the long-term viability of some of the smaller ones. Given their experience in the former conflictive zones, and connections with a variety of international donors, the popular NGOs seemed best positioned to expand their role in the postwar period. Since AID assumed financial responsibility for many of the key areas of national reconstruction, the question of whether or not to work with AID-sponsored programs quickly became a question of how to best participate in such programs.

Catholic Relief Services played a key role in this period by acting as an intermediary between AID and two dozen popular NGOs participating in an agricultural credit program. Several new NGOs, such as the *Fundación 16 de Enero* and PROESA were established to respond to the particular organizational and social needs of the former combatants of the FMLN.

As relationships slowly formed among the popular NGOs, the SRN, and AID, the bulk of reconstruction funding passed through NGOs with better political connections to ARENA and SRN Director Norma de Dowe.

Shortage of project funds was not, however, the biggest problem facing the popular NGOs. Much more problematic was their lack of technical capacity and experience in implementing development projects.[74] Wartime conditions had not always allowed full involvement of local constituents in project planning, and the lack of structures of popular participation created serious difficulties for the elaboration of any sort of postwar development plans.

Lack of coordination among NGOs serving the same function in the same area also caused problems, and the methods of financial administration developed by the NGOs during the war were inadequate for the peace period. Finally, much like the popular organizations, the effectiveness of NGOs suffered as the political connections that had allowed them to survive during wartime became obstacles to efforts to bring about organizational change after the war's end.

The popular NGOs devoted tremendous energy to securing project funding from the SRN. In retrospect some NGO leaders acknowledged that, given all the organizational challenges facing them in the immediate postwar period, it might have been better to have demanded a voice in SRN decisions rather than project money for individual NGOs.[75]

Cognizant of these difficulties, nearly all the popular NGOs embarked on processes of "reconversion" to better respond to the challenges of the postwar context. Technical staff received more and better training and administrative structures were decentralized and made more democratic. Also, the popular NGOs actively sought to develop strategies to allow themselves to become effective policy advocates with government institutions.[76] These changes resulted in real changes in even the largest NGOs, such as CORDES and FASTRAS, but the pace of change seemed slow and uneven against a backdrop of increasing impatience and social crisis in the communities served by the NGOs. The sacrifices made by the NGO personnel during the war created a deep reservoir of popular goodwill toward them, but that reservoir threatened to dry up in the mid-1990s as people demanded rapid answers to the economic problems left unsolved by the Peace Accords. In a definite departure with past practice, a group of NGOs worked to prepare a platform on national reconstruction to be presented to the June 1995 World Bank Consultative Group meeting in Paris.

These changes resulted in important transformations in even the largest and most established NGOs, such as CORDES and FASTRAS, but the pace of change seemed slow and uneven against a backdrop of increasing impatience and social crisis in the communities served by the NGOs. By the mid-1990s, new types of NGOs were being established to fill in what they saw as holes in the work of existing organizations. FUNDALEMPA was established to draw attention to the plight of the Lempa River, the nation's primary waterway. PROCAPP began promoting conflict resolution in the former zones of conflict and quickly assumed a variety of development tasks. FUNDASIDA sought to educate the Salvadoran population about the dangers of AIDS. All these NGOs shared a common claim to a technical mission of direct response to a given social problem. The lessening of social tensions in the postwar period appeared to be opening some space for the creation of an "independent" NGO sector not defined by its connections to one or another political institution.

The efforts of Salvadoran NGOs during the war had clearly established a permanent role for nongovernmental work at all levels of Salvadoran society. While NGOs would never recede to the anonymity of the pre-1980 period, the latter part of the 1990s promises to be a period of consolidation in which a smaller number of better-coordinated, more effective NGOs become a consistent voice for the interests of civil society in El Salvador.

Mass Media and Culture

Traditionally under the tight control of wealthy families from the Salvadoran oligarchy, the mass media in El Salvador have undergone important changes in the past fifteen years and, especially, since the end of the war. In the course of the war, the government mounted a well-funded and increasingly sophisticated apparatus to ensure the mass dissemination of the official version of the war. At the center of this apparatus stood the government communications department, which eventually became the National Communications Secretariat (SENCO), and the press and public relations committee of the Armed Forces (COPREFA). These communications experts worked closely with military and civilian intelligence operatives (both Salvadoran and international) and made extensive use of modern communications technology to subliminally attach notions of "terrorist" and "subversive" to all discussions and imagery of the FMLN.[77] The impact of twelve years of consistent implementation of such a strategy on the consciousness of all Salvadorans should not be underestimated when analyzing national events like the 1994 elections.

Even in the highly polarized environment of the war, certain media outlets (especially in radio and TV) became increasingly aggressive and balanced in their coverage, even to the extent of interviewing guerrilla commanders under certain circumstances. Especially under Napoleón Duarte, such approaches were given a certain space alongside the mass strategy outlined above. The limits of such a space were firmly established during the guerrilla offensive of 1989, when a well-prepared emergency broadcasting system filled all the country's airwaves with a week-long stream of invective against the FMLN and those foreigners and Salvadoran civilians accused of harboring pro-FMLN sympathies.[78]

From the beginning of the war, the FMLN and its allies saw the importance of developing a communications strategy to counter the government propaganda machine. The bulwark of this alternative strategy were the two guerrilla radio stations, Radio Venceremos and Radio Farabundo Martí, headquartered in the guerrilla strongholds of Morazán and Chalatenango, respectively.[79] Almost miraculously, these two stations—operated from portable transmitters carried on the backs of the guerrilla broadcasters—managed to present their view of the war almost without interruption. Aware of the importance of these communications outlets, the Armed Forces unsuccessfully invested enormous resources in trying to silence the rebel radios.[80] The postwar emergence of both Radio Venceremos and Radio Farabundo Martí as legal stations broadcasting from San Salvador was symbolic of the changes wrought by the end of the war.

Print Media

La Prensa Gráfica, founded in 1915, is El Salvador's largest and most technically advanced daily paper. A morning paper with a highly developed distribution network, La Prensa is owned, and its top management dominated, by members of the Dutriz family. Although his name does not appear as an editorial contributor to the paper, noted intellectual and former member of the government team in the peace negotiations, David Escobar Galindo is known to be the author of many of the paper's unsigned editorials.

A conservative paper, La Prensa has sought to broaden its appeal since 1992. By improving the quality of reporting, toning down its ideological content, and using high-quality color printing and modern graphic techniques, the paper has appealed to a more educated middle class seeking to be informed participants in a new world economy. These changes have in no way altered its unabashedly pro-business, pro-government outlook.

Those who seek to label La Prensa "moderate" can do so only in relation to its vitriolic competitor, El Diario de Hoy. That paper was founded in 1936 by the Altimirano family, a prominent and powerful grouping with interests in cotton and coffee. Always a voice of the extreme right in Salvadoran politics, in the early 1980s the paper became identified with Major Roberto D'Aubuisson and the then-nascent ARENA party.

During the worst of the political repression and human rights violations in the early 1980s, several prominent opposition figures were murdered or disappeared after having been denounced or threatened in El Diario de Hoy. As a result, the paper gained an identification with the rightwing death squads in the eyes of many Salvadorans.[81] Its rabid style of denunciatory journalism earned it the label of "ultraconservative" from the United States Information Agency (USIA) and *"El Diablo de Hoy"* ("Today's Devil" rather than "Today's Paper") from members of the country's political opposition.

After the signing of the Peace Accords—against which *El Diario* editorialized on a regular basis—the paper did not change as quickly as *La Prensa*. It consistently criticized what it saw as a "capitulationist" trend in the Cristiani government's dealings with the FMLN. While it supported Calderón Sol's bid for the presidency, it did not hesitate to criticize him after he took office. Columnist and ideologue Kirio Waldo Salgado's anticorruption campaign and his move to form a break-away party to ARENA's right both began on the pages of *El Diario de Hoy*.

El Mundo, founded in 1968, is an afternoon paper with more limited circulation and influence than its morning competitors. Nathan Borja, a wealthy coffee grower, owns the paper.

In the late 1980s, *El Mundo* began to accept paid announcements from opposition organizations such as trade unions and human rights groups as a way to buttress sagging revenues. The government halted these paid ads during the offensive of 1989, but the practice was quickly reinstated and became an important communications vehicle for the popular organizations—and a significant source of revenue for the newspaper.

Diario Latino, founded in 1892, is the nation's oldest newspaper. In 1989, former presidential hopeful Julio Adolfo Rey Prendes walked away from the paper citing its unpayable debt. In July of that year, a group of workers took over the paper and assumed its debts. The new *Latino* quickly earned the government's wrath for its "pluralistic" style of journalism which not only featured paid ads by opposition groups, but also represented such views in its news articles and editorials. In 1991 *Latino* began publishing a weekly literary supplement called *Tres Mil* which included poetry, essays, and short stories by many people who the war had long since condemned to silence.[82] With the war still in progress, the paper even went so far as to directly criticize the conduct of the Salvadoran military.[83]

For many on the Salvadoran right, *Latino* was nothing more than a journalistic facade for the FMLN. The paper and its staff, working out of a building that had been seriously damaged in the 1986 earthquake, were the constant targets of threats and intimidation. In February 1991, a firebomb further damaged the building housing the *Latino* and destroyed much of the paper's printing equipment. Given the precarious economic situation of the paper, the fire seriously threatened its existence, but, with support from the National University and other institutions, *Latino* was able to continue publishing without interruption. While it was continually facing both internal problems and external threats, the paper managed to stay alive and play an important role in providing information about the range of perspectives on the peace process.

Clearly, the broadening of freedom of expression in the postwar period has robbed the *Latino* of some of the uniqueness that sustained it in the early 1990s. Whereas it was enough to be willing to brave government repression during the war, the coming of peace has challenged the paper to improve the quality of its reporting and resolve its internal organizational problems in order to expand its readership and become economically viable.

The only other daily paper is *La Noticia*. This mid-day paper distinguished itself during the war for its sensationalistic news coverage and daily publication of a full-page "bon-bon"—a scantily-clad young woman in a demeaning pose. This orientation made *La Noticia* the prototype for what Salvadorans call "yellow journalism." In 1994, new ownership launched the paper on a new course designed to make it a respectable, high-quality alternative for educated Salvadorans. Within a few months, the bon-bons were gone and the paper had largely shaken its "yellow" past. Observers inside the newspapers suggested that the shift in *La Noticia* was really an attempt by the owners of *La Prensa* to test the market for a high-quality newspaper without the political history of the major Salvadoran dailies.[84]

The four most important weekly publications in the country are *Orientación*, *The El Salvador News Gazette*, *Primera Plana*, and *Proceso*. *Orientación*, the official organ of the Salvadoran Roman Catholic Church, gains a wide distribution through the country's local churches. Wealthy businessman Mario Rosenthal began publishing the *News Gazette* during the war as an extremely conservative bilingual weekly.[85] After the war, Rosenthal sold the paper to Ramón Quiros and his wife. The paper made a quick turn toward the political center and became a free-distribution weekly with a decidedly upscale orientation.

After a long period of preparation, *Primera Plana* emerged in 1994 as an attempt to provide the country with a genuine alternative newsweekly. Although much of the leadership of the paper has historical connections to the FMLN, *Primera Plana* has worked hard to project an image of political independence by viewing all of Salvadoran politics and society through the same critical lens.[86] While the paper was able to secure advance financing to support several months of production in an attractive, color format, financing will present a major challenge in the medium term. In its first few months of publication, readers were already criticizing *Primera Plana* for seeking access to the mainstream through the same sort of sensational reporting and exploitative imagery of women prevalent in the rest of Salvadoran journalism. This debate points directly to the difficulties faced by most of the new media emerging in the postwar period.

The University Documentation and Information Center of the UCA (CIDAI) has published since 1980 a weekly journal of news analysis and commentary called *Proceso*. It is progressive in its approach but careful to remain scholarly and objective. Many readers observe that personnel and other changes have resulted in a significant decline in the quality of the information in *Proceso* since the end of the war. Nonetheless, *Proceso* and the other publications emanating from the UCA remain one of the best sources for knowledge of contemporary Salvadoran society.[87]

Television

With the number of television sets in El Salvador growing faster than the population, television has become an increasingly important medium in the 1990s. All polls concur in the conclusion that television has surpassed radio as the primary source of information for educated Salvadorans.[88] Channels 2, 4, and 6 dominate TV ratings: All are owned by the Salvadoran government.

Prior to the war, television news was little more than a digest of official pronouncements and the latest tidbits from high society. Beginning in the mid-1980s, however, Salvadoran TV news, especially that of Channel 12, became one of the best in Central America.[89] The improvements at Channel 12 forced competitors at the state-owned stations to improve their coverage, as well. Channel 12 created a sensation in the mid-1980s when it began to program televised debates between government leaders and opposition figures. Perhaps the most celebrated of such debates occurred among Roberto D'Aubuisson of ARENA, Gerardo LeChevalier of the PDC, and Ignacio Ellacuría of the UCA. Such programs soon became a staple of Salvadoran TV.

The increasing popularity of television news created several well-known TV personalities. Among the best known of this new breed of national opinion-makers were: Roxana Lemus, who worked as a TV anchor woman at Channel 12 before marrying guerrilla commander Joaquín Villalobos after his return to civilian life; Antonio Miñeros, anchor at Channels 12 and 21 before becoming the press director for the ARENA party; and Mauricio Funes, an intelligent young reporter who hosted the popular interview program *Entrevista Al Día*. In the wake of the signing of the Peace Accords, labor difficulties led to sweeping changes at Channel 12, with many of the leading reporters moving to a new private channel, Channel 21. While the technology of news coverage continued to improve, the rapid improvements in news quality that occurred in the 1980s leveled off considerably during the first half of the 1990s.

As TV news coverage became more influential in the formation of Salvadoran public opinion, the importance of the medium in the political process grew by leaps and bounds. Beginning in the late 1980s, ARENA's access to resources allowed it to experiment with modern mass communications techniques in the development of its campaigns. The party's use of television greatly increased after it won control of the government in 1989. By the 1994 elections, ARENA had in place a TV-led communications strategy which was a major factor in its electoral victory.

Radio

Even as television gained significance as a communications medium among the Salvadoran middle and upper classes, radio, with 4.3 million daily listeners, remained the mass medium with the broadest national reach. The country has more than four dozen radio stations yet the airwaves are dominated by a small number of stations owned by wealthy supporters of the ARENA party. These stations, including YSKL (La Poderosa), Radio Sonora, and Radiocadena (YSU), attract large quantities of advertising dollars and dominate the ratings. The radio station of the Armed Forces, Radio Cuscatlán, also claims a significant audience.

The Catholic radio station, YSAX, broadcasts the Sunday homily of the Archbishop of San Salvador and other religious programming. In the late 1970s the station rose in prominence with the popularity of Monseñor Romero. It was said that one could walk through certain rural areas in El Salvador without missing a word of the Monseñor's homily because every house was tuned to YSAX. The station came under increasing attack and was bombed several times until 1984, when a new director took the station in a more conservative direction.

Even in the difficult conditions of the war, the determined efforts of a small number of young journalists led to efforts to provide more balanced news coverage. These changes, although not as dramatic as the developments in TV news, made their contribution to an openness in Salvadoran society that was an important precondition for peace.

During the war the FMLN challenged the government's effort to dominate the airwaves by establishing two guerrilla radio stations. Government jamming techniques severely limited the ability of Salvadorans in the capital to receive the guerrilla stations, but they were a significant communications presence throughout rural El Salvador.

On November 16, 1991, on the second anniversary of the Jesuit killings, YSUCA ushered in a new era of Salvadoran radio broadcasting with its first transmissions from offices just a few yards away from the garden where the massacre had occurred. In fulfilling a long-term dream of Ignacio Ellacuría, YSUCA began with a virtually noncommercial format combining protest music with religious programming, wide-ranging talk shows, and news coverage clearly in line with the Jesuits' critical view of Salvadoran reality. Although the war was still in progress, the situation in El Salvador had changed to the point where the government was loathe to move against YSUCA.

The narrow path opened by the launching of YSUCA became a well-paved road in the wake of the signing of the Peace Accords. Both Radio Venceremos and Radio Farabundo Martí gained legal status in the first weeks of 1992, emerging on the FM dial throughout the country. After the euphoria of the first few weeks, both began to experience the difficulties of the transition from rebel stations to commercially viable communications outlets in a highly competitive radio market. Both began with sufficient financing to assure operations for an initial period, but the stations felt the pressure to quickly establish market niches that would make them sustainable in the long run.

The search for a place within the market led to massive organizational and format changes at both stations. Many FMLN supporters expressed dissatisfaction with the changes and accused the stations of abandoning their commitment to the country's revolutionary process. Some even wondered if the market would do what the army had been unable to do during the entire war— destroy the rebel stations.

Soon both stations were accepting paid announcements from the government and electoral propaganda from all political parties. Protest music had been increasingly replaced by the *cumbias* preferred by most Salvadorans, and rock music from the United States even elbowed its way onto playlists. By the 1994 electoral campaign, the distance between Radio Venceremos, traditionally the voice of the ERP, and the political project of the FMLN had reached the point where the FMLN-supported campaign of Rubén Zamora angrily withdrew all advertising from Radio Venceremos when it refused to run an announcement about Armando Calderón Sol's reported physical abuse of his wife.[90]

By the mid-1990s, both of the formerly FMLN radios, YSUCA, and a new private station called *Mayavisión* remained formally committed to alternative broadcasting. While each of these stations continued to produce some excellent programs, it became more difficult to distinguish these "alternatives" from other commercial outlets.

The end of the war and the entry of rebel stations into legal broadcasting led to a broader diversity in Salvadoran radio and a substantial increase in freedom of expression in that medium. Gradually, market discipline tended to limit that diversity. Despite these obvious limitations, all observers acknowledged that peace had considerably broadened freedom of expression, not only in the Salvadoran media but throughout society. In 1995, reflecting on three years of peace, Salvador Samayoa of the FMLN went so far as to say:

> I'm not sure that there is another country in Latin America that has the level of freedom of expression that we now do, and that's not luck, it's part of a new culture of freedom of expression that didn't exist.[91]

Literature and the Arts

The general increase in freedom of expression after the war extended beyond the mass media to cultural expression, which had also been severely restricted in wartime. The increasing repression experienced in the late 1970s forced the vibrant culture of opposition that accompanied the growth of the popular movement underground.[92] Repression also stifled much artistic expression that never sought any particular political identification. Art that could be construed to have any sort of critical social content became a subversive act punishable, like all subversion, by death.

In the latter half of the 1980s, cultural workers began to cautiously test the possibilities of public presentation of music, visual arts, and literature associated with social protest. Groups such as the Association of Salvadoran Artists and Cultural Workers (ASTAC) were formed to support such work.

Cultural work expanded rapidly during 1991 in anticipation of the end of the war. The downtown National Theater, barely used for much of the 1980s, became a busy venue for a variety of cultural presentations, from protest music from the Latin American "New Song" tradition to classical piano sponsored by the United States embassy. Newly formed theater groups as well as established ones like *Sol del Río* also made use of the aging performance space. During this same time, *Diario Latino* began publishing its cultural weekly, *Tres Mil*, which surprised many observers by combining guerrilla poetry written in the mountains with the classical verse of David Escobar Galindo, an establishment intellectual who sat on the government commission to the peace talks.

The UCA publishing house also got an early start on the postwar literary era with the mid-1991 release of *Las mil y una historia de radio venceremos*.[93] A rousing success by Salvadoran standards, the collection of stories about life in the mountains with the "official voice of the FMLN" sold out the first run of five thousand copies before the conclusion of the war.

Immediately after the end of the war, cultural activity expanded rapidly as Salvadoran cultural workers and their audiences took advantage of their new found freedom. Musical groups like *Los Torogoces de Morazán* drew large, enthusiastic audiences. Several clubs/cultural centers were established in response to the perception that oppositional cultural activity would create viable economic opportunities. *La Luna*, an eclectic private center formed at the end of the war, emerged as the most popular and successful of the group.

In addition, several publishers either initiated or expanded their publishing activities in the postwar period. The books of *Sombrero Azul, Arcoiris, Istmo* and other small publishers joined those of the UCA and the National University on shelves not just in the universities, but in quality bookstores around the city.

Theater and other performing arts also experienced something of a postwar boom. Dance ensembles from the National University and the UCA made increasingly frequent presentations, and, in 1993, *Sol del Río* sponsored a regional theater festival that drew thousands of theater patrons to an entire week of presentations by accomplished troupes from several countries. ASTAC expanded its educational work and general support for the arts out of its *Centro Cultural La Mazorca* conveniently located across from the National University.

The postwar expansion of cultural activity continued into the mid-1990s and even accelerated in many areas. Despite this growth, nearly all cultural institutions encountered the same sorts of pressures faced by the new media enterprises. Several of the cultural centers started as businesses after the war were forced to close for economic reasons. *La Luna*, however, appeared to be thriving by offering a varied menu of activities. Those small publishers who did not overextend themselves in economic terms also seemed to be surviving, if not rapidly expanding.

On the third anniversary of the signing of the Peace Accords, Salvadoran writer Jacinta Escudos boldly stated that maybe it was time for Salvadoran writers to move away from what she indentified as a cultural fixation on the war.

> Salvadoran literature needs to break with the themes it is dealing with, especially with reference to the war, where we really seem to be stuck. We need variety, experimentation, and exploration of other than local themes or social issues of which, I repeat, the readers are tired. This fatigue could be one of the causes of disinterest in reading and culture, generally.[94]

Such opinions point to one of the most serious dilemmas faced by Salvadoran cultural workers searching for their place in postwar El Salvador.

Social Organizations and the Popular Movement

© Edgar Romero

Popular Movement

Analysis of the current situation in El Salvador is impossible without reference to the evolution of the country's popular movement. The word "popular" has quite a specific meaning in the Latin American context. According to Salvadoran activist and writer Mario Lungo Uclés, "...*popular* is characterized by an identification with transformation in economic, political, cultural, and social terms that benefits the marginalized. Those who act for social justice identify with and make up the popular movement. It is the political option, not their economic status, which defines the participants in the popular movement..."[1]

Popular Organizing in Historical Perspective

An extreme polarization of the social classes of Salvadoran society led directly to the outbreak of civil war there. These tensions eventually overwhelmed the limited ability of social and political institutions to mediate conflict and bring about necessary social reforms. The growth of the guerrilla movement in the 1970s represented a radicalization of a popular movement with deep roots in a long tradition of Salvadoran resistance.

Since the arrival of the Spanish in the sixteenth century, the occupants of the land now called El Salvador have organized, first to oppose the Spanish invaders and then to seek social justice within the new order. Historically, the groups holding power in the country—the Spanish *conquistadores*, their *criollo* descendants, and the "modernized" oligarchy of twentieth century El Salvador in the 1970s—have typically answered such movements with violent repression.

This dynamic reached an extreme in 1932 with the infamous *matanza*, in which the military massacred thousands of urban and rural opponents of the regime.[2] Although rural opposition almost disappeared after the *matanza*, the urban movements showed some strength, especially in the 1940s when nonviolent popular action played an important role in ending the dictatorship established after the 1932 massacre. It was not until the 1960s, however, that popular movements began to return to their place at the center of the national political stage.

During that decade, young activists with support from sources ranging from the Alliance for Progress to the new Christian Democratic party formed rural cooperatives to press for the interests of impoverished campesinos. The labor movement was similarly revitalized and important sectors of the urban middle classes began to demand social changes.

In part, this new popular movement had its roots in the traditional urban radicalism represented by the small, but influential, Salvadoran Communist Party. Especially in rural areas, the movement also had another, critically important impetus, namely, the transformation of the Catholic Church.

As early as the 1950s, the Salvadoran Roman Catholic Church had shown signs of shaking free of the staunch conservatism which had traditionally placed it at the side of the country's economic oligarchy.[3] Beginning in the mid-1960s, young nuns, priests, and other church leaders, many of them Salvadorans, were moved by the suffering around them to reconsider their role in society. This experience led them to a new and challenging reading of the Bible, which saw the future of the church in its service to poor people. This new vision insisted that poor Salvadorans did not have to wait until death to "inherit the earth," but instead, were entitled to their fair share of the fruits of human society.

Slowly, this new reading of the Bible began to form the basis of a deep transition in the world view of many Salvadoran campesinos, who formed organizations to demand a better future for themselves and their children.[4] The teachings of the Second Vatican Council and the Latin American Bishops' conferences at Puebla, México and Medellín, Colombia validated the church's shift toward a commitment to a "preferential option for the poor." Many clergy and lay people of the historical Protestant churches—the Lutheran, the Episcopal, and the Baptist, for example—soon joined the Roman Catholic Church on this new path. The theology which arose to describe and explain this new experience of the Latin American church became known as liberation theology.

This reinvigorated vision of the church spawned an organizational upsurge all over El Salvador. The "Christian base community," often built around a small group of people engaged in the study of the Bible in relation to their own reality, served as the basic building block of this movement. This movement quickly moved to challenge traditional structures of power and wealth in the name of the installation of the "Kingdom of God" on earth.

By the mid-1970s, both urban and rural movements had grown tremendously and had begun to inspire a vibrant political opposition. A unique and explosive relationship began between the urban-based left—undergoing its own process of transformation—and the new popular movements rooted in Christian base community organizing. The predictable response of the oligarchy was violent repression. In both 1972 and 1977 clear electoral victories for the opposition were vetoed by the military and protests drowned in pools of blood. Death squads, which were not a new phenomenon in El Salvador, became the preferred weapon for the elimination of the opposition, and the death toll mounted.

In the face of such repression, the popular movement quickly adopted more radical positions, demanding not only reforms but a revolutionary transformation of the society. Important sectors of the movements decided that, in the face of the intransigent repression of the Salvadoran power structure, only armed struggle could bring about the necessary changes.

Large popular mobilizations in January and March 1980 ended in massacres as the security forces fired on huge crowds in the streets of San Salvador. The second of these was the funeral procession for Monseñor Oscar Arnulfo Romero, the tremendously popular Roman Catholic leader who was assassinated while saying Mass in San Salvador. Later that year, the leaders of the opposition Democratic Revolutionary Front (FDR), the unified leading body of the popular movement, were taken from a meeting at the Jesuit high school in the capital and murdered. The formation of the FMLN and the outbreak of the civil war were direct outcomes of this cycle of repression and radicalization. The influence of external factors should not be minimized. Obviously, the July 1979 Sandinista triumph in neighboring Nicaragua turned up the heat on the pot of social protest in El Salvador. The pot, however, was already well on its way to boiling from the heat provided by internal contradictions in Salvadoran society. East-West factors had even less influence at this stage.

Popular Organizing in the 1980s

Whereas in the 1970s the government had responded to popular organizing with repression, by the early 1980s it had developed a two-pronged, carrot-and-stick approach. Reforms like political modernizations and agrarian reform served as the carrot, while brutal repression much more intense than that of the 1970s was the stick.

This combination of reform and repression seriously weakened the popular movement and facilitated the creation of pro-government worker and campesino organizations supported by U.S. aid programs.

The repression of the early 1980s wiped out the strong popular coalitions that formed in the previous decade. In the midst of the repression, only organizations linked to the government and the U.S. embassy could operate openly.[5] Activists from the older popular organizations had either fallen victim to death squad attacks, gone into hiding, or joined the ranks of the FMLN guerrillas. Its space for activity reduced to nothing, the above-ground popular movement virtually ceased to exist.

The progressive popular movement did not disappear for long. Labor organizations were among the first to reemerge.[6] Several labor federations and peasant associations had formed Democratic Popular Unity (UPD) in the early 1980s, but this organization was closely linked to the PDC and the American Institute for Free Labor Development (AIFLD). It was not until 1983 that a strongly anti-government labor movement started to organize. The first to form was the leftist MUSYGES federation, founded in 1983 but quickly cut down by repression. Soon thereafter, however, a powerful new confederation of labor unions and peasant associations rose up to challenge the economic policies and war-making of the Duarte government. This was the National Unity of Salvadoran Workers (UNTS), which was much broader than the UPD or any other existing alliance. This sparked the formation of a pro-government, U.S.-financed coalition called National Union of Workers and Campesinos (UNOC). UNOC was largely made up of rural associations and unions funded by AIFLD.

By the late 1980s an extraordinary variety of new popular organizations had surfaced. Most of these were quite closely tied to one or another of the component parts of the FMLN. The student, worker, and peasant movements that had been crushed in the early 1980s reemerged with different names and often with different leaders. They were joined by new organizations from every social sector. These included organizations of the displaced, squatters, earthquake victims, the unemployed, women, political prisoners, and families of the dead and disappeared.[7] During this period, the popular movement showed extraordinary creativity in adapting to the rapidly changing social situation of the country.

Most organizations began as expressions of social and economic demands specific to a particular sector, such as women or displaced people. The political differences resulting from affiliation with different organizations of the FMLN complicated these sectoral differences.[8] At the same time, since many organizations subordinated their sectoral demands to the overall goal of the revolution, the common relationship to the FMLN allowed a certain coherence behind the general FMLN project of revolutionary transformation. As a result, while the various organizations of residents of marginal communities, for example, might have had difficulties coordinating concrete community organizing activities, they largely agreed on the long-term goal of overthrowing the Salvadoran government. This agreement was critical in the late 1980s, when this broad, diverse popular movement was able to come together behind a political platform rooted in the demand for a negotiated peace based on structural changes to Salvadoran society. In 1988 Archbishop Arturo Rivera y Damas called a broad-based conference, billed as the National Debate for Peace. At that conference, the participants decided to create a Permanent Committee for the National Debate (CPDN) to act as an ongoing voice for the popular movement in the peace process. Although the CPDN was never formally recognized in either the dialog or negotiation phases of the peace process, the Permanent Committee played an important role through the signing of the peace agreement and beyond.

Facing an ARENA Government

The election of the first ARENA government in 1989 represented a serious challenge to the popular movement which had reestablished itself under the Duarte administration. The months after President Cristiani's assumption of power in June of that year saw a return to the dynamic of repression and radicalization. As the number of violent attacks on the popular movement surpassed that of the Duarte period, at least part of the popular movement adopted more radical tactics, such as militant street demonstrations in which buses were burned and other property destroyed. This change also responded to an increasingly aggressive posture by the FMLN, which assassinated several key government and ARENA party officials during this same period.

This spiral of violence culminated in October 1989 with the lunchtime bombing of the headquarters of the trade union federation, FENASTRAS. The bomb took the lives of FENASTRAS president Febe Elisabeth Velásquez and nine other union members. The FMLN withdrew from negotiations with the government and the November offensive took place within two weeks of the FENASTRAS bombing.[9]

The offensive ushered in a severe round of repression against the popular movement. Many activists took up arms and actively supported the FMLN offensive. UNTS leader Humberto Centeno insisted that, "For many, it was stay above ground and be killed [by the army] or incorporate."[10] Leaders who did not go underground were arrested;

all organizational offices were closed in San Salvador and their contents looted by military and security police. The military ended up with so much material from these raids that Col. Francisco Elena Fuentes of San Salvador's First Brigade was said to be using a facsimile machine as his office doorstop.

Much to the surprise of all observers, the popular organizations quickly reconstituted themselves after the offensive. The members of the Christian Committee of the Displaced (CRIPDES) boldly reentered their offices in February 1990 under the watchful eyes of a large contingent of Salvadoran soldiers accompanied by a menacing tank. Movement leaders used the occasion of the tenth anniversary of the death of Monseñor Romero in March 1990 to hold a dramatic public march which widened the space available to the movement. By mid-1990, the popular movement was up and running again—minus those who had lost their lives in the offensive.

This ability to recover quickly from periods of repression is one of the movement's defining characteristics. When describing this trait, Salvadorans often resort to the image of the country's aptly-chosen national flower, the *flor de izote*. The plant, whose small white blossoms are an important seasonal food source in some areas of the country, grows back quickly after being cut. Campesinos insist that if cut in the afternoon, a new plant will have blossomed again by noon of the following day.

In the wake of the offensive, the popular movement worked to broaden itself by becoming more unified. Since it could not hope to succeed at the PDC strategy of coopting an important sector of the popular movement, ARENA addressed the movement with policies, such as the subdivision of the agrarian reform cooperatives, that were antagonistic to all campesino organizations.

Such policies helped to foster unity between the more radical elements of the popular movements with close ties to the FMLN and those organizations that had been previously connected to the Duarte administration. The UNTS and UNOC united with smaller federations to form the INTERGREMIAL, the broadest worker-campesino alliance in recent Salvadoran history. Similarly, twelve campesino organizations formed the Democratic Campesino Association (ADC) uniting previously divided rural organizations. In 1990, for the first time, groups like UNOC began to join the call of the UNTS for popular demonstrations demanding peace. The first meaningful collaboration of this sort took place in the march organized for Independence Day, September 15, 1990.

With important exceptions—like the strike of Treasury employees in 1991—popular organizations during this period eschewed the radical tactics of the pre-offensive days, preferring instead to pursue their goals via peaceful street demonstrations, paid advertisements in the newspapers, and other actions well within the framework of Salvadoran legality.[11] Once the peace negotiations got back on track in early 1990, the popular movement clearly prioritized its role as a loud and consistent voice in favor of a peaceful solution to the conflict.

Clearly, the numbers of detentions of popular leaders and the scale of human rights violations against the popular movement declined in the early 1990s from the explosive situation that existed in the latter part of 1989. Nonetheless, relations between the ARENA government and the popular movement remained strained and abuses of the human rights of movement leaders continued to be a serious problem.

The signing of the Chapultepec Accord had as significant an impact on the Salvadoran popular movement as it did on the political parties and other institutions of society. Hopes ran high that the end of the military conflict would permit the strengthening of the institutions of civil society—including the popular organizations—and allow them to play a more protagonistic role in society. Similarly, organized Salvadorans expected that the end of the war would allow their organizations to downplay their political role in favor of an emphasis on promoting the economic and social interests of their constituents. The expectations for immediate improvements were tremendous.

Not surprisingly, the experience of the postwar varied greatly from organization to organization. Most popular organizations, however, have found it difficult to respond to this dizzying array of opportunities and challenges. While each social movement has had to develop its own approach to this situation, the various responses share a great deal.

Labor and Unions

Workers in El Salvador are known throughout the region for their industriousness and proclivity for organizing. According to a 1993 report, however, fewer than 100,000 Salvadorans were legally organized members of trade unions.[12] This number does not include public sector workers, who are legally prohibited from forming unions but are well-organized in employee associations. Even if state workers are included, this is not a large number of people in a country of more than five million people. The proportion takes on a different meaning, however, in the social and political context of Salvadoran society.

The economic situation of a country where over half of the "economically active" population is without a formal job, and where it takes 3.5 minimum wages to meet the basic needs of a family greatly limits the possibilities of a trade union movement.[13] Furthermore, even though the Legislative Assembly passed a reform of the country's Labor Code in April 1994, unions still face powerful legal obstacles to organizing. Salvadoran law, for example, explicitly prohibits all public workers and nearly all agricultural workers from organizing unions. The law recognizes a limited right to strike for all workers who can organize, but as of 1995 no strike had ever been declared legal under that law. Finally, the number of workers who belong to unions must be understood in the context of a long history of political repression of the labor movement, which became even more acute during the civil war of the 1980s.

A Brief History of Labor Organizing

The Salvadoran labor movement traces its history to the formation of the Central American Congress of Workers in El Salvador in 1911.[14] After the Regional Federation of Salvadoran Workers served as the primary vehicle of the rebellion of 1932, Gen. Hernández Martínez outlawed unions from 1932 to 1944. Unions quickly reappeared after the fall of the dictatorship but suffered a major setback with the failure of a general strike and the exiling of labor leaders in 1946. The constitution of 1950 was the first in El Salvador's history to concede the right of urban workers (excluding state workers) to organize, to bargain collectively, and to strike. As a group, agricultural workers have yet to receive even these basic freedoms.

These formal rights had little meaning to Salvadoran workers. The successive military governments attempted to control the incipient labor movement through bureaucratic manipulations of the Ministry of Labor and the outright repression of the forces of public security. The international operations department of the AFL-CIO and (after 1962) the AIFLD spent large sums in the effort to maintain moderate, pro-government unions like the Salvadoran General Confederation of Unions (CGS).

Neither repression nor buy-offs succeeded in containing the independent and often leftist-oriented organizing efforts of Salvadoran unions. The 1970s were an especially fruitful period for labor organizing. Internal demands for more militant positions on the part of union leaders caused the weakening of the CGS, with a significant part of its base departing to form FENASTRAS. That federation was destined to become a focal point of the radical labor movement of the 1980s.

Massive repression in the late 1970s and early 1980s all but closed the space available to the unions associated with the anti-government popular movement. Between 1980 and 1984 hundreds of labor leaders were openly murdered or disappeared. Although independent organizing was silenced, this was a period of rapid growth for AIFLD-sponsored groups not normally subject to the same repression. Several such organizations, most with ties to both the United States and the Christian Democratic party, gained prominence during this period but did little to improve the lot of Salvadoran workers. In 1988, the U.S. embassy gave unwitting testimony to the lack of effectiveness of the U.S.-supported unions by saying that, "Fully 77 percent of collective bargaining agreements were between employers and UNTS affiliates."[15]

In 1984 labor organizing increased markedly as the progressive labor movement began to take advantage of the "democratic opening" resulting from the election of President Duarte and increased international press coverage of El Salvador. This upsurge of organizing culminated in 1986 with the formation of the UNTS. Primarily a labor coalition, the UNTS brought together the progressive labor movement with like-minded campesino organizations and other popular groups. Although the repressive environment of the war made it impossible for the UNTS to openly declare its political sympathies, the radical orientation of the federation spoke to the influence of the FMLN within the popular movement.

The Christian Democratic government quickly responded by forming the UNOC as a counterweight to the UNTS. Not content with the formation of UNOC, AIFLD worked to counter the growing strength of the UNTS by creating parallel unions in an attempt to isolate the UNTS affiliates. UNOC and the UNTS were sharply at odds until after the election of the ARENA government in 1989 and the guerrilla offensive in November of that year. At that point, a common distaste for ARENA policy began to create the basis for the aforementioned new unity in the labor movement. Although UNOC firmly supported the PDC in the elections of 1989, and again in 1991, that federation began to cautiously applaud FMLN proposals for a peaceful end to the conflict. Broad unity behind the peace process within a traditionally divided labor movement served as one of many positive factors pushing the FMLN and the government toward Chapultepec.

Economic and Social Forum

The Peace Accords made little mention of the economic problems confronting workers in El Salvador, and contained even less in the way of solutions to those problems. The agreement did, however, establish a potential mechanism for resolving these problems in the form of a mutual commitment to a social consensus-building process called *concertación*. Specifically, problems in labor-management relations were to be resolved through the Economic and Social Forum (FES). The FES was originally conceived as a forum for the discussion of a broad range of popular concerns, but the agenda was quickly narrowed to focus on the concerns of the labor movement. The other social movements were forced to seek other avenues for dealing with their issues.

As outlined in the Chapultepec Accord, the forum was to involve a series of tripartite meetings between labor, business and government. The meetings were to "achieve a set of broad agreements tending toward the social and economic development of the country, for the benefit of all its inhabitants."[16] Specifically, the government was mandated to place before the forum a proposal for a new legal framework to govern labor relations and an analysis of the situation of the marginal communities. In addition, participants in the forum were to arrive at consensus on policies to alleviate the social costs of structural adjustment.

In the immediate postwar period, the labor movement was very hopeful about the possibility of resolving its problems through the FES but those hopes were quickly frustrated. The inauguration of the FES was delayed for months as the business representatives decided under what conditions they would participate.

When discussions finally began, progress was painfully slow. The agenda of the forum was further narrowed to a single point—an amended Labor Code for El Salvador that would remove the overwhelming legal obstacles to labor organizing. Labor ended up proposing that El Salvador ratify a series of international conventions regarding labor rights recognized by the International Labor Organization (ILO).

When the business and government representatives balked, UNOC and the UNTS formally petitioned the United States government to have El Salvador removed from the list of nations receiving special trade benefits under the Generalized System of Preferences (GSP). The petition based its demand on the consistent denial of basic organizing rights to Salvadoran workers. Among consistent violations of workers' rights, the labor petition highlighted the government's inability to resolve 200 longstanding labor conflicts, the Ministry of Labor's refusal to declare any strike legal, and the ministry's delay in legalizing new unions after ARENA assumed power in 1989. AIFLD, which during the war had blocked efforts to end U.S. military aid to El Salvador on similar grounds, actually endorsed the 1993 petition.[17]

In response to the petition, the U.S. government insisted that a new Labor Code be approved before El Salvador's GSP status came up for renewal at the end of 1993. With the deadline approaching and no agreement in sight, President Cristiani placed his own proposal for labor legislation before the Legislative Assembly. The Assembly quickly approved the legislation over the protests of Salvadoran unions who said that the new law did not even include the agreements that had been reached in the FES. The Salvadoran government, for its part, insisted that the new code had the support of the ILO representative Arthur Bronstein who sent the government a letter stating that "on the whole [the proposed changes] contain important advances."[18] Bronstein even went before the U.S. Congress to testify in support of the Salvadoran government's claim of improved labor rights.[19] In January 1994, the United States extended El Salvador's status under the GSP pending a full review of the labor law reforms.

The FES was suspended in late 1993 for the electoral period. After the elections, the government maintained that the Superior Labor Council established by the new Labor Code superseded the FES, making it redundant. By 1995, the FES showed few signs of life.

In early 1992, the labor movement had looked forward to participation in the FES with great hope. Three years later, that outlook had changed radically. The primary tool established by the Peace Accords for the harmonization of the interests of labor and business appeared to have disappeared with very little to show for its brief existence.

Main Labor Organizations

For a small country with less than 100,000 trade unionists, El Salvador has an inordinate number of labor federations and unions. The variety is related more to the attempts of various political projects to influence the labor movement than any simple consideration of the needs of Salvadoran workers. The immediate postwar period in El Salvador saw a great deal of restructuring of organizational alliances in the labor movement, and this trend can be expected to continue for most of the 1990s.

The UNTS, though weakened by its own internal problems, continued to group left-leaning unions and public worker associations, many with close connections to the FMLN. Major UNTS affiliates included the Federation of Associations and Independent Unions of El Salvador (FEASIES), the Coordinating Council of State and Municipal Workers (CCTEM) (between them, these two include many of the most important public sector workers' organizations in the country), and the United Labor Federation of El Salvador (FUSS). As of early 1995, the UNTS had embarked on an effort to restructure itself in a way that would offer member unions more control over the direction of the organization. Many traditionally progressive unions, however, had decided to remain independent of the UNTS.

UNOC survived the early 1990s as a rickety coalition of unions with historical ties to the Christian Democratic party. It disbanded, however, in 1994 in the context of major internal convulsions in the PDC. As of early 1995, the remnants of UNOC embarked on a new strategy to form three new sectoral federations. Conservative union leader Freddy Vásquez took the lead by forming a new federation which grouped together most of the private sector unions from UNOC and several previously independent unions.

In 1993 some previously independent federations joined with the remnants of the Popular Democratic Union (UPD) of the early Duarte period and others who had departed from UNOC to form the Democratic Labor Sector (SLD). The members of the SLD included the Federation of Construction Industry Unions (FESINCONSTRANS), the General Confederation of Workers (CGT) (mostly agricultural cooperatives), and the old, traditionally pro-government CGS. SLD support for the presidential candidacy of Armando Calderón Sol and for the Labor Code reforms proposed by President Cristiani in late 1993 showed this grouping to be a fruit of ARENA's determined effort to build support within the labor movement.

The decline of FENASTRAS is indicative of the overall problem faced by Salvadoran unions. Once the broadest and most effective sector of the movement, by 1995 FENASTRAS had become a shadow of its former self. In 1986, FENASTRAS reached a peak membership of over 24,000, representing 25 percent of the entire labor movement, but by 1995 it numbered no more than 1000 workers.

Political differences with the leadership of the UNTS led FENASTRAS to withdraw from the former in 1993. During the same period the organization broke decisively with the National Resistance (RN), the FMLN party with which it had associated during the war. The ensuing leadership battle led half of the federation's member unions (representing the majority of the membership) to withdraw. The corruption and divisions within FENASTRAS suggest that independence from the FMLN is no panacea for the union movement. In assessing the sad turn in the fortunes of FENASTRAS, it is important to remember that the federation lost the heart of its leadership in the October 1989 bombing and a series of other attacks in the same period.

The Salvadoran Worker-Management Foundation (FOES) became an important institutional presence in the Salvadoran labor movement in the postwar period. Founded in the early 1990s with the support of AIFLD and AID, FOES represents an effort to establish a new direction in labor-management relations. Rather than supporting labor-management collaboration to undermine unions, FOES is using its ample funding to involve labor leaders in investment projects that will turn them into small business people.

After denouncing the FOES as "company unionism," a broad cross-section of Salvadoran union leaders are making their peace with FOES. FENASTRAS, previously a virulent opponent of AIFLD's attempts to influence the Salvadoran labor movement, by 1995 received a significant part of its budget from FOES.[20] Given the financial crisis of Salvadoran unions and the unclear prospects of union leaders, FOES' capacity to provide funds appeared to be assuring a broad hearing for its message of labor entrepreneurship.

Hard Times for Labor

The ARENA program of deep structural adjustment with massive privatization and upward distribution of income directly challenged the ability of the labor movement to defend the interests of Salvadoran workers. Despite its many difficulties, the labor movement had emerged from the war with increased unity and an optimistic view that it had the answer to the government challenge. In the immediate postwar period, however, several widely publicized labor conflicts ended in defeat for the workers because of the obstinate opposition of employers to unionization.

Perhaps the most publicized of these efforts was FENASTRAS' attempt to organize the giant Soyapango facility of the ADOC shoe company through a strike in 1992. The union drive represented the fourth effort to organize the facility since 1969. The factory was owned by the Palomo family, a proud member of the country's traditional economic oligarchy. Roberto Palomo refused to recognize the union and threatened to move the factory's production to Costa Rica. Rather than enforce the rights of the workers, the government openly supported the owner and the strike was quickly defeated.

This pattern persisted at the Hotel El Salvador, Blokitubos, and other important companies where the workers showed interest in forming unions. ARENA pursued the same policy in its approach to labor conflict in the public sector. Employer obstinacy, firings, and intimidation largely replaced the "direct-action" repression of the previous two decades, but the result was much the same.

Privatization posed a major threat to the thousands of workers in the public sector. The Cristiani government achieved the privatization of the banking system and several small- to medium-sized government services, such as the National Coffee Institute and the institution responsible for the marketing of basic food crops under the Duarte administration.

Labor first expressed blanket opposition to privatization, but began to moderate its view in the face of the government steamroller and the limited public support for corrupt and inefficient state services. By 1993 labor was already supporting the privatization of some "nonessential" services as long as the interests of workers and consumers were taken into account. This change did not extend to the basic services like electricity, telephone, and water, or the health and education systems.

As one of its first programmatic initiatives, the Calderón Sol administration proposed a much more aggressive program of privatizations than that pursued by its predecessor. A massive publicity campaign claimed that huge savings would be realized and services improved by placing even basic services in the hands of the private sector. Labor's response to the government communications offensive was a communiqué presented to the president and the major media reiterating labor's willingness to talk about privatization and even support it under certain circumstances. The movement, however, maintained its determined opposition to privatization of basic services and its willingness to fight to prevent such actions. The communiqué, however, carried only the signatures of the leaders of several public sector associations; the more progressive members of the UNTS and UNOC did not sign it.

Fresh from its landslide electoral victory, ARENA showed little interest in discussing its privatization plans with labor or anyone else. Instead, ARENA regularly pointed to the support of the SLD unions for its positions as evidence of its work to build social consensus. Short of a highly unlikely return to the militant mass mobilization tactics of the 1970s, labor appeared to be without the resources to halt mass privatization. The inability of labor to respond decisively to privatization or to assert its basic right to collectively bargain on behalf of workers raises another key factor in the relative weakness of the movement in the postwar period—the movement's internal organizational health.

The experience of organizing during the war created some exceptional trade union leaders and also developed union members who were willing to sacrifice everything for their movement. At the same time, that experience left the movement with many organizational deficiencies that have become apparent only in the postwar period. Wartime repression turned unions into highly centralized organizations with rigorous security procedures as a necessary survival strategy. National staff took responsibility for almost all organizational tasks, and local and sectional organization faded from existence.[21] Such a structure created unions that could keep leaders alive in wartime and have a political impact at the national and international levels, but it did not create a democratic movement that could organize workers in the face of determined opposition from employers or defend workers unjustly singled out by their employers for union activity.

The complicated internal scenario of the labor movement outlined above surely limited its effectiveness. ARENA's political manipulation of the SLD did no small amount of damage, but other political relations also caused the labor movement harm in the postwar period. Many of the strong political ties of Salvadoran unions—be they to the FMLN or another political entity—were formed and nurtured under the extraordinary conditions of the war. In that highly repressive context—where even an accusation of collaboration with the FMLN was often tantamount to a death sentence—political ties to the Frente were, understandably, a taboo subject. Such ties, however, greatly influenced the organizational structure and programmatic orientations of Salvadoran unions.

Although union leaders have almost universally acknowledged the need for more autonomy from political parties, the movement's pattern of political relations has proven resistant to change. As the political parties began to experience the dislocations of the postwar period, the labor movement could not help but be affected by these changes. The fragmentation of the FMLN placed a powerful strain on labor unity.

Looking Toward the Future

The traditional 1994 May Day march took place in San Salvador just a week after ARENA's resounding victory in the second round of the presidential elections. During the latter stages of the war, large May Day marches offered an opportunity for workers and other Salvadorans to express their opposition to their government. In 1994, however, just a few thousand workers turned out to the alternative "swearing-in" of the newly elected deputies of the FMLN. Although demonstrations are often not good indicators of the vitality of social movements, this demonstration did reflect the somber outlook among many workers about the future of their movement.

It was fairly clear that the government-sponsored reform of the country's Labor Code created a legal environment that would not result in markedly better conditions for labor organizing. Furthermore, labor's internal difficulties suggested that building the unity and organizational vitality necessary to successfully confront the government's structural adjustment program would be a long-term project.

Although cloudy, the horizon for labor in the mid-1990s was not entirely dark. Only one month after the May Day march and on the same day on which Calderón Sol was inaugurated president, twenty-four labor organizations presented the president with a "United Labor Platform" for the second half of that year.[22]

The platform presented labor's position on four pressing national problems: unemployment, the high cost of living, the condition of public services, and the threat to privatize publicly-held assets. In a departure from past efforts of this nature, the platform was a coherent, proactive proposal of concrete solutions from labor's perspective. In addition, it represented an attempt to unify the social agendas of a range of unions. The SLD, of course, declined to sign the platform and the name of FENASTRAS was also sadly lacking from the list of signatories. Nonetheless, efforts like the United Labor Platform and other local initiatives could be the first small steps toward the emergence of the unified, democratic and active labor movement demanded and deserved by Salvadoran workers.

In January 1995, when the Calderón Sol government announced a package of economic measures that included the privatization of many of the largest public enterprises, labor took to the streets in large, spirited demonstrations. It was not clear that public workers had the broad support necessary to stop the privatizations—which remained prominent in later "consensual" versions of the economic package—but they certainly appeared prepared to put up a serious fight against the plan.

Around the same time, another often ignored sector of Salvadoran workers showed that they might be ready to breathe life into the movement. In early February, women workers at a *maquila* plant in the free zone in San Marcos succeeded in shutting down the entire complex in a dispute over lay-offs. The action, followed by another, smaller activity at a nearby free zone, drew national attention to the situation of the mostly-female workforce in the rapidly growing *maquila* sector. *Maquila* owners have used their special status to avoid even the minimal requirements of Salvadoran labor law, resulting in scandalous mistreatment of *maquila* workers.[23]

The experience of the workers at Mandarin International points to the difficulties in organizing maquilas. Mandarin, owned by Army Colonel Mario Guerrero, was at the center of the dispute in the San Marcos. When workers there organized a union in January 1995, Mandarin became an example of the protections offered by Salvadoran labor law.

In February, however, Mandarin began firing union workers and beefing up its security forces. Guerrero showed what he thought about unions and labor law by telling Mandarin workers that "I have no problem, but perhaps you do: the union will either behave or leave...or people may die." [24] As of 1995, Mandarin, which produces clothing for the GAP, Eddie Bauer, and J.C. Penny, had not been sanctioned by the Salvadoran Ministry of Labor. Given the prominent place occupied by the maquilas in the economic plans of the government, success in this sector will be crucial to the labor movement.

Campesino Organizing

Since the Salvadoran civil war was essentially a rural insurrection by large numbers of poor farmers, the war had a particularly powerful impact on rural organization. Campesino organizations and communities suffered the brunt of the repression of the early 1980s but resurfaced to help lead the push for a negotiated solution to the conflict a decade later.

After the war's end, these organizations—centered mostly in the cooperative sector and in the repopulated and repatriated communities of the conflictive areas—were forced to make the difficult transition from the highly politicized structures of the war years to instruments for the expression of new economic alternatives. The transition was a difficult one that illuminated the internal limitations of the organizations as well as the hostile terrain of neoliberal economic policy at the national level.

Historical Roots

Since the arrival of the Spanish, the Salvadoran countryside has been home to a large group of landless or land-poor farmers. The country's agroexport economy—whether the primary crop was indigo, cacao, or coffee—always depended on the availability of this mass of poor campesinos as a source of cheap agricultural labor at harvest time. The extension of export agriculture to every corner of El Salvador involved the removal of increasingly large tracts of land from the country's indigenous communities, and its concentration in the hands of a small number of powerful landowners. This dispossession reached its zenith in the 1880s with the laws passed to place land suited to coffee cultivation in the hands of potential planters.[25]

Rural organization, therefore, threatened the bread-and-butter of the Salvadoran oligarchy and was always strictly controlled. The National Guard was formed in the late-nineteenth century with the explicit purpose of maintaining social order in the countryside. Not even the National Guard could control dissent in 1932, however, when it was forced to call in the Army to assist in the infamous *matanza*.

In the wake of that unprecedented massacre, rural organizing, at least in the western part of the country where the 1932 uprising was centered, all but disappeared for decades.[26] Campesino unions were effectively outlawed, and the 1950 constitution upheld this prohibition. Cooperative associations, however, were legal under conditions dictated by the government, thus creating a space for some form of rural organizing.

Salvadoran campesinos began to take advantage of this space in the late 1960s and early 1970s in organizations closely related to the Roman Catholic Church and that church's emerging "preferential option for the poor." The best known of the new campesino organizations, the Federation of Christian Campesinos (FECCAS), was particularly strong in the area north of San Salvador around the Guazapa volcano and the cities of Suchitoto and Aguilares.[27]

The violent repression of this campesino movement touched off a long process of radicalization of those organizations that began with men sleeping in the hills to avoid nighttime raids by the National Guard and culminated with the formation of the predominantly campesino army of the FMLN. From 1977 to 1983, thousands of rural Salvadorans were killed—and as many as one million (fully one-fifth of the country's entire population) were forced to flee their homes—transforming much of the rural population into refugees and displaced people.[28] Survival during this time required high levels of organization, explaining why above-ground popular organizations like FECCAS all but disappeared. By the time above-ground organization returned to rural areas in the mid-1980s, there were two main organized sectors—displaced communities and the cooperative sector.

Return of Refugees and Displaced People

The experience of massive displacement completely changed the lives of as many as one million Salvadoran campesinos and, therefore, their organizations. When rural organizations (apart from those connected to the Christian Democratic government) began to resurface in the mid-1980s, they were dominated by organizations of displaced communities seeking to return to their places of origin and resume their lives even as the war raged on in those areas. The Armed Forces saw these communities as the civilian base of the guerrillas and sought to keep them out of the war zones at all costs.

As early as 1984 a few small communities were formed in the western part of the country by people seeking to leave the church-sponsored refugee camps in and around San Salvador. In 1984 the Roman Catholic Church, in cooperation with FUNDASAL, a Salvadoran NGO known for its sponsorship of low-income housing projects, began planning a model resettlement project in the town of Tenancingo. That same year, faced with the Catholic Church's decision to close the urban refugee centers, a group of refugee leaders formed CRIPDES. Despite threats and intimidation from the Duarte government and the army, CRIPDES organized the first mass repatriations of the communities of San José Las Flores, Chalatenango, and El Barillo, Cuscatlán in 1986. A year later, 1300 refugees from the Mesa Grande refugee camp in Honduras returned to five more communities.

War-related displacement continued to occur even as the resettlement movement got underway. As CRIPDES prepared for the first mass repopulations, the army launched Operation Phoenix to clear the remainder of the civilian population from the foothills of the Guazapa volcano, twenty miles north of San Salvador. As Operation Phoenix was finally winding down, a powerful earthquake struck San Salvador on October 10, 1986, displacing another ten thousand people.

Despite these setbacks, by the late 1980s the momentum was clearly in favor of the resettlement of at least part of the country's displaced population. Whereas many Salvadoran campesinos had traditionally lived an isolated, family-based existence, they returned in the late 1980s as highly organized, almost entirely collective communities.[29] In the repatriated communities, almost all production was collective and the refugee experience had caused the almost complete disappearance of a cash economy.[30]

Each community formed its *directiva*, or community council which made most of the decisions that governed everyday life in the communities. These councils were then further organized into a complex web of regional and national organizations. Alliances typically followed historical ties to refugee camps and political connections with the various parties of the FMLN.[31]

The government and the Armed Forces were forced to accept the existence of the resettled communities but did everything in their power to make life impossible for them. They established military checkpoints throughout the country at key points of entry to the conflictive zones, and soldiers strictly controlled the movement of people and goods into and out of those areas. Continued fighting between the army and the guerrillas made production almost impossible, and any social infrastructure which people managed to create became an easy target for army operations. As a result, the communities were almost entirely dependent on economic support from foreign sources, which flowed through a network of Salvadoran NGOs. This aid—coupled with their own organizational efforts—allowed the communities to survive during the war, but the dependency created major obstacles to the efforts to create economically viable, self-reliant economies in the postwar period.

From Displaced Person to Productive Campesino

In the immediate postwar period, the communities of displaced people and repatriates sought to turn their attention from the political and military demands of the war to questions of economic viability. In this context, much of the campesino movement struggled to become a rural development movement after years of acting as a political-military movement. Even though they were relatively well-organized and had access to external resources, the path to economic viability has been a painful one for these communities and their organizations as they seek to form a "new popular economy" (See New Popular Economy).

Many of the communities were located in the mountainous northern regions of Chalatenango, Cabañas, and Morazán, areas that had always been extremely marginal in economic terms. In general, the land is of poor quality with limited water resources and high degrees of deforestation. Under the best of circumstances, these areas have limited economic potential. In addition, the repopulated and repatriated communities found that the forms of organization that had allowed them to survive in wartime were often not the ideal structures for increasing production in a new context. Years of dependency on outside resources rather than their own production had created a contradictory work ethic that proved resistant to change. In a common response to such problems, the community of Copapayo, Cuscatlán gradually altered the almost entirely collective production structure of the war years to a combination of family-based and cooperative forms of organization. By 1995, collective production had all but disappeared.

As communities began to reorganize themselves to overcome these problems, they confronted other, equally daunting, obstacles to economic independence. First of all, the unstable situation of land tenure in the postwar period made people unwilling to invest time and resources in land that might not ever be theirs. In southern Usulután, for example, five communities were forced, as part of the Land Transfer Program (PTT), to abandon land that they had occupied during the war and farmed for several years.[32] As late as 1995, dozens of communities in Morazán and Chalatenango were still farming land to which they had no legal title.

These and other difficulties, such as lack of productive infrastructure and non-existent marketing connections for agricultural produce, placed a new series of demands on the organizational structures that had grown up to protect the communities from a hostile army in wartime. Not only did forms of community have to change, but the relations between communities and the nongovernmental organizations that served them also needed to be reevaluated. Some organizations changed more quickly than others, meaning that some communities fared much better than others during the transition period.

In Salinas de Sisiguayo the community quickly gained title to valuable salt works and shrimp ponds under the European Union reconstruction program in Usulután. By all accounts, the community—mostly former combatants of the FMLN and their families—had quickly organized in a way that placed it at the center of a new emerging coastal economy. Nuevo Gualcho, a much larger community located sixty miles to the north, did not fare nearly as well. Lack of access to credit and production difficulties on the marginal agricultural land acquired by the community caused severe problems. These factors, combined with internal political problems, drove nearly one-half of the residents to leave in the first three years after the signing of the Peace Accords.[33]

Most of El Salvador's repatriated and repopulated communities fall within the target zone of the National Reconstruction Plan (PRN). The deficiencies of that plan have, therefore, greatly impacted these communities. Through the first three years of PRN implementation, these communities and their organizations showed little capacity to influence government reconstruction policy or even to assure compliance with basic commitments.[34] The economic future of these communities depends on the development of this capacity as well as on improvements in internal productive organization.

Cooperative Sector

Despite the repression of the late 1970s, small organizations of agricultural cooperatives did survive. These so-called "traditional sector" cooperatives were formed in response to the legal opening presented by the 1950 constitution. A cooperative was established when a number of campesinos gained access to a significant piece of land—often through church connections—or decided to pool resources by organizing. Several organizations of such cooperatives formed during the 1970s, among them the Salvadoran Federation of Agricultural Cooperatives (FEDECOOPADES) which organized as many as two hundred traditional sector cooperatives and had the most influence.

The second Christian Democratic junta, placed in power after the "progressive" military coup in 1979, began promoting limited agrarian reform in hopes of preventing mass rural insurrection. A series of laws promulgated in 1980 established over five hundred agrarian reform cooperatives on many of the country's largest landholdings. The emergence of these cooperatives, which came to occupy more than 10 percent of El Salvador's arable land, greatly expanded the scope of cooperative property and similarly altered the map of rural organization. The Christian Democrats promoted the formation of the Federation of Salvadoran Agrarian Reform Cooperatives (FESACORA)—originally including 74 percent of the cooperatives—to assure the political fidelity of the cooperatives to the political project led by junta leader Napoleón Duarte.

Serious problems immediately confronted the agrarian reform cooperatives. Administrative problems and corruption combined with the military situation to make life economically difficult for the cooperatives. Many were abandoned during the mid-1980s, and most of the rest suffered serious economic problems.[35] The massive debt which the cooperatives assumed when they acquired the land went unpaid and became a huge threat hanging over the head of the entire movement.

Political divisions of the cooperatives were also a source of difficulties throughout the 1980s. In 1984, cooperatives more critical of the Christian Democrats and the leadership of FESACORA formed the Confederation of Salvadoran Agrarian Reform Federations (CONFRAS). The two agrarian reform federations lived a less-than-peaceful coexistence until the end of the 1980s when the rise of ARENA and the party's frontal attack on the agrarian reform forced FESACORA to reconsider its political alliances.

In 1989 nearly all the significant agrarian organizations in both UNOC and the UNTS—including FESACORA, CONFRAS, FEDECOOPADES and ACOPAI—had joined to form the ADC to oppose ARENA's policy of subdivision of the cooperatives (See From Agrarian Reform to the Land Transfer Program). Two years later FESACORA took a further step by affiliating with Salvadoran Federation of Cooperative Associations (COACES), an organization created in 1986 by a sector of the popular movement in hopes of unifying all cooperatives—agricultural, credit & savings, transportation, etc.—under a single, anti-government roof. The political complexity of the popular movement assured that this multiplicity of organizations would maintain their separate existences, but, during the last years of the war, the clear tendency was toward more unity in the search for a negotiated peace and real solutions to the social and economic problems facing all Salvadoran campesinos.

Postwar Efforts at Cooperative Integration

COACES and CONFRAS, the two major Salvadoran cooperative federations, took an unprecedented step in October 1991 when they jointly sponsored the First National Cooperative Congress in San Salvador. At that conference, representatives of a wide range of cooperative organizations agreed that the cooperative sector needed a renewed emphasis on economic vitality and viability if it was to fulfill its proper peacetime role as a contributor to the economic development of Salvadoran society. Without such economic renewal, the cooperatives would fall prey to a combination of economic competition and the government's political efforts to break up the cooperatives into individual parcels. Such a turn toward a new economic mission demanded more operational integration of the cooperatives, overcoming the organizational differences which had traditionally divided and weakened the sector.

The cooperative movement received support for a number of projects reflecting this new orientation. For example, COACES and CONFRAS founded the Integrated Cooperative Marketing System (SINCOMCOOP) as a mechanism for all cooperatives to gain control over the marketing of their products at a national and international level.

Old organizational rivalries proved difficult to overcome, however, and the optimism of October 1991 quickly dissipated. International donor agencies continued to support joint cooperative-sector projects, but the projects achieved little in the way of real integration of the sector. Because the various cooperative organizations retained close alliances with individual parties of the FMLN, the political differences within the FMLN that came to a head in the Legislative Assembly on May 1, 1994, sounded the death knell for any short-term vision of an operationally unified Salvadoran cooperative sector.[36] From that point forward, SINCOMCOOP and similar cooperative integration programs showed little dynamism.

Even with political differences intact, by the mid-1990s all sectors of the cooperative movement had embarked on programs of credit expansion, technical training, and marketing assistance. Although acknowledging the importance of the basic food crops of corn and beans, most training and credit programs focused on expanding production and opening up new commercial channels for export crops, such as coffee, sesame seed, and sugar cane.

In coffee, for example, the agrarian reform cooperatives moved to develop the capacity to process and export the 15 percent of national production which they controlled. In the western part of the country, SOCRA, an alliance of CONFRAS coffee cooperatives opened a modern coffee processing plant and secured licensing to export coffee just as world market prices recovered from the disastrous plunge of the late 1980s. COACES, working through its commercial arm, AGRODESA, sought to import large quantities of fertilizer as a means of lowering the price of that key agricultural input.

Such initiatives are clearly making progress that can be seen both in the improved economic situation of the cooperatives and the slowing of the momentum behind the ARENA government's effort to subdivide them. The cooperatives, however, continue to face a huge debt, a persistent lack of clarity concerning land titles, and many other difficulties. As a result, it is not yet clear that the cooperative sector will be able to flourish in the long run without much higher levels of coordination and integration and some measure of support from those governing the country.

Women's Organizing Takes a New Turn

Organizations to promote improvements in the situation of women have existed since the formation of the Salvadoran Women's Federation in 1957 under the auspices of the Communist Party.[37] Women's organizing expanded as part of the overall growth of the popular movement in the 1970s. Women also bore much of the burden of the community-level organizing efforts connected to the Christian base communities in the Roman Catholic and historical Protestant churches.

As the situation in the country worsened and the popular upheaval became a guerrilla war, women intensified their participation. The Association of Progressive Women of El Salvador (AMPES) and the Salvadoran Women's Association (AMES) were both formed during this period and did organizing work throughout the country.

Women also actively denounced the increasing human rights violations—murders, disappearances, torture. With the help of Monseñor Romero, the Salvadoran Committee of Mothers and Family Members of the Disappeared (COMADRES) was formed in 1977 and became the first group to take to the streets to publicly protest the human rights abuses of the early 1980s.

The women's groups of this period were formed around the need for rapid structural transformation of Salvadoran society. Concerns about the specific needs and interests of women were addressed only insofar as they were consistent with the overall revolutionary project. The Women's Platform of 1994 goes so far as to say that "The few who raised the banner of the women's struggle were harshly criticized by the parties, both traditional and revolutionary."

The reappearance of the popular movement in the mid-1980s led to the growth of several new women's organizations. The National Coordination of Salvadoran Women (CONAMUS) was the first explicitly feminist organization in El Salvador. Other women's organizations quickly formed, and many popular organizations organized influential women's committees.

These organizations did significant organizing work with women around women's concerns. These efforts made women's health services more accessible, promoted the establishment of child care centers, undertook new research on the problems of women, and created many local committees offering women support in resolving myriad day-to-day problems. While the war was still in progress, however, this work occurred within the framework of the overall orientation of the FMLN. In describing the weaknesses of that reemerging movement, Isabel Guevara of the Salvadoran Women's Movement (MSM) says, "We had not yet defined ourselves as a movement...We were not clear about our role."[38]

Women's organizations certainly made critical contributions to the great wave of popular pressure which helped make the Chapultepec Accord a reality. But the attention of the movement quickly shifted to ensuring that Salvadoran women share equally in whatever benefits peace might bring. The time had passed when women's needs could be seen in the context of a contribution to some greater good.

The *Concertación de Mujeres* was formed in 1991 as a forum in which women's organizations could openly discuss the challenges facing women and compare their different organizing approaches. Soon after the war ended, some organizations began to openly question whether or not they could effectively advance the cause of women without achieving more independence from political parties. Women for Dignity and Life (*Las Dignas*) decided that they needed to be able to choose on which issues they would work and how they would work on them. After the end of the war, *Las Dignas* broke their connections, as an organization, to the FMLN.[39] Other organizations, such as the Melida Anaya Montes Women's Movement (MAM), decided not to make such a break but exerted pressure within political structures for more emphasis on their organizational priorities.[40] Women's organizations, both inside and outside of larger political structures, also sought to control their own financial resources and develop their own contacts with international funding agencies. The existence of forums like the *Concertación de Mujeres*, for all their growing pains, greatly enhanced changes in women's consciousness after the war. International contacts also helped in the redefinition of the movement.

In March 1992, soon after the signing of the Salvadoran Peace Accords, five hundred women gathered at Montelimar, Nicaragua for the First Congress of Central American Women. Women from each of the Central American countries discussed a wide range of topics, including the meaning of political autonomy and the advantages and disadvantages of staying within the region's often male-dominated political structures. Nicaraguan women with long experience in that country's Sandinista movement cautioned Salvadoran and Guatemalan women not to expect that "dedication, sacrifice and heroism would automatically guarantee women's interests in the peace process, or women's leadership in the new civil institutions and organizations being established."[41]

At Montelimar, Morena Herrera, a leader of *Las Dignas*, told an interviewer that "We have come from a very long war, a difficult process in which our needs and demands have been postponed by both the war and the specific circumstances we have faced. Now we face the familiar argument that national reconstruction and the upcoming elections in 1994 are important and that women's concerns should wait until after the elections. This conference has allowed us to say 'No more.' We are not going to keep postponing our needs, our demands, and our struggles."[42]

In January 1993, the *Concertación de Mujeres* was expanded to include more than forty women's groups and was renamed *Mujeres '94*. The primary task of *Mujeres '94* was to develop a women's agenda for the 1994 elections. After eight months of intense and sometimes contentious meetings, "The Salvadoran Women's Platform" was released at a public meeting in August 1993. No other sector of society was able to place such a comprehensive set of policy positions before the political parties and the nation. The platform generated considerable discussion throughout the pre-electoral period.

At the Montelimar conference, El Salvador had been chosen as the site for the Sixth Latin American Feminist Conference. Despite death threats against the organizers, massive logistical problems, and announcements in the local press decrying a "congress of lesbians, homosexuals, bisexuals, and queers," 1300 women met at the Tesoro Beach Hotel in November 1994.[43] The conference, the first of its kind to take place anywhere in Central America, gave a huge boost to the new-found strength of Salvadoran women's organizations.

In March 1995 women from all over Central America and the Caribbean met once again in El Salvador, this time to discuss the challenges of organizing women in the *maquila* plants. The chance to review strategies pursued by more experienced women's groups and labor unions from other countries advanced the dynamic work being undertaken in El Salvador to organize the growing number of women employed in *maquila* facilities. Participants even discussed the possibility of enforcing regional standards that would remove the threat of *maquila* owners simply closing up shop and moving across the border.

The conferences and political platforms, of course, reflected profound changes in the vision and organizational programs of Salvadoran women. All women's organizations were struggling to keep up with the new demands on their energies—the other side of the coin of greater autonomy. Internal training and organizational development became immediate priorities for women's organizations.

The movement acknowledged the role of international cooperation in supporting its work but also demanded that international organizations update their visions of women's participation in the development process to reflect the changing situation of Salvadoran women. Much of the international community became accustomed to working with women's organizations through intermediary NGOs, but many in the women's movement now question that mechanism. According to one activist, "[International NGOs] should leave it up to women's groups, with all their limitations and potential, to assume responsibility for the design, administration and execution of a project."[44] Fully incorporating a gender perspective requires that international organizations also examine the participation of women within their own structures of project approval and evaluation. Projects developed "for women" without such a perspective can and have worsened the position of Salvadoran women.

The degree to which changes in the women's movement will affect the lives of Salvadoran women in lasting ways remains to be seen. The roots of male dominance are deep in Salvadoran society and women are not immune from the problems affecting all sectors of the popular movement in El Salvador. Women's organizing in El Salvador has, nonetheless, undergone more change than perhaps any other social movement since the war's end. Issues like reproductive rights, the condition of women workers in *maquila* factories, and domestic violence may not be on the national agenda, but the Salvadoran women's movement is determined to put them there. As Verma Zamora of *Las Dignas* put it, "We're not going to wait until they give us space on their agenda. We're demanding it right now."[45]

Other Women's Organizations

Many Salvadoran women—mostly from the middle and upper classes—participate in social and political organizations outside of the popular movement. During the war, women's groups of the extreme right like Crusade for Peace and Work, the Salvadoran Feminine Front, and the Women's Civic Association (funded by the U.S. government through the National Endowment for Democracy) held a highly public profile mostly through inflammatory paid advertisements in daily newspapers. This tradition has been kept alive by the

Association of Salvadoran Women which published defamatory ads about the Latin American Women's Conference in 1994.

Wealthy women in El Salvador also have a long tradition of service work in support of charitable organizations. The president's wife often takes the lead in this regard. The impact of such work in relieving the immediate suffering of some less privileged citizens cannot be overlooked, but Salvadoran charities are also known to be even more plagued by corruption and misuse of funds than their northern counterparts. Furthermore, the charities, by their nature, do not attempt to alter the structures which give rise to the desperate need of so many Salvadorans. Few charitable organizations exist to directly respond to the immense needs of women.

Women's participation across the political spectrum has also increased markedly in the last decade. Although ARENA is clearly a male-dominated structure, it is well known that the party's impressive electoral machine relies on a large core of female party activists. Gloria Salguero Gross was chosen by the party to be President of the National Assembly, and ARENA women also occupy the key posts of Minister of Education, Director of the Social Investment Fund, and Director of the National Reconstruction Secretariat.

Towards a New Popular Project?

From the time of its rebirth in the 1960s through the end of the war, the Salvadoran popular movement showed tremendous resilience and creativity. It was able to recover from periods of brutal repression and repeatedly change its organizational character and methods as the war transformed Salvadoran society.

Although consistently plagued by divisions along political and sectoral lines, the movement was able to come together behind a unified "popular project" for at least two periods. First, the movement united behind the FMLN's revolutionary project of radical transformation of Salvadoran society; subsequently, in the late 1980s, it united behind the demand for a negotiated end to the armed conflict.[46] In both cases, the unity of the movement made it an important actor on the national stage.

Such unity has been difficult to achieve in the postwar period. The "common enemy" is not nearly as clear as it was in the war years, and as the organizations of each sector have focused more directly on the particular needs of their constituents—probably a healthy shift for the individual organizations—the common threads have been less apparent. The fissure in the FMLN has also had major repercussions for the popular movement.

The issue of political independence has been at the heart of the postwar transition in the popular movement. Survival in the polarized context of the war demanded a set of relations between the popular organizations and political movements that sometimes bordered on dependency.[47] Although it would be a mistake to view the wartime popular movement as a series of "facades" of political organizations, political concerns often overshadowed the direct interests of constituents in the establishment of organizational priorities.

Many movement leaders acknowledged the need for these relationships to change in the postwar context, but relations formed over two decades could not be transformed overnight. The tendency to shift scarce human and economic resources from the popular organizations to the 1994 electoral campaign highlighted the need for more progress in this regard.[48] As of the mid-1990s, its pattern of political alliances remained an unresolved issue for the Salvadoran popular movement.

Much has been made of the postwar weakness of the popular movement, and, indeed, the popular movement entered the latter half of the 1990s with more freedom of action yet less influence than at any point in the last ten years. Conditions have changed and the movement has been slow to adapt, but it may also be true that, after two decades of intense organizational activity and twelve years of war, the Salvadoran people need a rest from politics and organization. Opinion polls conducted by the UCA and other institutions consistently illuminated such fatigue as well as a general antipathy toward politics.

One campesino activist from Cabañas explained the malaise of the popular movement in similar terms. "It's like we campesinos after a long day at work in the fields. When we come back into the house, we're tired. We sit down in the chair or lay down in the hammock for a long *sentón*. That doesn't mean that we won't go to work the next day, or that we won't go visit a relative after dinner. It just means that we know when we need to rest." The Salvadoran popular movement may be enjoying just such a *sentón*. The question is how long it will rest and what it will do when it gets up out of the hammock.

Ecology and Environmentalism

© Edgar Romero

Bulldozers make way for luxury housing on hillsides around San Salvador.

Environment

An ecological crisis of major proportions has been brewing in El Salvador for at least a century. The majority of the forests that once covered almost all of the country had been destroyed by 1900.[1] As the expansion of export agriculture pushed campesinos onto steep hillsides and rocky crags, erosion became generalized to the point that today well over half of all arable land suffers some degree of erosion. When thousands of Salvadorans were forced to return to El Salvador from Honduras after the Soccer War of 1969, pressure on the land increased—especially in the mountainous northern area of the country—and such pressures were an important factor in the crisis which led to the war.

The war worsened the crisis in many ways, and the environmental impact of the war should not be underestimated.[2] Many areas of guerrilla activity were bombed with white phosphorus, thus turning vegetation to cinders. Similarly, displacement often left concentrations of the rural population adjacent to or within forested areas.[3] In a more generalized way, the war lead to a major shift in the country's population, from the north and east to the central and southwestern section of the country. The presence of 3.4 million people in that small an area greatly increases pressure on land, water, and other resources.[4]

The decline of productive activity and other improper patterns of land use in some areas of the country helped to relieve ecological pressures in important ways. The coastal plain, where the war and market factors led to a decline in cotton plantations from 200,000 to 15-20,000 acres, provides a good example of this phenomenon. Lower cotton acreage required less application of pesticides, thereby allowing marine, animal, and human life to make a dramatic recovery.[5]

A few environmental groups sought to educate the public and raise environmental issues during the war, but these activists were often seen as elitist or out of touch with the overriding need to end the war. The public failed to identify ecological degradation as a serious problem.[6]

Although the Peace Accords did not directly address the ecological crisis, in the postwar period environmental problems quickly became part of the national consciousness as never before. Many nongovernmental organizations sought to integrate ideas of "sustainable development" into their proposals to international agencies as well as their educational work in El Salvador. Major international supporters of the Salvadoran government like the Inter-American Development Bank (IDB), the World Bank and AID—which, in 1988, spent almost 200 times as much to fight the war as it did to protect and restore the environment—suddenly made environmental action a program priority.[7]

No longer are environmental concerns dismissed as elitist or reformist by the political left. Instead, an increasing number of analysts and activists see environmentalism and sustainable development policies as the foundation for a new social movement that can challenge El Salvador's unjust social and economic structures. Nor is the environmental crisis simply an issue of the left. Salvadorans from all political viewpoints have realized that, as one analyst put it, "El Salvador is a limits case." Absolute environmental limits are being reached and unless something is done quickly to harmonize economic development with pressing needs of ecological restoration, the viability of the nation is in doubt.

The Case of El Espino

The end of the war released a huge wave of pent-up development energy in El Salvador, which, in the absence of intelligent land use planning, was often damaging to the environment. Peace opened a sort of land rush on the wooded hillsides around San Salvador as the bulldozers raced to clear land for new dwellings in the suddenly speculative luxury housing market. Property values surged as soon as the bullets stopped flying.

Finca El Espino is a one-thousand-acre coffee plantation covering just such a hillside between San Salvador and the large suburb of Santa Tecla. The agrarian reform took the land from the Dueñas family—one of El Salvador's richest and most influential—and turned it over to a cooperative of coffee workers. The area was so conflictive during the war that, even though it abutted the exclusive residential area of San Benito, no one cared to develop it. The CETIPOL police training academy, located in the middle of El Espino, was attacked so often by the guerrillas that one radio announcer suggested in 1990 that it might be better to run a news story on those nights when the

FMLN *did not* attack in the area. Not even the notoriously daring Salvadoran taxi drivers cared to make night trips past the academy.

As soon as the fighting stopped, the land value of El Espino increased several times. The Dueñas family quickly stepped back into the picture, and the cooperative became a battleground between those arguing that the national interest required developing this fabulously located strip of land and those arguing that the forest cover of El Espino constituted the "lungs" of San Salvador and needed to be preserved.[8]

By mid-1995, consensus had been reached that one part of the land would be used for commercial and residential development and another made into a park by the city of San Salvador. Environmentalists like Ricardo Navarro of the Salvadoran Center for Appropriate Technology (CESTA) continued to battle the city over the degree to which the park would protect the forested land of El Espino.[9]

Water: The Ecological Lifeline

The debate concerning El Espino focused on the land rights of a cooperative versus the economic and political power of El Salvador's oligarchy, but the question of water lay beneath the debate like an underground spring. Environmentalists and other critics of the plan to construct on El Espino pointed to the critical role of the forest cover there in the recharging of the aquifers providing much of San Salvador's water supply.[10] By the mid-1990s El Salvador was finally recognizing that it had a water problem of troubling proportions. A careful consideration of that problem exposes its links to other difficult issues, such as energy, soil degradation, and threats to biodiversity.

The most obvious problem is the pollution of 90 percent of all surface water sources in El Salvador. The major sources of the pollution are sewage, wastes from agroindustrial plants, other industrial wastes, fertilizer and pesticide run-off, and solid wastes washed off of municipal dumps.

At most, 30 percent of Salvadorans have access to sewage connections, and even that piped sewage is dumped, untreated, into waterways. Agroindustries, especially coffee, create huge amounts of organic waste, and government has shown itself unable to force these industries to treat their wastes.

Clearly water quality is a major public health problem, but the quantity of water available may eventually pose an equally difficult challenge. The danger of collapse of the country's water system is, at first, puzzling given that, "With an average rainfall of 1,850 mm., an ample system of streams and rivers, and some excellent groundwater recharge areas, El Salvador is not an arid country and its inhabitants need not experience water shortages." [11] Part of the water crisis resides in the incompetence and neglect that characterizes ANDA (the National Water and Sewage Authority), but forces like erosion and deforestation pose a more serious, long-term problem.[12]

The patterns of land use that create erosion and deforestation leave the soil without the capacity to absorb the copious rains that fall annually between the months of May and November. Studies find that between 50 and 89 percent of the country's land suffers the effects of erosion. The rapid run-off of rain water carries away more topsoil thus intensifying the cycle of environmental degradation. The process has reached the point where some areas of the country—especially in the northern mountains where cultivation of hillsides has become generalized—are undergoing a process of desertification.

The Land Transfer Process demanded by the FMLN as part of the Peace Accords may, unwittingly, be worsening this situation as expanded cultivation of marginal agricultural land increases the erosion problem. Even before the initiation of the PTT, land use in and around the Upper Lempa watershed endangered that critical ecosystem, and both cattle grazing and small-scale corn cultivation in the area have increased markedly since 1993. Mark Smith, a volunteer with the Mennonite Central Committee in the Upper Lempa area, reported in January 1995 that the campesinos in the region were aware of the negative impact of growing corn on steep hillsides but saw no alternative: "They see the deforestation and erosion and notice that there is less water around every year, but if they don't plant the hillsides, their families starve. Given the choice between starving today and dying of thirst in the future, people keep planting on steeper hills." [13]

These threats to the water system are also intimately linked to the country's serious energy problems. Efforts to recharge the water table through reforestation run headlong into the poverty of most rural Salvadorans, which leads them to use firewood as a primary energy source. The burning of wood provides between half and three-fourths of the country's energy, and, in many areas, campesinos in search of economic survival strip the hills bare more quickly than forest resources can recover.[14]

Salvadoran industry and commerce, as well as those citizens with access to electricity, rely heavily on the two huge hydroelectric dams located on the Upper Lempa. The runaway erosion in that zone has washed millions of tons of topsoil into the artificial lakes that serve the dams, thus limiting their effectiveness. When the Salvadoran public complained about increased electric rates in the postwar period, they were feeling the direct effects of inadequate land use patterns in rural areas.

Many of El Salvador's water problems lead directly to the Lempa River, the largest river in Central America. FUNDALEMPA, a Salvadoran NGO established to promote urgent action to save the entire Lempa River Basin, summarizes the state of El Salvador's largest watershed as follows:

> The situation of the Lempa is very bad. We face an environmental emergency due to the high levels of pollution of the water, the air, and the soils of the basin. This pollution is directly transferred to the foods produced in the area and consumed, daily, by millions of us. The river has been overutilized since the beginning of the 1950s, but the actions taken to protect and recover the basin's natural resources have in no way corresponded to the intensity of its exploitation.
>
> If urgent and immediate measures are not taken, the environmental crisis of the Lempa River, which can still be successfully solved, could become an irreversible situation as early as the beginning of the next century.[15]

Such pronouncements were once considered to be the ravings of doomsayers, but by the mid-1990s more people were beginning to approach the environmental problem with just such urgency.

As water and other problems destroy entire ecological zones, biodiversity is threatened. The indigenous name of the San Salvador volcano is *Quetzaltepec*, "place of the quetzal," but the quetzal disappeared along with its habitat, the cloud forest. The department of Usulután is named after the ocelot, which once roamed the area in abundance. Few *usulatecos* have, however, ever seen such an animal. Coastal savannahs and stands of old-growth ebony, cedar, mahogany, and granadilla have been lost to the onslaught of the agroexport economy. The country's howler monkeys, anteaters, and white-lipped peccaries did not survive these ecological losses.[16]

Pesticide Overuse: A Silent Killer

Pesticide contamination of water and soils is probably the country's second most pressing environmental problem after soil erosion and deforestation. These contaminants have moved well up the food chain to affect animals and human beings. Thousands of people are poisoned annually by pesticides, and this number can only increase as pesticide use increases in those areas of the country that were not farmed intensively during the war.

Excessive use of pesticides and the subsequent absorption of harmful chemicals by people and animals remains a severe problem in El Salvador. The use of pesticides increased dramatically in the

1960s and 1970s, especially in the cotton-growing areas on the country's coastal plain. Increasing pest resistance led to a tripling of the use of DDT between 1970 and 1977. By the end of that decade, pesticide costs represented one-half of the cost of cotton production.

By 1980, the Ministry of Health reported an annual average of 2500 hospitalizations for acute pesticide intoxication.[17] No reliable figures exist regarding the numbers of birth defects, chronic illnesses, or fatalities related to pesticide poisoning, but levels of organochlorine pesticides three to five times the maximum allowed by the World Health Organization (WHO) have been found in women living in the coastal area.[18] Harmful pesticide levels have also been found in cattle and other animals, marine life of all sorts, and on vegetables for sale in local markets. Beef shipments to the U.S. were turned back in the late 1970s when it was found that they contained 722 times the permissible levels of organochlorides.[19]

As detailed above, the decline in cotton production resulting from the war gave certain coastal areas a respite from pesticide poisoning. Total pesticide imports did not, however, decline during this period as applications increased in other areas of the country. Given the lack of control over pesticide importation and use, a postwar expansion in the area of export agriculture will only worsen the pesticide problem.

The high cost of pesticides is creating an openness in many campesinos to alternative farming techniques that use fewer pesticides and other agrochemicals. Small-scale programs designed to educate farmers in organic and other alternative pest control and soil conservation methods exist in every one of El Salvador's fourteen departments, and in the former conflictive zones experimental projects were being carried out in the production and marketing of organic coffee, sesame seed, and several other crops. Finally, government programs through the Ministry of Agriculture and the Executive Secretariat for the Environment (SEMA) were also attempting to integrate the new discipline of agroecology into educational and extension programs.

Nonetheless, these programs remain at the margin of the agricultural economy, and AID's warning was as applicable in 1995 as it was when issued as part of a 1989 study on pesticide use:

> If no positive action is taken to correct the situation, it is reasonable to conclude that El Salvador will lose export markets because of pesticide residues, that the environment will continue to be contaminated, leading to the potential loss of existing industries (e.g. fish and shrimp), and that pesticide intoxications will increase as organochlorine use declines in favor of organophosphates and carbamates, some of which pose a greater direct threat to human health.[20]

San Salvador: A Less Than Livable City

As late as the 1960s, visitors to San Salvador regularly described it as a lovely city with wide, clean streets and a wonderful climate. Few visitors to San Salvador would offer the same observations today. Apart from the crime wave, which makes personal security a constant worry, the city has become an ecological disaster area.

War and the decline of subsistence agriculture in the countryside caused a population explosion in San Salvador, with population increasing from 200,000 in 1950 to 1,500,000 in the 1990 census.[21] Almost half of that population is crowded into substandard housing in the ravines that crisscross the city and in the "belts of misery" that surround it.

The road system in and around the capital was already inadequate during the war when vehicle traffic was relatively light, but the number of vehicles appeared to double almost immediately after the signing of the Peace Accords. The impossibility of movement causes inconvenience, but the vehicular snarl has led to spectacularly poor air quality in San Salvador. Few studies are available on the impact of worsened air quality on respiratory disorders and other health problems but North American visitors to San Salvador routinely report burning eyes, headaches, and breathing problems after their first day of breathing the diesel cloud that blankets downtown San Salvador.

Trash disposal creates another huge environmental problem for San Salvador. Only half of the tons of trash created each day in San Salvador is picked up and removed to landfills. While modern garbage trucks roll through upper class neighborhoods as many as three times a week, most Salvadoran children never see one on their streets.[22] Most trash on the streets is burned—adding to the air pollution problem—and improper landfill techniques and garbage dumping may contribute to groundwater pollution.

In El Salvador, as in much of Latin America, economic necessity forces large numbers of people to live in garbage dumps where they survive by picking the city's trash. Never were the tragic connections between El Salvador's environmental and social problems more clearly drawn than in June 1993 when heavy rains caused a landslide that buried dozens people under mountains of trash in a dump on the outskirts of San Salvador. Twenty-five people, all residents of the community of Santa Eduviges built on and around the landfill, perished in the landslide. In the wake of the disaster, the Sanitation Battalion of the military admitted that the government had been slow to respond because the site was contaminated with toxins and the military was unsure how to handle the situation.[23]

Compared to the Latin American megalopolises like Mexico City or Lima, the problems of San Salvador seem minor, but for Salvadorans, the conditions of their capital will soon begin to approach dangerous limits.

Responding to the Crisis

The increasing ecological awareness in El Salvador owes its existence to many factors. Among the most important of these factors were:

- Severity of the crisis and the degree to which environmental factors began to impose limits on economic growth.
- Determined efforts of a core of Salvadoran environmental activists to place environmental issues on the national agenda.
- Bold steps by major international actors like AID and the Inter-American Development Bank (IDB).
- A general increase in awareness of the environmental challenges facing developing countries as expressed in the "Earth Summit" held in Rio de Janeiro in 1992.

Efforts to make substantive changes in Salvadoran environmental policy still confront both opposition and apathy, but each of the above factors has opened space for the ecological debate.

Although the journal *Proceso* was certainly exaggerating when it wrote that "The concern about the environment was originally introduced into Central America by AID, which promoted studies of the possibilities of adapting institutional and legal structures to the necessity of articulating an environmental protection strategy," international institutions like AID and IDB have played an important role.[24]

Beginning with an exhaustive 1989 study of environmental conditions, AID began to express a serious interest in Salvadoran environmental affairs. In 1991, President Bush's Enterprise for the Americas explicitly proposed a scheme whereby debt-relief could become a new source of U.S. aid to Latin America. The U.S. signed a formal agreement in December 1992 whereby it forgave $464 million in debt in return for a Salvadoran commitment to make quarterly interest payments into a special fund. The agreement established the Enterprise for the Americas Fund (FIAES) to receive these payments and then make the money available to projects designed to alleviate El Salvador's environmental crisis. The Salvadoran government was to pay $41 million into FIAES over twenty years.[25] The Canadian government established the Canadian Environmental Fund (FCMA), a similar fund designed to produce $8 million over three years.

These environmental funds set out from the start to avoid earlier problems by encouraging the participation of Salvadoran NGOs from across the political spectrum. By all accounts, they did this quite successfully, including four NGO representatives on the council which would make decisions about project allocations.[26]

In December 1994, initial projects were awarded to 48 of the 112 NGOs that had presented projects. Although the projects were excessively weighted toward reforestation projects and many lacked sufficient technical preparation, the participants were generally happy with the outcome. The original fears that only NGOs close to the ARENA party or the government would be chosen were apparently calmed by the selection of a broadly representative group of NGO applicants.[27]

FIAES made up only part of AID's support for environmental programs in El Salvador. The Salvadoran Environmental Protection Project (PROMESA) was launched in the early 1990s with the promise of $20 million in grants.

AID funding created a series of new institutions including the SEMA. The Secretariat was charged with coordinating all public institutions working on the environment and all government efforts toward new environmental legislation.[28]

Financial strains on AID's program place the future of its environmental work in doubt. The IDB launched an even larger program of $50 million in credits for environmental projects. The IDB package includes a major project for the environmental renovation of the Lempa River Basin. The project's price tag (more than $30 million) seems large at first glance but shrinks when compared to the magnitude of the problem it confronts. One very important difference between PROMESA and the IDB program is that the latter takes the form of loans that will, one day, have to be repaid.

Environmental Compensation?

Since the end of the armed conflict, AID and other donors have put in place an impressive array of institutions to respond to the worsening environmental crisis. These new institutions and funds have much more effectively incorporated the participation of Salvadoran civil society than previous efforts like the PRN. Nonetheless, they have little in the way of new legislation or successful programs to show for their efforts. One explanation for this lack of success is that environmental efforts consistently run up against the orientation of the neoliberal economic program that heads the social agenda in El Salvador. That model seeks to make the market the rector of all economic decisions, regardless of the environmental consequences. In that context, serious efforts to change the behavior of businesses and individuals will confront powerful political and economic foes.

For FUSADES, poverty is the main cause of environmental degradation. Consequently, further economic growth is the only solution to the ecologic problem. Such growth can only be achieved by a more rational and efficient use of resources, which, of course, only the market can determine.[29]

Agricultural Minister Antonio Cabrales sounded a more cautionary note in 1992 when he declared that "...the market economy doesn't work for natural resources...If we do not take sufficient care over the next ten years, we could cause an ecological disaster even worse than that of the past thirty years."[30] Unfortunately, the Calderón Sol administration appears not to have heeded Mr. Cabrales' warning.

In that context, programs like PROMESA and the IDB loans can be seen as projects to deal with the negative environmental side effects of neoliberal economic programs, in much the same way that the FIS and other "social compensation" programs seek to alleviate the negative social consequences of structural adjustment (See Economy). As preconditions for the establishment of the Enterprise of the Americas Fund, the United States required that the Salvadoran government complete a stabilization agreement with the IMF and a structural adjustment agreement with the World Bank.[31] Programs like FIAES are every bit as much a part of the neoliberal plan as the FIS and other social compensation programs.

As "environmental compensation" programs, these projects are unlikely to challenge the model of accumulation that sits at the basis of environmental degradation in El Salvador. They are, therefore, unlikely to produce enduring solutions. Salvadoran NGOs have proposed a much more thorough evaluation of the country's economic vision as a way of combating environmental degradation. These proposals share the following elements:

- Need for a national social and economic plan that incorporates "environmental sustainability" into patterns of land use and industrial reconversion.
- Concern for population concentration and a willingness to consider offering economic incentives for major relocations.
- A biological conservation plan that makes maintenance of the country's biodiversity a priority.

Whatever measures are adopted, El Salvador's environmental crisis promises to pose a major challenge to all of the country's social groups well into the next century.

U.S.-El Salvador Relations

U.S. Foreign Policy

The U.S. military and economic presence in Central America since the beginning of the twentieth century had established a strong U.S. influence in El Salvador. Jimmy Carter's 1979 decision to approve the delivery of military aid, however, marked the beginning of a radical change in the relationship between the two countries. During the 1980s the United States assumed a preponderant role in Salvadoran internal affairs and international relations. The scope of U.S. influence led one analyst to conclude that, "There are few examples in the world where the aid of one country has become so intimately related to the politics, the economy, and the institutionality of another country as in the case of United States - El Salvador relations." [1]

During the period 1980-92, covert and formal United States aid of all types to El Salvador approached $6 billion, making El Salvador one of the top five recipients of U.S. foreign aid during that time.[2] Although most of the assistance was nominally considered economic aid, the Arms Control Caucus of the U.S. Congress determined that 75 percent of U.S. aid was "war-related."[3]

Little mystery existed about the basis of U.S. policy in the 1980s. The State Department outlined the main principles and features of that policy in its January 1989 statement "El Salvador: The Battle for Democracy." [4] Against all logic, the "Soviet menace" continued to guide the policy and there was no mention of the necessity of a negotiated solution to the war. The policy was "driven by the American obsession, given new impetus by the Reagan Doctrine, to draw the line against [communist] gains throughout the Third World." [5] When the Bush administration took office, official U.S. policy still called for the defeat of the FMLN through a combination of unrelenting, if limited, military power and democratic reforms. This combination formed the basis of U.S. "Low-Intensity Conflict Strategy" (LIC).[6]

Much had changed by late 1994. At that time, the State Department circulated a tepid document simply entitled, "U.S. Policy Toward El Salvador." Under the heading "Key Goals," it offered the following summary:

> U.S. objectives in El Salvador include promoting complete implementation of the 1992 peace accords between the Government of El Salvador (GOES) and the Farabundo Martí National Liberation Front (FMLN); supporting the rule of law, judicial reform and democratic institutions; encouraging national reconciliation; and helping El Salvador achieve national reconstruction and economic growth.[7]

Such a reformulation of policy required not only the electoral defeat of a Republican administration but the implicit acknowledgment that the $6 billion policy of the Reagan years had been a dismal failure.

Building Bipartisan Consensus

Although the aid levels of the 1980s were unprecedented, U.S. support for military-controlled regimes in El Salvador was nothing new. During the Alliance for Progress era of the 1960s the United States had backed economic and military aid programs designed to modernize the country and block the rise of a leftist alternative.

AID reported to Congress in the mid-1960s that El Salvador was continuing on its "course of steady progress" and praised the military government as "a model for other Alliance countries." In its 1967 annual budget presentation, AID asserted: "El Salvador has been pushing social reform and economic development on a broad front" and "has taken a leading role in the Central American Common Market and fostered a good climate for foreign investment." Military aid was used to establish a civil-affairs program within the armed forces. According to one U.S. military adviser, the U.S. military aid in the 1960s resulted in "a high degree of expertness and a strengthening of corporate loyalty" within the Salvadoran army.[8] The consistency of U.S. support for democracy in El Salvador can be gauged by the way in which both the Nixon administration (in 1972) and the Carter administration (in 1977) ignored elections that were clearly stolen from the opposition candidates.

In the late 1970s military aid was cut off from the hard-line regime of Gen. Carlos Humberto Romero as a consequence of the Carter administration's human rights policy. Nevertheless, some $8 million in annual economic aid continued to flow to the military government and the 18 U.S. military advisers assigned to the Salvadoran army remained in the country.[9] In 1978 the *New York Times* reported that the U.S. embassy was still "closely identified with the military government." [10] Once it became apparent that the destabilized military government was being seriously challenged by a left-of-center opposition, Washington renewed its direct military aid to El Salvador.

During the early 1980s presidential requests for increasing military aid proved a contentious issue in the U.S. Congress. In the wake of the killings of two U.S. agrarian reform advisers, four religious workers, an archbishop, and tens of thousands of Salvadorans, Congress made some effort to hold onto the reins of El Salvador policy. From 1979 to mid-1984 Congress required that the president semiannually certify that the Salvadoran government was making progress on the problem of human rights. [11]

From the beginning, the certification of the human rights progress was an exceptionally weak restriction on the Reagan administration's ability to support the war. Certification served more as a face-saving measure for the congressional Democrats than as any real lever to improve the human rights situation. In 1980 thousands of Salvadoran civilians were murdered by death squads. Congress, however, acted on human rights only after the murder of the four U.S. churchwomen, and even more so after the deaths of the two U.S. land reform officials, one of whom worked for the CIA.

The 1984 election of José Napoleón Duarte and the release of the recommendations of the National Bipartisan Commission on Central America (Kissinger Commission) created a solid bipartisan consensus on El Salvador. Duarte's presence gave a certain validity to the notion that democratic reforms could win Salvadoran hearts and minds even in the context of a violent civil war.

With a civilian government and an economic stabilization plan in place, El Salvador lost importance in Congress, where attention had switched to the contra war against Nicaragua. Duarte's election was a major success for the U.S. counterinsurgency strategy. In the State Department's view the election demonstrated that there was indeed a political center in El Salvador worth defending.

The forging of congressional consensus did not, however, guarantee a successful policy. Although Duarte was elected on a platform of peace and reforms, neither dialogue nor reforms were on the agenda of the Salvadoran oligarchy or the military establishment that had been greatly strengthened by the war (See Military).

Faced with this contradiction between its dual goals of democratic reform and military victory, the Reagan administration consistently decided in favor of the latter. As one analyst put it, "The reformist *appearance* of the Duarte regime was more important—and easier to contrive—than the real thing...In fact, it is clear that the policy makers in Washington never fought the political war very seriously." [12]

For example, the Reagan administration soon dropped its insistence on the full implementation of the agrarian reform. Instead, it began to place new emphasis on projects aimed at supporting the private sector. The war against the FMLN, however, continued to be the overriding priority of Washington. In its second term, the Reagan administration counted on bipartisan support for a prolonged war of attrition aimed at wearing down and isolating the FMLN. Constant military pressure would sap the FMLN of its strength while successful elections would increasingly isolate the FMLN politically. If elections could sufficiently increase the legitimacy of the government, negotiations with the FMLN would become unnecessary.

The elections of the 1980s certainly did not represent either a perfection of democracy or the political isolation of the FMLN, but they did alter the country's political map in important ways. The military did not participate directly as candidates, and the extreme right—represented by ARENA—had to learn a new approach to politics. By the end of the decade, the return of Rubén Zamora and the "democratic left" made it more difficult for the FMLN to reject the elections as a farce. The pressure to reevaluate the approach to the elections was clearly a factor in the FMLN's proposal to join the 1989 balloting.

With its support for discussion of the FMLN's dramatic negotiating proposal of January 1989, the Bush administration had shown a certain openness to considering basic changes in U.S. policy.[13] This opening, however, had not translated into a new policy by the time negotiations began between the FMLN and the Cristiani government in September 1989.[14]

Two months later, the November 1989 offensive tore huge holes in what remained of the Reagan policy. On the one hand, the widely held view that the FMLN was incapable of significant offensive actions was put to rest, as was the fantasy of an imminent military victory by the Salvadoran army.[15] Even more importantly, the offensive succeeded in driving home the fact that nine years of training and logistical support had failed to turn the Salvadoran army into a professional army capable of respecting human rights. Ironically, while hundreds of atrocities against unnamed Salvadoran civilians and aerial bombardments of the most populous neighborhoods failed to make this point, the brutal murder of six Jesuits, their housekeeper, and her daughter brought the true nature of the Salvadoran military to the world's attention. The failure of U.S. tutelage could hardly have been more obvious. The unit of the Atlacatl Battalion that carried out the assassinations had received U.S. Special Forces training only a few days before the attack.[16]

More than any other single act, these eight deaths ensured that the military as an institution would become a serious subject of the peace negotiations.

The Bush administration first tried to portray the offensive as a "desperate move" and to suggest that the military was firmly in control.[17] In the immediate aftermath of the Jesuit killings, William Walker, the U.S. Ambassador parroted the military's absurd contention that the FMLN might have been responsible. The State Department condemned the killings and called for a full investigation, but, even after President Cristiani ordered the detention of the killers, the administration insisted on exonerating the government from these "aberrations" committed by extremists.[18] An effort to consider withholding 30 percent of 1990 military aid was narrowly defeated in Congress as the offensive was winding down.

Despite these "damage-control" reactions, the offensive and the Jesuit murders had set the stage for irrevocable changes in U.S. policy. According to one U.S. diplomat present in El Salvador at that time, "There was a shift in emphasis from supporting the counterinsurgency to supporting a negotiated settlement."[19]

In January 1990, even as he was defending the continuation of the military aid program, Under Secretary of State Bernard Aronson was telling the House Subcommittee on Western Hemisphere Affairs that, "El Salvador needs peace, and the only path to peace is at the negotiating table,...[L]et both sides come to the bargaining table to stay and negotiate in good faith until the war is over."[20]

Congress also did its part to redirect the policy. After a long debate, the House and Senate agreed in October 1990 to cut the $85 million military budget by half and conditioned the other half on progress on the Jesuit case. Bush later renewed part of the aid on a flimsy pretext, but the bipartisan consensus on the importance of military aid to El Salvador had clearly evaporated.[21] In Congress, Senator Joseph Moakley (D-MA) stands out among those who tried to get to the bottom of the Jesuit case and change policy in its wake. The Salvadoran press and public generally acknowledge Moakley's pressure as a key factor in the government's decision to bring the Jesuit case to trial.

A decade of actions by U.S. opponents of the Reagan policy also influenced the slow shift toward support for a negotiated solution to the war. Although it never succeeded in breaking the bipartisan consensus on aid to El Salvador during the 1980s, critics of the policy did develop the constituency in Congress that seized the initiative and helped alter policy after 1989.

Groups advocating a different U.S. attitude toward El Salvador carried out their own policy based on solidarity with popular movements in El Salvador and sanctuary for undocumented Salvadoran immigrants in this country.[22] The moral and political force of such actions not only influenced events in El Salvador but countered the voices of those in Congress and the Bush administration, such as Secretary of Defense Richard Cheney, who continued to support a large military aid program to El Salvador even after the Jesuit murders.[23]

While U.S. policy remained ambiguous for most of 1990, the administration by 1991 had begun to speak with one voice on the need for a negotiated solution.[24] All observers acknowledge the importance of the U.S. pressure on the government in the difficult final stages of the negotiations.[25] Predictably, the State Department hailed the Peace Accords as a victory for U.S. policy, in particular, and the cause of democracy, in general.

President Bush sent Vice-President Quayle to the ceremony marking the end of the war on February 1, 1992. After that event, however, the diplomatic mission in El Salvador was led by the embassy's political officer for six months. The fact that a new ambassador was not assigned to El Salvador until October 1993 speaks to the country's dramatic decline in importance after the signing of the Peace Accords.[26] El Salvador slipped back to the lower reaches of the State Department priority list, to much the same place it had occupied before the war. An embassy official later explained that, "There was a general feeling after January 16 (the date the Accords were signed) that things would fall into place. People didn't realize how ambiguous the accords, especially land, were."[27]

Evaluating the Reagan-Bush Policy

The furor created by the release of the Truth Commission report in March 1993 led Secretary of State Warren Christopher to convene a special State Department panel to investigate the conduct of U.S. diplomatic personnel in El Salvador from 1980-1992. The panel's report, released in July 1993, declined to discuss the merits of the policy being carried out by U.S. diplomats, and concluded that U.S. personnel acted in a "laudable fashion and even with personal courage at times, defending the cause of human rights."[28] Some errors were acknowledged, as in the case of the failure to fully investigate the massacre at El Mozote in 1981 but, in the end, all U.S. officials got high grades for effort.[29]

Congressional response was swift and less than favorable. Senator Patrick Leahy commented that the report "glosses over...the lies, half-truths and evasions that we came to expect from the State Department during that period." Christopher Dodd called it "sloppy, anemic, basically a whitewash."[30] In El Salvador, *Proceso* insisted that the report represented an attempt by the State Department to "wash its hands" of its responsibilities for the suffering caused by 12 years of conflict in El Salvador. Astonishingly, for the Salvadoran commentator, the report even tried to deny that the Reagan administration had downplayed the importance of human rights in El Salvador in favor of a military solution to the conflict. *Proceso*, however, ended its evaluation highlighting two positive aspects of the report:

> The first is that the U.S. foreign policy establishment at least recognizes that it committed errors. In El Salvador, neither the government, nor the army, nor the judicial system has had the courage to do the same. The second is the recommendation to open, with only the indispensable security restrictions, the El Salvador files of the State Department so that all may have access to this part of our reality.[31]

The State Department report came on the heels of a less publicized but much more damning report issued on January 16, 1992. Those who had been consistent critics of U.S. policy had noted the change after the 1989 offensive and attributed the new course to an implicit acknowledgment of the failure of the Reagan policy. The 1992 RAND Corporation report, *American Counterinsurgency Doctrine and El Salvador: The Frustrations of Nation Building*, surprised many observers by drawing conclusions very similar to those of administration critics.

The report assumed that the Reagan and Bush administrations did, indeed, seek to defeat the FMLN through a combination of military action and democratic reform, but that they had only one weapon against the recalcitrant Salvadoran right that opposed reform—the threat to withdraw aid. Salvadoran leaders learned early on that U.S. desire to defeat the FMLN was much stronger than its support for democratic reform, so the aid card was not a credible deterrent to human rights abuses. U.S. pressure for reform succeeded only after the Jesuit murders, when the U.S. Congress was truly ready to withdraw support.

U.S. foreign policy in El Salvador, therefore, suffered from the same delusion of arrogance that led to defeat in Viet Nam, "namely, that it is relatively easy to ensure that an ally does what American policymakers deem necessary to eliminate an insurgency."[32] Faced with the failure of its policy, the United States was left with two options which might have led to the defeat of the FMLN—support for unmitigated repression, "total war" by the Salvadoran army; or direct occupation by U.S. troops. In 1989, neither of these options was politically viable for the Bush administration, so they slowly moved to cut losses by supporting a negotiated settlement.

Research for the RAND report was completed in September 1991, after the New York Agreement had pointed the way toward a final settlement of the conflict. The report evaluated the settlement as follows:

> This situation, however, is no occasion for the United States to congratulate itself, since such a settlement was anathema to the architects of U.S. policy toward El Salvador in the 1980s. Until 1990, America did not seek a compromise brokered by the United Nations but pressed for a clear victory through a combination of military and reform measures. In these terms, American policy failed.[33]

The State Department "whitewash" must be seen in the context of this devastating internal critique of the conduct of U.S. policy.

If the State Department report sought to sanitize the diplomatic history of the 1980s, the November 1993 release of previously classified State Department and CIA documents vindicated even the most vocal critics of U.S. policy. The documents were released only after publication of the Truth Commission report gave added strength to pressure by Senator Moakley and other members of Congress. In the words of the *New York Times*, the 12,000 documents "show that the Bush and Reagan administrations received intelligence reports that the Salvadoran military, which received $1 billion in United States military aid between 1980 and 1981, was dominated throughout the decade by officers who either ordered or took part in death squad activities at some time in their careers." [34]

No small amount of self-congratulations accompanied the release of the information as the Clinton State Department fulfilled a deep ideological need to appear as the "good guys" vis-a-vis the Republicans. According to the State Department, the documents were released "in keeping with the president's and the secretary's interest in providing the public with a full accounting of U.S. government involvement in El Salvador." [35] Such a "full accounting," however, will have to wait for another day as the release included none of the critically important documents from the White House, Justice Department, FBI, or National Security Council (NSC). Another 600 State Department and CIA documents (6 percent of the total) remained classified and unreleased.

The documents were damning of U.S. policy not because of what they revealed about Salvadoran involvement in death squads but because of what they revealed about how much the U.S. government knew about that involvement and declined to make public. Even some opponents of U.S. policy were surprised by the scope of the deceit:

We've known for a long time that the [Reagan] administration suppressed the information it had about human rights abuses by the Salvadoran government. What has only now become evident is the depth and breadth of the lie.[36]

Absent from the fanfare accompanying the release of the documents was an acknowledgment that they serve as a vindication of the critique of U.S. policy advanced throughout the 1980s by solidarity groups, human rights monitors, advocacy groups, and international aid organizations. For their insistence on telling the truth about the "big lie" in El Salvador, more than one hundred groups opposing U.S. policy became targets of an FBI campaign of infiltration, surveillance, and intimidation.[37]

Salvadoran critics did not ignore the role of the United States in the pushing and shoving that led to the signing of the Chapultepec Accord. This effort does not, however, balance 10 years of support for a military solution on the scales of history. As one Salvadoran analyst put it in his assessment of the possibilities for a new Clinton policy:

Even if the ultimate responsibility for the conflict rests with us, the Salvadorans, the United States was the only actor capable of achieving a peaceful settlement ten years ago, thereby avoiding so much death and destruction in our nation. The decisive role played in the war and, then, in the negotiations does not redeem the historical responsibility of that country, of Republicans and Democrats, in our now eternal suffering.[38]

In Search of a Clinton Policy

The election of Bill Clinton as U.S. president in late 1992 led to much speculation among Salvadorans about future directions in U.S. policy toward their country. Armando Calderón Sol, then still mayor of San Salvador and a leading presidential hopeful, did not conceal his distaste for a potential Clinton presidency. On the night of the U.S. elections, Calderón Sol complained that a Clinton victory would hurt El Salvador and even went so far as to accuse Hillary Clinton of donating to the Committee in Solidarity with the People of El Salvador (CISPES), thereby, in Calderón Sol's view confirming the Clinton's leftwing extremism.[39] Clinton took office right after that critical moment in the peace process when the FMLN completed its formal disarmament.

When, in his inaugural speech, the new President made only a single reference to Latin America—and that to Mexico and the Free Trade Agreement—Salvadorans felt certain that their country was well on its way along the slippery track from "the maximum priority to the almost forgotten."[40] Their only hope was that the new president and the Congress would recognize the potential symbolic value of active support for El Salvador during the consolidation of its peace and would respond out of a sense of moral responsibility.

The president and his administration have disappointed the Salvadorans on this score. The elimination of trade barriers has stood at the front of the Clinton agenda in Latin America, but the tiny Salvadoran market will certainly not make the country a priority for a trade-driven policy. Large countries like Brazil and, of course, Mexico receive more attention.[41] Chile, because of its relative prosperity and the purity of its structural adjustment program, stands next in line for NAFTA membership.

In emphasizing the importance of free trade, Clinton followed a path already well-worn by the Bush administration. In June 1990 President Bush launched his Enterprise for the Americas. The Enterprise rested on three pillars: investment promotion, aid via debt reduction, and the elimination of trade barriers. Latin Americans correctly saw the third pillar as the meat of the matter, and the sluggish process of Central American integration immediately picked up steam (See Free Trade and Regional Integration).[42]

Even before the end of the armed conflict, El Salvador led the push for Central American economic integration on the assumption that only as a unified block could the Central American countries gain access to the emerging trade bloc of the Americas. At the Caribbean Basin Initiative meeting in late 1993, and again at the Summit of the Americas, El Salvador and the other Central American nations sought an opening that might offer them the possibility of more access to U.S. markets.

In both cases, Clinton lectured the Latin Americans about the importance of eliminating tariff barriers but offered no assurance of NAFTA-type arrangements to any but the strongest and most stable economies. The collapse of the Mexican economy in 1995 will probably make the U.S. Congress extremely reticent to accept any expansion of NAFTA, at least in the short run.

The free trade craze in the United States has had some impact on trade and investment patterns in El Salvador, but the increase in exports to the U.S. can not be the basis for economic stability in El Salvador.[43] The U.S. complaint to GATT concerning Salvadoran textile exports clearly showed the limits of the Clinton view of trade liberalization for a small economy like El Salvador (See Free Trade and Regional Integration). In the mid-1990s the United States, which dominates the country's foreign trade economy, enjoyed a trade surplus with El Salvador of about $400 million annually (Figure 8a).

Salvadorans and other Central Americans closely connect U.S. trade policy with its immigration policy. Given the number of Salvadorans in the U.S. and the importance of their dollar remittances to the Salvadoran economy, a change in U.S. immigration policy could lead to social and economic disaster in El Salvador (See Economy). At the end of the war, nearly 200,000 Salvadoran immigrants were accorded Deferred Enforced Departure (DED) as a sort of stop-gap measure while officials found a long-term solution to their immigration problems. Under pressure from anti-immigrant sentiment similar to that expressed in California's Proposition 187, Clinton was ready to terminate DED when it expired at the end of 1994.

An emergency meeting between President Calderón Sol and Vice-President Gore in Mexico City on December 1, 1994, led to a reversal of the decision to end DED. President Clinton signed an order extending the special status through September 30, 1995. Most undocumented Salvadorans were expected to apply for full legal status in the interim. Under U.S. immigration law, undocumented immigrants may avoid deportation if they can show that they have lived in the United States for seven years, or that returning to their homeland would cause severe hardship.[44]

The administration went out of its way to assure Salvadoran authorities that there would be no mass deportations, but in a context where laws like Proposition 187 are possible, people take such assur-

Figure 8a

Direction of Trade, 1993

Foreign Suppliers	% of total
United States	44.2
Guatemala	10.8
Mexico	5.9
Japan	5.1
Venezuela	5.0
All Others	29.0
Foreign markets	
United States	29.9
Guatemala	22.0
Costa Rica	9.0
Germany	7.2
Honduras	6.5
All Others	25.4

SOURCE: Economist Intelligence Unit, *EIU Country Report: El Salvador*, 1995.

ances with a large grain of salt. Many expect an increased rate of return of undocumented Salvadorans from the United States over the second half of the 1990s.[45]

The State Department policy paper quoted above makes no mention of immigration policy and includes only a passing reference to the importance of global trade to the economic future of El Salvador.[46] Successful implementation of the Peace Accords and the strengthening of democratic institutions occupy center stage. In the interest of maintaining political stability, postwar U.S. diplomacy in El Salvador prioritized the implementation of the Peace Accords that it helped broker.

On at least two key issues in the peace negotiations—land and the structure of the PNC—the U.S. exerted high-level pressure on the Salvadoran government to help break a deadlock. After Chapultepec, however, the U.S. exerted such diplomatic pressure less frequently and effectively as El Salvador slipped lower on the foreign policy agenda. During a series of Washington meetings between AID officials and NGO representatives in 1993 and 1994, AID staff regularly expressed frustration at their inability to draw the attention of top administration officials to the problems of the Salvadoran Peace Accords.

Military defeat of the FMLN was the overriding priority of the Reagan administration in El Salvador. Circumstances drove the Bush administration to reconsider that priority to the point that ending the war became its primary goal. The Clinton administration's policy has emphasized a completion of the Peace Accords leading to political stability, but against a regional emphasis on trade which leaves El Salvador with a very low profile. Barring a complete breakdown of the peace process and a resumption of the armed conflict, El Salvador is likely to stay on the back burner of the foreign policy establishment.

The State Department policy statement notes that, "During his fall 1993 meeting with Central American leaders, President Clinton emphasized the importance of broadening trade contacts and working closely with international financial institutions to offset declining aid levels."[47] Some observers suggested that Clinton was moving toward a "trade-not-aid" posture in relation to Central America. Given their place in the international economy, the Salvadorans fear that they may well end with very little of either.

U.S. Economic Aid

The U.S. government classified well over 50 percent of the assistance which it sent to El Salvador during the 1980s as economic assistance (Figure 8b). The AID program pursued the three interrelated goals of stabilizing the Salvadoran economy, defusing organized opposition to the government through direct pacification and through structural reform of the economy, and modernizing and diversifying the country's private sector. Almost two-thirds of all aid arrived as Economic Support Funds (ESF) designed to solve the country's balance of payment problems, with the rest divided between development assistance and PL480 food aid.

Although the living standards of poor Salvadorans plummeted during the 1980s, the U.S. economic stabilization efforts are seen as one of the most successful aspects of the program. Huge infusions of ESF funds kept the economy afloat and allowed El Salvador to enter the 1990s with fewer debt problems than most Latin American countries.[48]

Similarly, AID was relatively successful at both modernizing the political outlook of a significant portion of the private sector, and preparing it to play a leadership role in the planning of the structural adjustment program implemented by the Cristiani government. The private sector orientation supplanted an earlier emphasis on reforms designed to improve the situation of poor Salvadorans and build the "centrist alternative" represented by Duarte and the Christian Democrats.[49]

The millions of dollars intended to control and "pacify" the population of the conflictive areas showed few results. The sale of ESF dollars created large government institutions like the National Commission for the Restoration of Areas (CONARA) and the National Commission for Aid to the Displaced (CONADES) for the expressed purpose of "challenging the guerrilla presence not through military strategies, but by creating positive images of the government in the minds of the population."[50] These agencies were able to carry out major civic-military campaigns like "United to Reconstruct" and "Chalatenango 88," but, despite much public fanfare, the campaigns won few hearts and minds for the counterinsurgency project.

Immediately after the end of the war AID re-oriented its program toward postwar reconstruction via the Salvadoran government's National Reconstruction Plan (PRN). In March 1992, AID signed an agreement with the Salvadoran government to support a five-year, $161 million Peace and National Recovery Project (increased to $191 million three months later). This project, combined with local currency contributions from ESF dollar sales and existing projects, amounted to a promise of $300 million from AID for national reconstruction in El Salvador (See National Reconstruction).[51]

Although AID's immediate support for the PRN allowed the Salvadoran to "jump-start" its reconstruction program, the agency's effort was plagued by a multitude of difficulties almost from the start. A program of such scope and complication as the PRN—the program projected the provision of emergency aid, land, credit and technical

Figure 8b

U.S. Economic Aid to El Salvador

In millions of U.S. $

Year	DA	ESF	PL480 Tit. I	PL480 Tit. II	Peace Corps	Total
1983	58.8	140.0	39.0	7.8	—	245.6
1984	41.2	120.2	49.0	5.5	—	215.9
1985	91.1	285.0	49.0	8.8	—	433.9
1986	86.3	181.9	44.0	10.4	—	322.6
1987	133.0	281.5	42.0	6.4	—	462.9
1988	70.7	195.0	35.5	12.9	—	314.1
1989	62.3	190.9	40.0	13.8	—	307.0
1990	63.3	136.4	40.2	6.8	—	246.7
1991	55.7	124.0	34.0	14.1	—	227.8
1992	108.9	125.5	29.4	4.9	*	268.7
1993	78.0	94.3	33.4	8.0	0.4	214.1
1994	31.0	25.4	—	—	0.7	57.1

* less than $50,000
DA=Development Assistance
ESF=Economic Support Funds
PL480=Food for Peace Program
SOURCE: U.S. Overseas Loans and Grants and Assistance from Interantional Organizations July 1, 1945-Sept. 30, 1983, 1987, 1990, 1993, 1994.

assistance to thousands of former combatants and civilian landholders—was bound to face both technical and political problems.

AID, however, made matters worse by putting all of its 300 million reconstruction eggs in the same basket, that of the newly created National Reconstruction Secretariat (SRN).[52] Since in its early stages the SRN was nothing more than a reincarnation of CONARA with new letterhead, the FMLN and the popular organizations quickly came to view it as a politically motivated extension of wartime counterinsurgency. In its first two years of operation, the SRN did precious little to dispel such perceptions.[53] By January 1994, AID's own, internally commissioned evaluation of the Peace and National Recovery Project recommended a series of major changes.[54]

The victory of Bill Clinton brought new leadership to AID in Washington in early 1993. Key members of this new leadership—notably Chief of Staff Richard McCall and Latin American Director Mark Schneider—expressed a special interest in El Salvador and a determination to make the program there reflective of a new vision of development assistance. Almost immediately, tensions mounted between the Washington leadership and the veteran staff responsible for the program in San Salvador.

In testimony before Congress in July 1993, Bryan Atwood, the new administrator of AID in Washington, outlined a new direction for the agency based on the promotion of "sustainable development." Atwood also acknowledged the need for a consolidation of AID operations in the wake of the end of the Cold War.[55] Even in the context of major international transformations, economic assistance was still justifiable on the basis of the existence of certain disturbing trends that represent strategic threats to the United States and its allies. Among the most pressing of these trends, Atwood listed overpopulation, environmental degradation, endemic poverty, and massive migration.

By late 1993, the new thinking in Washington had coalesced into a new set of program objectives in El Salvador. These included:

- Assist the country in making the transition from war to peace.
- Promote enduring democratic institutions and practices.
- Increase equitable economic growth.
- Improve the health and education of all Salvadorans.
- Improve environmental and natural resource management.[56]

Although rhetorical flourishes mean little in El Salvador, after 12 years of support for counterinsurgency the proposal of such goals at least held out the opportunity of a change in the terms of the debate about AID's work in El Salvador. Before such a debate could develop, however, it was overshadowed by major cuts in the program budget.

After receiving $233.6 million in 1991, $275 million in 1992, and 252.2 million in 1993, AID in El Salvador received appropriations of $80.7 million in 1994, and the 1995 budget is sure to be significantly less than that of 1994.[57] The above cuts occurred before the 1994 election of a new congressional leadership committed to slashing the foreign aid budget even more radically.

By January 1995, AID had spent $172.5 million of the $300 million which it had promised to the SRN. Program officials in San Salvador saw little chance that they would ever be able to provide the $300 million, and even doubted the availability of the $254.7 million that had already been committed to specific projects.[58] The same sort of calculations pertained to all AID programs designed in the early 1990s.

As of early 1995, feeling in Congress was running decidedly against the bilateral foreign aid program managed by AID. The cuts in El Salvador were indicative of a global trend toward a radically reduced AID budget, and several foreign aid reform proposals contemplated the elimination of AID as an autonomous government agency. Multilateral institutions like the World Bank and IDB had already become more significant financial supporters of Salvadoran government programs than AID.[59] Despite these changes, the institution administering the United States economic aid program in El Salvador will continue to be an important presence in El Salvador, and the debate about that program will be an important one for the country's future.

The new rhetoric at AID was accompanied by some programmatic changes in the postwar period. For example, the agency's much maligned Judicial Reform Project received high marks from knowledgeable observers for its efforts to place major civil and criminal code reforms before the Legislative Assembly.[60] Similarly, while many NGOs continued to criticize the exclusionary practices of the SRN, others, such as the FMLN's Fundación 16 de Enero, played an increased role in AID-sponsored programs.

Although it was clear that AID's El Salvador program would be smaller in the late 1990s, whether or not the new discourse at the agency would produce enduring programmatic changes in favor of human development in El Salvador was much less certain. The presence of new programmatic thinking in many areas was undisputed, but the very connection to U.S. foreign policy that gave AID its importance in El Salvador made such lasting change look doubtful—at least in the short term.[61]

U.S. Military Aid

From the beginning of the Reagan era, U.S. policy was caught between the administration's need to defeat the FMLN militarily and the political impossibility of a massive troop commitment. The military was anxious to put into practice the lessons of the U.S. defeat in Viet Nam, but political considerations made the FAES the principal instrument of this strategy. Here, again, the solidarity movement in the United States played an important role in the development of the war. Policymakers were fully aware that the U.S. organizations, such as CISPES, would immediately respond to any escalation of the war that involved the participation of U.S. troops. Without such a threat, the policy calculations in moments of great frustration with the conduct of the Salvadoran Armed Forces could well have been different.

Even by the U.S. State Department's narrow definition of military aid, the FAES received over $1 billion in official U.S. military assistance between 1980 and 1992 (Figure 8c).[62] Covert aid of $500 million and other assets also reached the Salvadoran military through the CIA.[63] Much of the covert aid to the military went to the National Intelligence Directorate (DNI), the large military intelligence and special operations center.[64] The Peace Accords specifically called for the dismantling of the DNI.

United States law limited the number of U.S. military advisers to 55, but this was routinely violated. U.S. military sources place the total closer to 150. In addition, Salvadoran military sources estimated that for each U.S. military adviser there was at least one other U.S. adviser connected to the CIA, Defense Intelligence Agency (DIA), or NSC working in intelligence or security operations.[65]

Although the Pentagon constantly suggested that it could see the "light at the end of the tunnel," by 1988, a group of U.S. Army colonels published an extensive study that called the El Salvador counterinsurgency war "a fertile ground for teaching Americans" how to avoid similar mistakes in future low-intensity conflicts elsewhere in the world.[66]

It was not until 1990, after the Jesuit killings, that public opposition was able to force Congress to begin to cut the military aid budget. After 1990, the military aid budget, which had hovered around $100 million for most of the 1980s, dropped steadily—$66.9 million in 1991, $22.7 million in 1992, and $11.3 million in "nonlethal" assistance in 1993, the first year after the signing of the Peace Accords. In 1994 and 1995, U.S. assistance to El Salvador contained only marginal amounts of military assistance—$400,000 in 1995 for military training.[67] U.S. aid, then, supported the trend toward the demilitarization of Salvadoran society in the wake of the signing of the Peace Accords, and the loss of aid dollars was another way in which the military was the big institutional "loser" in the peace process (See Military).

A separate issue concerning the U.S. military arose in September 1993 when U.S. army personnel joined the FAES in a civic-military campaign called *Fuertes Caminos* (Strong Roads). In its first stage,

Figure 8c

U.S. Military Aid to El Salvador

In millions of U.S. $

Year	IMET	FMF/ FMS	MAP	Total
1983	1.3	46.5	33.5	81.3
1984	1.3	18.5	176.8	196.6
1985	1.5	10.0	124.8	136.3
1986	1.4	—	120.4	121.8
1987	1.5	—	110.0	111.5
1988	1.5	—	80.0	81.5
1989	1.4	—	80.0	81.4
1990	1.4	79.6	—	81.0
1991	1.0	65.9	—	66.9
1992	1.4	21.3	—	22.7
1993	0.3	11.0	—	11.3
1994	0.4	—	—	0.4

IMET=International Military and Education Training
FMF=Foreign Military Financing
FMS=Foreign Military Sales
MAP=Military Assistance Program
SOURCE: U.S. Overseas Loans and Grants and Assistance from International Organizations July 1, 1945-Sept. 30, 1983, 1987, 1990, 1993, 1994.

450 U.S. military engineers, officers, and troops were assigned to construction and water projects at several sites around the country. Many social groups and the FMLN opposed *Fuertes Caminos* on the basis that it violated the Salvadoran Constitution which prohibits the stationing of foreign troops on Salvadoran soil "under any pretext, in any situation."[68] Archbishop Arturo Rivera y Damas expressed the opposition of the Catholic Church when he asked in his Sunday homily, "Why do we need more soldiers in the country when we have peace?"[69]

The Salvadoran Supreme Court—still under the leadership of Mauricio Gutiérrez Castro—refused to consider the constitutionality of the program, and *Fuertes Caminos* continued through the end of 1993, with a second session after the elections in 1994-95.

Since the Peace Accords promoted constitutional changes limiting the role of the military to the defense of the national territory, many Salvadorans saw the U.S.-sponsored civic-military action campaign as a means of justifying the continuation of such actions on the part of the Salvadoran military. The decline in U.S. military aid to El Salvador did not necessarily bring an end to U.S. military influence.

Reference Notes

Introduction

1. Cristina Equizábal, et. al., *Humanitarian Challenges in Central America: Learning the Lessons of Recent Armed Conflicts* (Providence: Thomas J. Watson Jr. Institute for International Studies, 1993), p. 3.

2. Whether or not the notion of fourteen families ever had validity, it is surely an exaggeration in El Salvador of the 1990s. Nonetheless, it is still possible to identify a few dozen interlocking families that retain control of an important percentage of the country's resources. Ex-president Cristiani is from one of those families.

Part 1: Politics and Government

1. Academics have debated how many were killed, with estimates ranging from 8-10,000 in Thomas Anderson's study to 25-30,000 in several other studies. W.H. Durham's estimate of 17,000 is often considered the most reliable figure. Durham surmised that, whatever the exact number dead, there was sufficient killing to create a labor shortage which set the stage for large-scale migration to coffee areas for the rest of the 1930s. See W. H. Durham, *Scarcity and Survival in Central America* (Palo Alto: Stanford University Press, 1979).

2. United Nations, *De la Locura a la Esperanza: La Guerra de 12 Años en El Salvador* (The Report of the Truth Commission), (New York and San Salvador: United Nations, March 15, 1993) p. 132.

3. The United States placed tremendous importance on these elections. One measure of that importance was the massive press and propaganda campaign orchestrated from the United States to generate international interest in the elections. According to Jack Spence of Hemisphere Initiatives, media attention created coverage of the Salvadoran elections on a scale never seen previously for elections outside of the United States.

4. The establishment of some form of proportional representation at the local level appeared on the list of priorities of the Special Electoral Reform Commission agreed to by candidates Armando Calderón Sol and Rubén Zamora before the 1994 elections. A year later there was still no indication as to when the issue would be addressed.

5. Philip L. Russell, *El Salvador in Crisis* (Austin: Colorado River Press, 1984), p. 90.

6. Ibid., p. 91.

7. ARENA won 19 additional seats in the Assembly while the PDC lost 11, and ARENA gained control of 178 municipalities while the PDC lost 174.

8. See, for example, the confession of a then PDC insider that his party could not have consummated such an agreement in "Impunidad y falta de administración de justicia: obstáculos al proceso de paz," Interview with Abraham Rodríguez in *Tendencias*, January 1994, p. 18.

9. Transcript of Roberto D'Aubuisson's speech at the celebration of the tenth anniversary ARENA party.

10. *Latin American News Update*, January 1990.

11. FUSADES became known in the United States through a "60 Minutes" report which exposed an AID-supported FUSADES program to entice U.S. business to leave the United States and take advantage of cheap labor costs in El Salvador. A storm of controversy followed the airing of the program.

12. The FIS is a fund created in 1990 with the support of the Inter-American Development Bank, the German government, and other foreign donors to alleviate some of the economic side-effects of structural adjustment with small-scale social projects. The position was ideal for a presidential aspirant as Murray Meza appeared in the newspapers on an almost weekly basis at the dedication of one or another project or the signing of an agreement with a foreign entity providing money to his organization.

13. Interview with Carlos Ramos, University Documentation and Information Center (CIDAI), in San Salvador, March 1993.

14. Given the vast sums of reconstruction, structural adjustment, and other foreign aid funds—all conditioned, in some way, on compliance with the Peace Accords—a failure to publicly commit itself to compliance would have had a high price tag for the ARENA government.

15. The traditional faction dominated the new executive committee, which was led by Calderón Sol loyalist José Domenich and includes Raúl García Prieto, a younger conservative who had threatened to leave the party.

16. The administration had already been shaken by the departure of two ministers for supposed opposition to the policies of Calderón Sol. See A. Hernández, et. al., "Dos favoritos de Calderón quedan fuera del gabinete," *Primera Plana*, December 2, 1994.

17. Celia Cabrera, "Entre abandonos y críticas, surge el PLD," *Primera Plana*, October 14, 1994, p. 6.

18. This same image appeared in articles in *Primera Plana* in October 1994, and *Diario de Hoy* in January 1995 and was used by high-ranking AID officials in a January 1995 interview.

19. Felix Ulloa, a prominent leftist lawyer who was later elected to serve on the TSE, sounded this concern in a Channel 12 interview on the evening after the second round of the elections.

20. Morris J. Blachman and Kenneth E. Sharpe, "Things Fall Apart: Trouble Ahead in El Salvador," *World Policy Journal*, Winter 1988-1989, p. 118.

21. Gianni Beretta, "Todos Contra ARENA," *Pensamiento Propio*, August 1989.

22. *Entrevista Al Día*, Fidel Chávez Mena on Channel 12, December 11, 1991.

23. Interview with ex-PDC member in San Salvador, January 1995.

24. Both the Popular Social Christian Movement (MPSC) of Rubén Zamora and the Authentic Christian Movement (MAC) owe their origins to such schisms.

25. In January 1995, the Salvadoran press reported serious discussions between the MRSC and both the Unity Movement (MU) and the ERP.

26. CIDAI, "PDC: Crónica de una ruptura anunciada," *Proceso*, November 30, 1994, p. 5.

27. In his first highly publicized speech after the end of the war, Joaquín Villalobos took responsibility on behalf of the ERP for the killing of Dalton and apologized to Dalton's

family and the RN for the error. The ERP also promised to deliver Dalton's remains to the family but failed in its efforts to do so.

28. Joaquín Villalobos, "El Estado Actual de la Guerra y sus Perspectivas," *ECA*, March 1986.

29. For a fascinating discussion of these internal debates and their impact on the war effort in the late 1980s, see Sara Miles and Bob Ostertag, "The FMLN: New Thinking" in *A Decade of War*, Anjali Sundaram and George Gelber, eds. (New York: Monthly Review Press, 1991).

30. Frank Smyth, "Salvadoran Abyss," *Nation*, January 8/15, 1990.

31. One FMLN leader, Mauricio Chávez, published an intriguing novel *Fin del Siglo* in which the offensive of 1989 is portrayed as the end of an authoritarian century in El Salvador. The novel concludes with the author's journal of the offensive. Mauricio Chávez, *Fin del Siglo* (San Salvador: Editorial Arcoiris, 1993).

32. Most sources anywhere near the negotiations have also emphasized the FMLN's hard-boiled assessment of the difficulties of maintaining an armed guerrilla force in the absence of significant external assistance.

33. This information circulated as a rumor for months before it was publicly confirmed in the televised debate between Joaquín Villalobos and Orlando Quinteros in May 1994.

34. The FPL's plan to fashion a ticket out of Zamora and former commander Facundo Guardado was shelved when the press and the government publicly connected Guardado with the huge arms cache that exploded in Managua in mid-1993.

35. All parties agreed on the choice of Lima as vice-presidential candidate on the presumption that he would attract business support and centrist votes. Post-election analyses questioned how many votes Lima actually drew to the ticket.

36. Lee Winkleman, who worked for the FPL electoral information center during the campaign, insists that FMLN electoral strategists wanted to run in more municipal races with the CD, but that the Convergence often chose to run separately in hopes of drawing more votes to its Legislative Assembly ticket.

37. Interview with ERP leader, San Salvador, April 1994.

38. See Xavier Obach, "¡Patria o gente...! Análisis de la campaña televisiva de ARENA y de la Coalición," *ECA*, March/April 1994.

39. There is no comprehensive reporting of campaign spending, but ARENA's base among the country's wealthiest people surely gives them a huge advantage in this regard. In addition, ARENA also had access to much more of the public money in a special electoral fund because of its victory in 1991. According to analyst Xavier Obach, in the first round of the 1994 voting ARENA spent over $1 million on TV advertising alone, only slightly less than the amount spent by the other seven contenders combined. In the final round, they outspent the coalition by a three-to-one margin.

40. Eugenio Chicas, a former RN member who struggled up to the last minute to keep the FMLN together makes this argument in Edgardo Ayala, "El FMLN se rompe en tres facciones," *Primera Plana*, October 7, 1994, p. 5.

41. The PCN joined the opposition for the first time on this vote, giving the opposition the majority necessary to defeat the ARENA initiative.

42. A rather pessimistic view of the post-split prospects for the Salvadoran left is presented in CIDAI, "La salida de la ERP del FMLN," *Proceso*, December 7, 1994.

43. "El Salvador: Presidential Election News Notes," *Update* (Central American Historical Institute), November 21, 1988.

44. These bombings also coincided with a string of assassinations of ARENA members by urban guerrillas of the FMLN.

45. United Nations, *De la Locura*, p. 104.

46. A reliable source insists that the CD failed to meet the filing deadline because the party leader entrusted with the task of delivering the list got drunk and failed to make it to the TSE by the deadline.

47. Jack Spence, et. al. *The Salvadoran Peace Accords and Democratization*, (Cambridge: Hemisphere Initiatives, March 1995), p. 27.

48. Interview with ONUSAL official in San Salvador, April 1994.

49. The party was plunged into another crisis in the immediate aftermath of the 1994 elections as party factions that managed to come to some understanding during the elections fought each other, once again, for control.

50. Serrano was forced from power in 1993 after a failed effort to dissolve the Guatemalan congress and assume extraordinary powers as President.

51. Jack Spence, et. al., *El Salvador: Elections of the Century*, (Cambridge: Hemisphere Initiatives, July 1994), p. 25.

52. On a colón-per-vote basis, the MU was the most effective party in the first round of the presidential election. See Xavier Obach, "¡Patria o gente...! op. cit., p. 254.

53. USCEOM, *Free and Fair?: The Conduct of El Salvador's 1994 Elections*, (Washington, D.C.: June 1994), p. 3.

54. Ibid., p. 10.

55. CIDAI, "El fiasco del siglo," *Proceso*, No. 604, March 23, 1994, p. 2.

56. The limited extent of the changes represented by the new TSE should have been indicated by the fact that Rutilio Aguilera and Eduardo Colindres, two of the leading magistrates on the TSE, had served the same function on the CCE. To make matters worse, the "independent" member was clearly connected to the ARENA party.

57. According to the UN, 74,000 applications for electoral cards were denied outright, often because mayors had failed to turn in copies of the applicants' birth certificates to the TSE. On March 20, there were over 160,000 applications that had been approved but never turned into cards. USCEOM, op. cit., pp. 12-13.

58. Jack Spence, et. al., *El Salvador...* op. cit., p. 6.

59. USCEOM, op. cit., p. 3.

60. This summary draws heavily from the excellent analysis presented in Carlos Acevedo, "Las elecciones generales de 1994: consolidación de la hegemonía de ARENA," *ECA*, March/April 1994, pp. 205-208.

Part 2: Military

1. William Stanley, *Demilitarization in El Salvador: Harbinger or Exception?*, paper presented at the International Studies Association Meeting in Acapulco, México, March 23-28, 1993.

2. The analysis concerning the erosion of the military-oligarchy alliance owes much to the arguments presented in Stanley, op. cit., and Knut Walter and Philip Williams, *The Military and Democratization in El Salvador*, paper presented to the Latin American Studies Association Congress, September 24-27, 1992, Los Angeles, CA.

3. Interview with ex-FMLN commander Antonio Gutiérrez in San Salvador, July 1993.

4. The charges appeared as part of a publicity campaign designed to force President Cristiani to act against the list of officers named by the Ad Hoc Commission.

5. Tommie Sue Montgomery made this assessment of Corado's performance as Minister of Defense in a telephone interview in May 1995.

6. U.S. military advisers have described the pre-1980 Salvadoran armed forces as "a militia of 11,000 that had no mission" which "acted historically as a blight on the political system."

7. The FAES total of 62,000 included both of the eliminated security forces (National Guard and Treasury Police). The FMLN protested this maneuver as a violation but eventually

accepted the reduction to 31,000 for the FAES. By 1995, the FAES had reduced troop levels significantly below the 31,000 level. It is not clear that the civil defense structures totally disappeared. The 1995 mobilization of former civil defense members to demand severance benefits suggests that some level of coordination continued to exist.

8. Figures from the Ministry of Treasury, cited in Alexander Segovia, "Límites y Dilemas de la Política Económica en un País en Guerra: El Caso de El Salvador," *Realidad Económico-Social*, November-December 1988.

9. After a receiving a 6% budget cut in 1993, the military was level-funded in 1994 and 1995. While the actual budget outlay was constant in those years, the military budget declined in real terms and as a percentage of both GDP and the national budget as a whole.

10. According to William Stanley, during the early stages of the war a number of officers in the security forces worked their way up through the ranks and had no military school training. Similarly, many officers trained in the early 1980s passed through a highly accelerated course that included participation in U.S. programs in Honduras, El Salvador, and the United States.

11. At the time of the passage of the law, many human rights advocates argued that the military should not be given such a blank check to maintain an institutional presence all over El Salvador.

12. The United States has attempted unsuccessfully to reform the officer corps, while also attempting to develop a cadre of noncommissioned officers which are regarded as essential for small unit operations. But the concept of noncommissioned officers is alien to the military establishment, which "consists of the commissioned officer elite above and short-service peasant conscripts below." Only 10 percent of the noncommissioned officers trained in the United States reenlist for another term. Ltc. A. J. Bacevich, Ltc. James Hallums, Ltc. Richard White, and Ltc. Thomas Young, John F. Kennedy National Security Fellows, "American Military Policy in Small Wars: The Case of El Salvador," Paper presented at the John F. Kennedy School of Government, March 22, 1988.

13. Ibid.

14. Several of the best articles on the death squads are collected in *Los escuadrones de la muerte en El Salvador* (San Salvador: Editorial Jaraguá, January 1994).

15. Together with Green Beret instructors, the CIA conceived and organized ORDEN (National Democratic Organization), the network described by Amnesty International as a movement designed to "use clandestine terror against government opponents." Several of the early death squads had connections to ORDEN. Several sources document the regular sharing of intelligence on leftists and popular leaders between the CIA and the U.S. embassy, on one hand, and the Salvadoran military and police intelligence units on the other.

16. Joya Martínez later fled to the U.S. where he was jailed by the INS and, eventually, extradited to El Salvador. He was immediately jailed there but was released under the amnesty law and given political asylum in a third country. As of November 1993 (interview by the Australian *Revista Farabundo Martí*) he still insisted on the veracity of his claims.

17. United Nations, *De la Locura*, p. 144.

18. Kidnapping was nothing new for the Army. Groups within the Armed Forces had operated kidnapping rings since at least the early 1970s.

19. This discussion on military corruption draws largely from an excellent article by Joel Millman, "El Salvador's Army: A Force Unto Itself," *New York Times*, December 10, 1989.

20. Ibid.

21. Grupo Conjunto..., *Informe del Grupo Conjunto para la Investigación de Grupos Armados Ilegales con Motivación Política en El Salvador*, San Salvador, July 1994, p. 25.

22. This might be considered a modest sum by the standards of U.S. pension funds but in El Salvador $100 million equals just under a tenth of the national budget or, coincidentally, the annual government military expenditure at war's end.

23. Stewart Lawrence, *Postwar El Salvador: An Examination of Military Issues Related to Reconstruction*, (Unitarian Universalist Service Committee, 1991), pp. 6-7.

24. When, in January 1994, demobilized members of the Armed Forces carried out a series of militant actions to demand severance and other benefits, they took over the IPSFA building, holding staff and management hostage for many hours in what demonstration leaders said was an act to symbolize the lack of support they received from the military.

25. Lawrence, op. cit., p. 9.

26. United Nations, *Acuerdos de El Salvador: En el Camino a la Paz*, San Salvador: United Nations, p. 47-8.

27. Several are detailed in Peter Sollis, *Reluctant Reforms: The Cristiani Government and the International Community in the Process of Post-War Reconstruction*, (Washington Office for Latin America, June 1993), p. 37.

28. Quoted in Sollis, op. cit., p. 41.

29. In early 1995, U.S. soldiers working on a construction project in the eastern part of the country reported that they were fired upon by unknown assailants. No injuries were reported.

30. According to Ray Lynch of AID, that agency organized a number of visits to countries like Nicaragua and Colombia in late 1991 and early 1992 for the personnel of the National Reconstruction Secretariat and leading NGOs, in hopes that the problems faced by those situations could be avoided in El Salvador.

31. This was true from the very beginning of the demobilization process as FMLN leaders fought to have many people who had been only irregular participants in the war classified as excombatants with full rights to benefits.

32. Interview with EU Director, Jaap van der Zee, in San Salvador, March 1994.

33. One ex-commander of the FMLN in Usulután lamented, in early 1994, that some of the younger *muchachos* who had fought with him had become involved in criminal gangs in that area as a result of economic desperation and a sense of abandonment by those who had offered them direction and hope during the war.

34. Jim McGovern, who as an aide to Congressman Joe Moakley of Massachusetts led the congressional effort to expose the cover-up in the Jesuit case, returned from a visit to San Salvador in 1995 convinced that this problem represented the single greatest threat to the country's stability.

35. In one case, the PNC fired on an ADEFAES crowd near the National University and one demonstrator was killed, but there was remarkably little violence given the militancy of the actions and the numbers of police and demonstrators involved.

36. The ADEFAES crisis occurred exactly at the same time that ONUSAL was attempting to mediate a solution in the strike of anti-narcotic officers of the PNC and led to much discussion in the local press of how the country would resolve such tensions after the departure of the UN mission.

37. CIDAI, "The political meaning of a violent week," *Proceso*, February 1, 1995 (English translation).

38. Saul Mirón, of ADEFAES, quoted in Edgardo Ayala, "Gobierno acosado por críticas y demandas," *Primera Plana*, January 27, 1995, p. 5.

39. In public speeches at the UCA and in the pages of *Proceso*, Rudolfo Cardenal expressed the popular theory that ousted ex-members of the military High Command (Ponce, Zepeda, Elena Fuentes, etc.) were behind ADEFAES in an effort to destabilize conditions to the point of creating the conditions for a military coup. Such a coup would be the vehicle for the restoration of the military to its traditional place in society. CIDAI, "The political meaning..." op. cit.

40. Before and after the signing of the Peace Accords, soon-to-be presidential candidate Rubén Zamora gave several speeches in which he emphasized that freedom from dependence on a "progressive sector" of the military was the key distinguishing feature of the democratic opening created by the peace process.

41. See, for example, Mario Lungo Uclés, "Los Obstáculos a la Democratización en El Salvador," in *El Salvador en Construcción*, August 1993, p. 25.

42. When ex-members of the PN and Immediate Response Batallions threatened the Legislative Assembly in late January, the Assembly President personally called out the army to protect the Assembly. In denouncing this action, the FMLN said that the apparent violation of the Constitution reflected "the existence of a destabilization plan which is directed, organized and financed by recalcitrant rightwing groups opposed to peace, with the goal of discrediting the PNC and thereby justifying the presence of the army in public security affairs; they also wish to see a state of emergency, thereby reversing the democratic progress initiated with the signing of the Peace Accords."

43. The analysis here owes much to the vision presented in the concluding section of Walter and Williams, op. cit.

Part 3: Justice, Human Rights, and Public Security

1. To cite only one example, four directors of the nongovernmental Human Rights Commission were assassinated during the 1980s.

2. In 1991 then-Colonel Francisco Elena Fuentes gave a group of U.S. visitors a startling explanation of the high body counts. The Colonel, himself accused of massive human rights abuses by the Ad Hoc Commission and the Truth Commission, insisted that taxi drivers, upon seeing a cadaver, would rush to the Camino Real Hotel to bring international journalists to the scene. After returning the journalists to the hotel, a driver would return to the scene, load up the cadaver and move it to a different site, and then repeat the whole process. In this way, according to Elena Fuentes, international observers arrived at their inflated statistics.

3. Cited in Margaret Popkin, "Human Rights in the Duarte Years," in *A Decade of War: El Salvador Confronts the Future*, (New York: Monthly Review Press, 1991), p. 60.

4. United Nations, *De la Locura*, p. 190 (Author's translation).

5. "Impunidad y falta de administración de justicia," Interview with Abraham Rodríguez, *Tendencias*, December 1993-January 1994.

6. Another often-overlooked factor in the decline in the numbers of murders and disappearances was the shortage of even vaguely suspicious people to kill. By 1984, the majority of people associated with the popular movement had either already been killed, had left the country, or had joined the FMLN.

7. Americas Watch, *Nightmare Revisited* (New York: 1988).

8. Ibid.

9. Two books have been published in English on the massacre and the subsequent cover-up and trial: Martha Doggett, *A Death Foretold* (New York: Lawyers' Committee for Human Rights, 1993), and Teresa Whitfield, *Paying the Price: Ignacio Ellacuría and the Murdered Jesuits of El Salvador* (Philadelphia: Temple University Press, 1995).

10. Both sides at the negotiating table signed the UN-drafted protocol that created the Truth Commission without amendment. The consensus was, nonetheless, "reluctant" because some social sectors, notably the military and the right wing of the ARENA party, only accepted the existence of a Truth Commission because they had no alternative. Other sectors, such as all branches of government and parts of the FMLN, showed their reluctance by providing the Truth Commission with incomplete information, pub-

licly questioning the legitimacy of the final report, or blocking compliance with the commission's recommendations.

11. For a more complete account of the twists and turns of government compliance with the Ad Hoc Commission recommendations, see Margaret Popkin, et. al., *Justice Impugned*, (Cambridge: Hemisphere Initiatives, June 1993).

12. CIDAI, "Se van los generales, permanece la impunidad," *Proceso*, June 7, 1993.

13. The Truth Commission report investigated the murders of eleven mayors but maintained that the total number of victims was higher.

14. The report specifically criticized the Chief Justice for his personal role in blocking the effort to investigate the 1981 massacre by the U.S.-trained Atlacatl Battalion of hundreds of unarmed civilians at El Mozote, Morazán.

15. Reportedly, the names of civilians with possible death squad connections were published in a secret annex to the report that went to the Secretary General and the Salvadoran President.

16. Legal experts raised serious constitutional and international law questions about the law at the time, but the Supreme Court declined to review the amnesty decision. See Organization of American States, Inter-American Commission on Human Rights, *Report on the Situation of Human Rights in El Salvador*, OEA/Ser. L/V/II. 85, Doc. 28 FCU, February 11, 1994 at 69-77.

17. For example, while finding the Truth Commission report to be an important advance in human rights protection, the Americas Watch report *Accountability and Human Rights: The Report of the United Nations Commission on the Truth for El Salvador*, suggests that the commission might have provided more information on some cases of abuses by the FMLN and should have held the Salvadoran government to its responsibility to prosecute those responsible for abuses.

18. See Margaret Popkin, "El Salvador: A Negotiated End to Impunity?", in *Impunity and Human Rights in International Law and Practice*, Naomi Roht-Arriaza, ed. (New York and Oxford: Oxford University Press, 1995).

19. While popular groups covered the walls around the Hotel El Salvador with graffiti welcoming ONUSAL and claiming its presence as a popular victory, clandestine groups made veiled threats against "foreign interference" and circulated flyers in posh restaurants threatening those who would cater to UN personnel.

20. Interview with Celia Medrano, Non-Governmental Human Rights Commission, in San Salvador, September, 1991.

21. CIDAI, "Los derechos humanos según ONUSAL: su X informe (III parte)," *Proceso*, May 25, 1994.

22. Popkin, *Justice Impugned*, p. 6.

23. We are grateful to Tommie Sue Montgomery for this observation about the early stages of Velásquez' leadership of the PDH.

24. ONUSAL, *Report of the Director of the Human Rights Division of ONUSAL covering the period from 1 March to 30 June 1994*, July 28, 1994.

25. Human Rights Watch/Americas, *Darkening Horizons: Human Rights on the Eve of the March 1994 Elections*, (Washington, D.C.: March 1994), pp. 16-17.

26. The Peace Accords state that excombatants of the FMLN and ex-National Police each will make up no more than 20% of the recruits to the PNC. At least 60% of recruits were to be civilians.

27. For example, in Tierra Blanca, Usulután, the arrival of the PNC in December 1993 was marked by a well-attended dance paid for by local community organizations. A few months later, the PNC was present at the discovery of human skeletal remains in a well located in a house that had been used by the Treasury Police during the war.

28. William Stanley, *Risking Failure: The Problems and Promise of the New Civilian Police*, (Cambridge: Hemisphere Initiatives, September 1993), p. iii.

29. Washington Office on Latin America, *Recent Setbacks in the Police Transition*, February 4, 1994.

30. A controversial move in this regard was the appointment of Major Oscar Armando Peña Durán who served as PNC Chief of Operations for six months during the initial deployment of the new police. Because Peña Durán had previously served as a military officer, his appointment to such a high position in the PNC was seen as a threat to the civilian character of the institution.

31. ONUSAL received 147 such reports between November 1, 1993 and June 30, 1994. Nearly one-third of these involved excessive use of force or torture. A previous report (the 11th Human Rights Report) verified two cases of torture.

32. Margaret Popkin, et. al., *Justice Delayed: The Slow Pace of Judicial Reform in El Salvador*, (Cambridge: Hemisphere Initiatives, 1994), pp. 10-11.

33. In another example of the smooth functioning of the Salvadoran justice system, a lower court judge later released Coreas for lack of evidence.

34. In late 1994, President Calderón Sol called out military units to support the PNC in dealing with a protest by bus owners near the city of San Miguel. With the situation threatening to get out of hand, the soldiers fired on the crowd, killing three and wounding another twenty people. Despite the controversy surrounding this incident, the President insisted on his right to call out the military in emergency situations.

35. For a rigorous analysis of the Constitutional Reforms of 1991 and the judicial reform process, in general, see Lawyers Committee for Human Rights, *El Salvador's Negotiated Revolution: Prospects for Legal Reform*, New York, June 1993.

36. Popkin, *Justice Delayed*, op. cit., p. 5.

37. "Domingo Mendes Presidente Corte Suprema," *La Noticia*, July 28, 1994, p. 6.

38. Jack Spence, et. al., *The Salvadoran Peace Accords...*, op. cit., p. 11.

39. Information provided by Margaret Popkin in April 1995.

40. Overcrowding and inhumane conditions in Salvadoran jails contributed to a series of violent prison riots in the years following the end of the war. The worst occurred in 1993 at the prison in San Francisco Gotera, Morazán, in which over two dozen inmates were hacked to death with machetes and many more seriously injured.

41. See, for example, Instituto Universitario de Opinion Pública (IUDOP), "La opinión de los salvadoreños sobre las elecciones. La última encuesta pre-electoral," in *Estudios Centroamericanos*, No. 545-6, p. 168. While crime was the number one concern of those polled, the four main concerns ranked after crime were all of an economic nature.

42. The Working Group appointed by the Secretary General of the United Nations was made up of Diego García-Sayán, the head of the Human Rights Division of ONUSAL, Carlos Molina Fonseca, the Salvadoran Human Rights Ombudsman, and two government lawyers, Juan Gerónimo Castillo and José Leandro Echevarría. Mario López, the third FMLN ex-commander killed in late 1993, was actually killed on December 9, the day after the announcement of the formation of the Working Group.

43. Grupo Conjunto..., *Informe..*, p. 25.

44. New York Times, *Unfinished Business in El Salvador*, August 12, 1994.

45. Gene Palumbo, "Report exposes renewed death squad violence," *National Catholic Reporter*, August 12, 1994.

46. Reliable crime statistics do not exist in El Salvador, but in 1994, one-third of Salvadorans polled reported that they or a member of their immediate family had been a victim of a violent crime.

47. In October 1993, President Cristiani ordered the army to undertake foot patrols in response to the threat to the security of the coffee harvest.

48. Young Salvadorans deported from the U.S. for criminal activities have apparently recreated their gangs upon returning to El Salvador. Mike O'Connor, "A New U.S. Import in El Salvador: Street Gangs," *New York Times*, July 3, 1994.

49. Francisco Díaz of The Center for the Study of Applied Law (CESPAD) quoted in Guillermo Mejía, "Rezagos en la post-guerra," *Tendencias*, October 1993.

50. Juan Hernández Pico, "La seguridad, la impunidad, la justicia," *Envio*, July 1994.

51. Alfredo Cristiani's September 1993 address to the United Nations, quoted in IDHUCA, "Tercer Informe de la Procuraduría para la Defensa de Derechos Humanos," in *Proceso*, October 13, 1993, p. 14.

52. Quoted in Jack Spence, et. al., *A Negotiated Revolution: A Progress Report on the Salvadoran Peace Accords* (Cambridge: Hemisphere Initiatives, 1994), p. 8.

Part 4: Economy

1. This growth also needs to be understood in the context of the drastic decline in income during the war. As of 1995, real per capita income had still not reached prewar levels.

2. The main growth in textiles came from the expansion of the so-called *maquila* sector in which foreign capital establishes mobile production facilities for the assembly of imported cloth into garments for export. Because of the war, El Salvador was a late entry into this market, but the sector showed dramatic growth rates in the mid-1990s.

3. Hernán Darío Correa, et. al., *Neoliberales y pobres*, (Bogotá: CINEP, 1993), stands out among the growing literature on this theme. IDB and UNDP, *Reforma Social y Pobreza: Hacia una agenda integrada de desarrollo*, (New York, 1993) summarizes the discussions at an international conference held in Washington, D.C. in February, 1993 on the persistence of poverty in Latin America in the context of structural adjustment programs.

4. CEPAL, *Centroamérica: el Camino de los Noventa* (CEPAL, LC/MEX/R.386 (SEM 53/2)), January 1993.

5. For a discussion of the impact of structural adjustment on income levels and income distribution throughout Central America, see Guillermo Mejía, "¿Ajuste o desbarajuste?", *Tendencias*, December 1994-January 1995, p. 6.

6. The Ministry of Planning reports that the percentage of urban Salvadoran families living in extreme poverty declined from 31.1 percent to 23.25 percent during the period 1988-1992.

7. CIDAI, "Poverty in El Salvador", *Proceso* (English translation), November 9, 1994.

8. See Mitchell Seligson, et. al., *El Salvador Agricultural Policy Analysis Land Tenure Study*, (AID Contract Nos. DAN-4084-Z-11-8034-00 and LAG-4084-C-00-2043-00), September 1993.

9. The excellent newsletter *Salvanet* draws on a 1989 study by the UCA to compare, in a very concrete way, the essential expenses of a campesino family with that same family's possible income sources. It finds that even a mildly properous family needs a lot of luck to avoid a period of critical shortages just before the first corn harvest. "The Miracle of Survival," *Salvanet*, February-April, 1995, p. 11.

10. The popular education group, *Equipo de Maíz*, produced a pamphlet on the persistence of poverty in the context of economic growth. See Equipo de Maíz, "El Salvador y el Crecimiento Económico," (San Salvador, 1994).

11. The causes of this increase were many. One important factor was that much of U.S. aid had to be spent on goods produced in the United States. In addition, the massive aid program began to broaden the Salvadoran middle class who used their increased income to buy large amounts of consumer goods from the United States. Increased migration of Salvadorans to the United States also had a direct impact on imports. Salvadorans living in the United States purchased millions of dollars worth of consumer goods there and shipped them to El Salvador.

12. This is quite a large deficit given that the country was only exporting $500 million that year. El Salvador would have had to double its exports in order to wipe out its deficit.

13. In the early 1990s, *maquilas* had to be located in one of the nation's free zones in order to receive tax benefits. Those regulations were relaxed to the point that such plants could receive most of these benefits regardless of where they were located. By early 1995, President Calderón Sol was widely quoted as saying that it was time to "turn all of El Salvador into one big free zone."

14. Interview with Lic. Mirna Liévano de Marqués in San Salvador, March 1994.

15. As part of the corruption scandals of the Calderón Sol administration, Legislative Assembly President Gloria Salguero Gross was accused, in January 1995, of evading $1 million in taxes by neglecting to claim the full value of her considerable real estate holdings. After viciously accusing her accuser, Kirio Waldo Salgado, of unfounded defamation, Salguero Gross concluded her public denial by saying that the accusations were, after all, irrelevant because "no one declares their properties at their real value." See CIDAI, "Las acusaciones contra Gloria Salguero Gross," *Proceso*, January 25, 1995, p. 5. In reference to the cost of bank privatization, the then-Vice-President of the Central Reserve Bank, Gino Battaglia, said that it cost the Salvadoran government just under $300 million to put the banks in the hands of the allegedly more efficient private sector.

16. The limits of Salvadoran nationalism were revealed in a Gallup poll published in the conservative *Diario de Hoy* on October 3, 1994. The poll reported that 47 percent of Salvadorans believe that tax evaders should not be punished while 46 percent believe that they should. For many Salvadorans, the idea that the homeland must be preserved at all costs does not include the cost of paying income taxes.

17. See Benjamin Schwarz, *American Counterinsurgency Doctrine and El Salvador* (Washington, DC: RAND Corporation, 1992), p.2. Schwarz adds $850 million in unsubsidized credits to arrive at a total aid package of $6 billion.

18. This figure includes both loans and grants. Although much of the $845 million pledged for the PRN was not received by the end of 1993, other funds—like World Bank and IMF loans—did become available during that period. The $800 million estimate was made by a UNDP official in March 1994.

19. AID, *May 1994 Report*.

20. Statistics from the *World Bank Development Report 1994* and the Salvadoran Treasury Ministry.

21. The nationalization of international trade in coffee and the banking system were both highly unpopular policies because they limited the investment options of the oligarchy. On the impact of the coffee policies, see Tropical Research and Development, Inc., *El Salvador Coffee Technology Transfer Project Paper*, 1990, p. 3-8.

22. Ironically, some of this capital flight represented investment decisions concerning capital provided directly to the Salvadoran private sector through the U.S. aid program. Rather than invest aid money in production, Salvadoran capitalists opted to recycle it back to U.S. banks.

23. Data provided by FUSADES in *La Prensa Gráfica*, "Martes Económico," December 7, 1993.

24. Data from Central Reserve Bank of El Salvador, summarized in CENITEC, "Propuesta de un Programa Económico-Social de Consenso para El Salvador," *Política Económica*, March-April, 1993. p. 10.

25. William C. Thiesenhusen, *How Agriculture has Effected Social Change in El Salvador*, Paper prepared for delivery at the University of Wisconsin, February 2, 1984.

26. This was supposed to have been a loan to be paid back when coffee prices recovered, but coffee producers have been reticent to repay the advance.

27. A frost destroyed millions of coffee trees in Brazil. These trees will have to be replanted and presumably will be at full productive capacity in 3-5 years.

28. FMLN activists from the early period of the war still talk about the day when guerrillas set fire to the giant mountain of cotton near Zamorán, Usulután as the "point of no return" for the war in that area.

29. Bean harvests increased to the point that, in 1993, the government decided to export massive amounts of beans. Later that year, domestic bean prices rose sharply as bean wholesalers hoarded supplies to improve prices. Farmers received very little of the price increase which devastated the urban poor, and, ironically, beans had to be imported from Asia on an emergency basis at a high price.

30. Foreign Agricultural Service/U.S. Department of Agriculture, *El Salvador: Agricultural Situation Report*, March 31, 1989.

31. According to Seligson, op. cit. p. 3-4, the cooperatives continue to greatly underutilize their land, but still use it slightly more efficiently than their private sector counterparts. Although 28 cooperatives were totally abandoned during the war and overall land utilization declined sharply, this trend was reversed in the postwar period by the Land Transfer Program and the expansion of cooperative cultivation.

32. Only 25 percent of the agrarian reform cooperatives received bank credits in the 1980s (mostly those engaged in export production), but even this limited coverage has resulted in a huge accumulated debt.

33. Jonathan Kandell, "Conservatives' Victory in El Salvador Signals End to Land Reform," *Wall Street Journal*, March 22, 1989.

34. Although it was clearly a result of political pressure and manipulation by ARENA, the decision to opt for subdivision can be interpreted as the deepening of a trend toward individual use of cooperative land. Already by 1987 about 28% of the land of the cooperatives was farmed on an individual basis, 72% collectively.

35. Kandell, *Wall Street Journal*.

36. This was the essential thrust of the First Cooperative Congress held in San Salvador in October 1991. At that time, it even appeared that the need for viability as a sector was compelling the agrarian reform cooperatives to put aside the sectarian political divisions that plague the entire Salvadoran popular movement. That tendency was much less pronounced by early 1995, but the momentum for organizational development and economic viability remained strong (See Campesino Organizing).

37. ARENA was active in the formation of MAIZ, a well-organized group of landowners who stubbornly opposed the Land Transfer Program, especially in Chalatenango and Morazán.

38. On the potential problems inherent in the combination of credit programs included in the government program, see El Salvador Information Project, *Land Transfers: 'Til Debt Do Us Part?*, March 1994. In interviews in early 1994, the director of the European Union program for ex-combatants in Usulután questioned whether or not the package offered by the government was viable, and claimed that the design of the EU program had been tailored to overcome this limitation. See Kevin Murray et. al., *Rescuing Reconstruction: The Debate on Post-War Economic Recovery in El Salvador* (Cambridge: Hemisphere Initiatives, 1994), pp. 45-49.

39. The General Secretary reported that, between April and August of 1994, only 351 beneficiaries received title to land.

40. Michael Hoffman, *Update on Land Issues in El Salvador*, (The SHARE Foundation, October 4, 1994), pp. 4-5.

41. As of the end of the second year of PRN implementation, FEDISAL, a Salesian-run NGO with heavy board-level participation from the Salvadoran oligarchy, had been assigned $17 million, one-third of all funds made available to NGOs as a whole. At that time, direct project approvals to NGOs with historical connections to the FMLN totalled less than $300,000, although another $1.5 million had probably been assigned to these NGOs through intermediaries.

42. Ironically, the actions of demobilized members of the FAES and the paramilitary civil defense units most dramatically highlighted the failures of reintegration programs. Or-

Reference Notes

ganizations demanding severance benefits for these groups seized the Legislative Assembly building and held deputies hostage on three occasions during 1994.

43. During the war Sra. de Dowe was a leading figure in the National Commission for the Restoration of Areas (CONARA), a key element in the government counterinsurgency effort. She brought that perspective to the SRN and ran the secretariat in such a way as to block the emergence of any sort of consensual vision of the PRN.

44. Vice-President Jorge Borgo Bustamante accompanied FMLN leader Leonel González on a visit to the UN in December 1994 to request that the Secretary General help them raise that amount to assure full compliance with the Peace Accords.

45. According to El Salvador-based AID officials Mark Scott, John Sullivan, and Tom Hawke, interviewed in San Salvador in January 1995, Economic Support Funds for El Salvador had been diverted when the Clinton administration needed to find funds for the reconstruction of Haiti in the wake of the military action there in late 1994.

46. During the 1950s, CEPAL developed the idea that Latin American economies were being crushed by continually worsening terms of trade with the developed countries, especially the United States. Central American planners used elements of the work of CEPAL to fashion their integration model, but definitely took the process in the direction which responded to their immediate political interests. The United States also used its influence to form the vision of the CACM, which was less ambitious than that of CEPAL. See Alfredo Guerra Borges, "Desarrollo e Integración en Centroamérica: Del Pasado a las Perspectivas," Mexico, *Cultura Popular*, 1988.

47. See Carlos Orellana Merlos, "El Nuevo Modelo de Integración Centroamericana y la Armonización Regional de Políticas Macroeconómicas," (CENITEC, 1993), pp. 2-3.

48. CIDAI, "Balance regional," *Proceso*, December 30, 1993, pp. 28-29.

49. Costa Rica raises several questions about integration. As a country without an army, it is concerned about the persistence of large armed forces in the other Central American countries. The more pressing issues, though, are economic. What would free mobility mean between a country with up to 60 percent unemployment, like Nicaragua, and neighboring Costa Rica, which has an official unemployment rate under 10 percent? All the integration agreements to date allow for each country to participate to the degree it sees fit. Guatemalan political scientist Carlos Sarti calls Costa Rica the "apple of discord in the integration process."

50. *La Prensa Gráfica*, November 2, 1993, p. 40.

51. CIDAI, "El NAFTA: nuevas relaciones entre E.U. y Centroamérica," *Proceso*, December 15, 1993, pp. 10-11.

52. Quoted in Trish O'Kane, "Central America still eating bitter fruit," *Latinamerica Press*, March 24, 1994, p. 3.

53. *La Prensa Gráfica*, August 21, 1994.

54. Quoted in Carlos Sarti, "Centroamérica: Entre la competencia y la cooperación," *Tendencias*, May 1993, p. 17.

55. Economist Aquiles Montoya developed the term "new popular economy" to refer to this social experiment being carried out in El Salvador. Montoya analyzed this notion at length in two books: *La nueva economía popular: una aproximación teórica* (San Salvador: UCA Editores, 1993) and *La nueva economía popular: una aproximación empírica* (San Salvador: UCA Editores, 1994).

56. As one measure of the problem of productive incentives, people from all over El Salvador reported that a significant percentage of excombatants receiving the reintegration loan of just under $2000 declined to invest those funds in productive activities.

57. In one case, an organization that had worked effectively as a community organization supporting land occupations during the war suddenly had close to $1 million in development projects when the war ended. Needless to say, the organization had tremendous difficulty implementing the projects in a way that benefitted any of the participating communities.

58. Interviews with representatives of Oxfam UK/Ireland, Jesuit Development Service, and Swedish Diakonia in San Salvador, January 1995.

59. Many Salvadoran analysts connect the failure of reconstruction to stimulate the new popular economy to the primacy of structural adjustment in the government's thinking. In a market-driven scenario, the government need only set the stage for the market to take over. See Alfonso Goitea, quoted in Oxfam America, *The Impact of Structural Adjustment...*, op. cit., p. 9.

60. In southern San Vicente, one of the former areas of conflict with the most productive potential, FUNDE sponsored quite an ambitious participatory evaluation of the organizational model in place in the area. See Alberto Enríquez, et. al., *Diagnóstico Socioeconómico y Propuesta de Desarrollo Sostenible para el Municipio de Tecoluca, San Vicente*, (San Salvador: FUNDE, January 23, 1995).

61. *InterPress Service*, "El Salvador estremece a los vecinos," February 3, 1995.

62. Ibid.

63. In February 1995 meetings with U.S. NGOs, State Department official Anne Patterson also spoke favorably of the plan, as amended.

64. The opposition of the popular movement and the FMLN were predictable, but Juan Héctor Vidal of the National Association of Private Enterprise publicly called the plan, as originally proposed, "a grave risk to national production and employment."

65. CIDAI, "An Economic Adventure," *Proceso* (English translation), February 8, 1995.

66. Even as this proposal was being debated in San Salvador, Mexico was reeling from the economic disaster resulting from its efforts to implement a similar policy.

67. The best example in the recent period is the difficulty faced by the government of Roberto Reina in Honduras.

68. In its August 1993 report recommending a second structural adjustment loan for El Salvador, the World Bank spoke of the existence of "a general consensus across the political spectrum" on the necessity of combating poverty by deepening the structural adjustment process. Furthermore, the need for continued international support of the reconstruction process would serve as a powerful incentive for any government to continue with the economic reform program.

69. FUSADES' plan was called "Social Solutions and Economic Reforms." In the version of the plan prepared for mass consumption and published in *La Prensa Gráfica*, FUSADES presented a plan for "breaking the back of poverty" which included increased social spending, decentralizing services and making them more participatory, promoting efficient public administration and focusing social assistance where it is needed most. The foundation insisted, however, that "economic growth is the most efficient way to fight poverty." Clearly, social reform is good, but only so long as it stays within the limits imposed by economic reform. Nonetheless, the emphasis on social reform represented a break with the 1989-94 plan which became the framework of ARENA economic policy.

70. One of the most comprehensive of these proposals is contained in FUNDE's, "New National Economic Agenda for El Salvador," published in late 1994.

71. Obviously, there is a sizable language problem within the debate over structural adjustment. FUSADES and the other spokespeople of structural adjustment have adopted much of the language of the opposition. Notions like "participation" in social services, "decentralization" of public administration, and "self-reliant" economic development all permeate the official literature without impacting a reality that can be quite authoritarian, corrupt, and centralized.

72. One study by an economist at the UCA concludes that, in 1990, for example, 61 percent of GDP went to capital as profit or rent, 35 percent to workers in wages, and only 4 percent to the government in net taxes.

73. The Peace Accords established the Social and Economic Forum to promote discussions among labor, business, and the government that might lead to such changes. The Fo-

rum was the least effective of the various institutions created in Chapultepec (See Social Organization and the Popular Movement).

Part 5: Society and Social Policy

1. Much of the money had been spent on increased administrative costs at the Ministry of Education and the construction of educational infrastructure. In programmatic terms, technical and vocational education were emphasized based on the expected demands of regional economic integration. When integration collapsed, these skilled graduates became superfluous and many of them were among those that left for the United States in the 1980s.

2. Political activism was nothing new for Salvadoran teachers and students. Students and faculty at the University of El Salvador initiated a general strike which helped bring down General Maximiliano Hernández Martínez in 1944. The teacher's union, ANDES, led a dramatic strike in 1972 which placed it at the head of the emerging popular movement of that era.

3. Since a tiny minority of rural Salvadorans advanced beyond sixth grade, rural education was far from a model system but the war brought it to a complete halt.

4. Joaquín Samayoa, "Problemas y perspectivas de las universidades privadas en El Salvador," *Estudios Centroamericanas*, May-June 1994, p. 471.

5. Anthony Dewees, Elizabeth Evans, and Carlos King, "La educación básica y parvularia," *Estudios Centroamericanos*, May-June 1994, p. 419.

6. "La Educación en El Salvador: Presentación," *Estudios Centroamericanos*, May-June 1994, p. 405.

7. América Rodriguéz, "Inversión en Recursos Humanos y Nuevas Modalidades de la Política Social en El Salvador: El Programa EDUCO," *Política Económica*, July-August 1993, p. 6.

8. CCR-CIDEP, *La Educación Popular en Chalatenango: Un Diagnóstico*, (San Salvador: 1993), pp. 10-12.

9. Interview with Any Masin, Jesuit Development Service, in San Salvador, September, 1994.

10. This vision of popular education has generated a broad descriptive and interpretative literature. Brazilian pedagogue Paolo Friere is among its best-known theorists, and his book *Pedagogy of the Oppressed* contains many of the basic concepts of the approach.

11. One of these literacy groups, CIAZO, sponsored a visit by Paolo Freire to the eastern part of the country in 1993.

12. This does not mean that Maíz events were never interrupted by acts of repression. Soldiers surrounded and forced the early conclusion of a fall 1989 music workshop in the town of Teotepeque, accusing the participants of hiding arms for the FMLN.

13. Although the Ministry's statistics show that EDUCO is growing quickly and bringing educational services to many new areas, few EDUCO resources have been directed to the former areas of conflict. Program funds cannot be used to pay popular teachers.

14. "Reforma educativa: nueva crisis," *Primera Plana*, Sept. 23, 1994, p. 9.

15. The Human Development Index was developed by UNDP as a comparative measure of well-being based on three criteria: longevity, intelligence, and purchasing power. Longevity is measured by life expectancy, intelligence by a composite of two-thirds adult literacy and one-third mean years of schooling, and purchasing power by real GDP per capita adjusted for the local cost of living. See United Nations Development Programme, *1994 Human Development Report*, (New York: Oxford University Press, 1994), p. 91.

16. ANSAL, *La reforma de salud: hacia su equidad y eficiencia*, San Salvador, May 1994.

17. Quoted in IDHUCA, "Privatization, impunity and other ills," *Proceso*, October 26, 1994 (English translation).

18. Studies show that, even with the end of the war, between 15 and 30% of the Salvadoran population lack effective access to health care and/or the resources to pay for those services to which they do have access.

19. This was not always the case. One 24-year-old Salvadoran woman now living in the United States reports that, when she was born in Rosales in 1970, the hospital was a respected institution even among the country's middle classes.

20. For a glimpse of conditions inside Rosales Hospital, see Pablo Cerna, "Privatizar el Rosales podría ser un mal negocio," *Primera Plana*, October 28, 1994, p. 6.

21. When the survivors of the October 1989 bombing at FENASTRAS ended up at Rosales, their union and supporters had them moved to a nearby private hospital, La Policlínica, as soon as possible. Several believe that they would not have survived in Rosales, not because of negligence or malpractice, but because of the lack of availability of sufficient blood for transfusions.

22. José Eliseo Orellana, "¿Por qué somos tan ineficientes?" *Tendencias*, December 1994-January 1995, p. 37.

23. For example, as of early 1994, the only CAT-scan machine available outside of the Military Hospital was at the Hospital Diagnóstico. A single scan of the upper-spinal area cost the equivalent of 18 months wages at the legal minimum wage.

24. Since this system emphasized primary health care, it faced a serious problem securing treatment for those cases beyond its capacity to treat. On the one hand, the system set up formalized regional clinics like the one in Guarjila, Chalatenango to provide some secondary care. At the same time, a few international NGOs, like the Jesuit Refugee Service and Medical Aid to El Salvador, established politically sensitive programs to gain access to the Salvadoran health system and to connect people to international sources of health care services.

25. "El Salvador: Picking up the Pieces," *Links*, Summer 1992, p. 16.

26. "AIDS and Sexuality in Central America," *Central America Report*, July 1, 1994.

27. Ibid.

28. In January 1995, a man arrived at the church in Tierra Blanca, Usulután with his baby girl in his arms and a look of terror in his eyes. The baby was suffering severe dehydration. The day before the man had buried the baby's twin sister who had died of dehydration a few days before. He had taken her to the regional hospital, but they had said that she did not need intravenous rehydration. She died on the trip home. The Catholic sister working in Tierra Blanca gave the man the princely sum of $60 to have the second baby treated at a private clinic in Usulután. With intravenous rehydration and antibiotics to treat a stomach infection, she quickly recovered.

29. Daniel Bausch, "From the Trenches: Post-War Health Care," *Links*, Summer 1992.

30. Cerna...op. cit.

31. Guardado was fired from his position at Rosales after he supported a 1993 strike by hospital residents demanding that the Ministry provide Rosales with an adequate budget. Quoted in Cerna, op. cit.

32. Orellana, op. cit., p. 35.

33. *Central America Report* (London), Summer 1989.

34. For a highly readable chronicle of that violence and the reaction of the Salvadoran church hierarchy, see James R. Brockman, *Romero: A Life* (Maryknoll: Orbis Books, 1990).

35. In María López Vigil, *Piezas para un Retrato* (San Salvador: UCA Editores, 1993) the author captures the human essence of this transformation.

36. Quoted in Gene Palumbo, "Paying tribute to Rivera y Damas," *Latinamerica Press*, December 22, 1994, p. 2.

Reference Notes

37. Phone interview with journalist Gene Palumbo, April 1995.

38. Miguel Huezo, et. al., "La división amenaza a la Iglesia salvadoreña," *Primera Plana*, April 28, 1995.

39. Colum Lynch, "Salvadoran Church, State Tensions Rise," *Washington Post*, June 24, 1989.

40. Jesuit Provincial José María Tojeira, quoted in Palumbo, "Paying tribute...," op. cit.

41. Ana Arana, "Salvador Church Relations with Military Grow Tense," *Miami Herald*, May 21, 1989.

42. *Directory and Analysis: Private Organizations with U.S. Connections—El Salvador* (Albuquerque: Resource Center, 1988).

43. *World Christianity: Central America and the Caribbean*, Clifton L. Holland, ed. (MARC/World Vision International, 1981).

44. Speech given by theologian Francisco Calles to a group of U.S. visitors to the Lutheran University of El Salvador in San Salvador, February 1991.

45. Interviews with religious workers in San Salvador, Suchitoto, Cuscatlán, and Tierra Blanca, Usulután, in January 1995.

46. The statistics in this section are drawn from *La Plataforma de las Mujeres Salvadoreñas*, Central America Reports, March 19, 1993, *Diagnóstico de la Situación de la Mujer Salvadoreña*, (CEPAL, 1988), and U.S. State Department, *Submission to the Senate Foreign Relations Committee on Human Rights in El Salvador*, (Washington, 1985). The statistics on women's participation in various professions are the oldest and these percentages have certainly increased.

47. Cecilia Cabrera, "Cuando el hogar es un nido de violencia," *Primera Plana*, December 2, 1994.

48. Paul Jeffrey, "Salvadoran women work for new revolution," *Latinamerica Press*, September 2, 1993; "Women in War and Peace," *Central America Report*, March 19, 1993.

49. Cabrera, "Cuando el hogar...," op. cit.

50. Vivien Altman, "El violador de la Miramonte," *Tendencias*, July-August 1994, p. 6.

51. "El aborto, una realidad unocultable," *Primera Plana*, September 16, 1994.

52. "Gathering Strength," (London: El Salvador and Guatemala Human Rights Committees).

53. Marilyn Thomson, *Women of El Salvador*, (Philadelphia: Institute for the Study of Human Issues, 1986), p. 27, which cites: T. Montreal, et al., "Abortos Hospitalizados en El Salvador," *Salud Pública en México*, May-June 1977, pp. 387-95.

54. Thomson, *Women of El Salvador*, op.cit., pp. 36-38.

55. Nelson González, "Los ambulantes no desalojarán sus puestos," *Primera Plana*, January 6, 1995.

56. "Free Trade Zones and Textiles: Abuses against women and labor rights," *El Salvador Information Project*, San Salvador, February 1995.

57. James Roush, et al., "Evaluation of the Peace and National Recovery Project (519-0394) El Salvador," (Arlington: Development Associates Incorporated, 1994).

58. Maria Torrellas, "Las mujeres policias prefieren el peligro," *Primera Plana*, November 4, 1994.

59. Besides support for the private sector, the AID program in El Salvador identified pacification of the population (political demobilization and control) and political and economic stabilization as its primary goals.

60. Deborah Barry, "Una herencia de AID en El Salvador: Andamiaje institucional empresarial en la sociedad civil," *PRISMA*, October 1993.

61. FUSADES, *Memoria*, 1986.

62. PRISMA reports that the first of these local foundations was established in Tepecoyo, La Libertad, where the Executive Director of FUSADES was a major coffee-grower.

63. Barry, op. cit., p. 6.

64. In 1993, AID officials insisted that the agency no longer supported the specific programs mentioned in the "60 Minutes" broadcast, but money continued to flow to FUSADES and like-minded organizations. One credible explanation of the creation of FEDISAL and the inclusion of groups like FUSADES and FEPADE in the projects of the National Reconstruction Plan is the intent of members of the El Salvador mission of AID to continue funding business NGOs in the wake of the "60 Minutes" disaster.

65. Martha Thompson, "Repopulated Communities in El Salvador," in *The New Politics of Survival: Grassroots Movements in Central America*, Minor Sinclair, ed. (New York: Monthly Review Press, 1995), pp. 112-4.

66. Cristina Eguizábal, et. al., "*Humanitarian Challenges in Central America: Learning the Lessons of Recent Armed Conflicts,* (Thomas J. Watson Jr. Institute for International Studies, 1993) p. 11.

67. Here the distinction between popular organizations and NGOs is important. Whereas the popular organizations, like CRIPDES, worked on organizing people to demand their rights, the NGOs, like DIACONIA, are similar to mini-foundations that receive money for projects and channel it to popular organizations. In most cases, the work of the NGOs is more technical and administrative than organizational. In the beginning, the distinction had much to do with the requirements of international funders.

68. The ability to put aside their differences to create a structure like DIACONIA differentiated Salvadoran NGOs from those set up to respond to the repression in neighboring Guatemala.

69. CORDES, REDES, FUNSALPRODESE, FASTRAS, and ASDI were all established in response to the need for mechanisms to channel aid to the country's repatriation communities.

70. The El Salvador Information Project (ESIP) was created by a group of international NGOs in 1989 to monitor the obstacles to humanitarian work in El Salvador. ESIP published monthly reports as well as a major study on government harassment of humanitarian workers before, during, and after the 1989 offensive of the FMLN.

71. Through CIREFCA, the NGOs gained access to more and larger projects. By the war's end, individual NGOs were managing budgets of several millions of dollars.

72. Barry, op. cit., p. 3.

73. See Sollis, *Reluctant Reforms...*, op. cit., and Murray, et. al., *Rescuing Reconstruction...*, op. cit.

74. The SRN used this lack of capacity as a pretext for excluding the popular NGOs from government projects, but the NGOs that received large SRN projects in this period were no more prepared to carry them out.

75. Statement by the Director of Fundación 16 de Enero Sonia Aguiñada at a San Salvador meeting sponsored by an international NGO, February 1994.

76. Since the popular NGOs had always been seen as enemies by the government, the whole notion of policy advocacy was a new idea in the postwar climate. Many international NGOs like OXFAM UK-Ireland reoriented their postwar programs in El Salvador to build advocacy capacity.

77. The communications system bungled no small number of public relations challenges but became increasingly sophisticated over the years. In the late 1980s, the owner of the "Pop's" ice cream chain reportedly received a government subsidy to print patriotic slogans and poetry on each of the thousands of paper bags in which Pop's products were packaged.

78. Prominent among the individuals reviled and threatened by these broadcasts were the Jesuit priests that governed the Central American University. The emergency broadcasting system was still in place when those same men were murdered by Salvadoran military units on November 16.

79. For an engaging narrative of the story of Radio Venceremos, see José Ignacio López Vigil, *Rebel Radio: The Story of El Salvador's Radio Venceremos* (translated by Mark Fried), (Willimantic: Curbstone Press, 1994).

80. Col. Domingo Monterrosa, perhaps the best known Salvadoran military commander of the early 1980s, was killed in 1984 just at the moment when he was sure that he had captured the famous Viking transmitter of Radio Venceremos. This fascinating tale of the struggle to control mass communication is told in López Vigil, op. cit., and in Mark Danner, *The Massacre at El Mozote*, (New York: Vintage Books, 1993), pp. 140-154.

81. In November 1993 unknown assailants murdered Heleno Hernán Castro, a former ERP commander, in what appeared to be a classic death squad killing. At Castro's funeral, Joaquín Villalobos publicly denounced *El Diario de Hoy* and wealthy businessman Orlando de Sola for their historical and continuing connections to the death squads. That same afternoon, an angry group of FMLN supporters demonstrated outside the paper's offices, causing the shutdown of newspaper production for that day. De Sola later charged Villalobos with defamation of character, but *El Diario de Hoy* limited itself to printed denunciations of the "lawless brigands" who had unjustly targeted the paper.

82. Almost every week, *Tres Mil* combined the work of establishment cultural figures like David Escobar Galindo with that of exiled writers like Manilo Argueta and poets of the "Committed Generation" like Alfonso Hernández and Amada Libertad, who had lost their lives in the war.

83. The paper regularly published accounts of human rights abuses by the military. Much riskier was the decision to publish internal letters allegedly originating from younger officers upset with the way their superiors were conducting the war. The Armed Forces, which had begun to purchase some paid space in *Latino*, cancelled one large publication for "The Day of the Soldier" over disputes concerning the paper's coverage of internal military affairs.

84. Interviews with international journalists, San Salvador, January 1995.

85. The *News Gazette* regularly published the work of "journalists" like Bruce Jones. As an expatriate rancher in Costa Rica in the 1980s, Jones was an important cog in the CIA's cross-border operation in support of the Nicaraguan contras. After being deported from Costa Rica for violations of Costa Rican law in the course of contra aid efforts, Jones reappeared in El Salvador in the 1990s as a "document researcher" analyzing the Salvadoran agrarian reform and contributing regularly to the *News Gazette*.

86. In its first few months, the weekly covered with considerable balance such stories as the break-up of the FMLN, the allegations of corruption against the political establishment, and the street actions of excombatants of the Armed Forces.

87. Other UCA publications include *Estudios Centroamericanos*, *Realidad Socio-Económico*, and *Revista Latinoamericana de Teología*.

88. U.S. Embassy, San Salvador, *Country Data: El Salvador*, January 1, 1989.

89. Lindsey Gruson, "Salvador TV Dares to Tell the News," *New York Times*, September 27, 1988.

90. A fascinating debate concerning the decision ensued on the pages of *Tendencias*. In describing the station's position, new director and ex-guerrilla Marvin Galeas explained the need to leave the "legendary" period behind and change the station's relationship to the FMLN. "We struggled for the transformation of the society, and so stations like ours could exist. I didn't fight so that the FMLN could win an election. I could care less if the left wins or not...it doesn't interest me." See Any Cabrera, "La Venceremos vs. Coalición: Discordía o Sobrevivencia?", *Tendencias*, May 1994, p. 9.

91. Salvador Samayoa, "Un Cambio Político Estructural," *Tendencias*, December 1994-January 1995, p. 33.

92. In 1975, political violence took the life of Roque Dalton, perhaps the best known Salvadoran poet and essayist of his generation. As opposed to many later attacks on cultural workers, Dalton's assassination resulted from a dispute within the ranks of the ERP in which his opponents wrongly accused the poet of being a CIA agent. His kill-

ing—an open sore for the Salvadoran left twenty years later—stands as a tragic reminder of the paranoia and fanaticism that fed divisions in the revolutionary movement of that era. It also robbed the country of one of its most creative artistic voices.

93. Published in English as José Ignacio López Vigil, *Rebel Radio: The Story of El Salvador's Radio Venceremos* (Willimantic: Curbstone Press, 1994).

94. Jacinta Escudos, "Guerra y Literatura: ¿Trauma histórico o histérico?" *Tendencias*, December 1994-January 1995, p. 45.

Part 6: Social Organizations and the Popular Movement

1. Mario Lungo Uclés, "Building An Alternative: The Formation of a Popular Project," in Sinclair, *The New Politics...*, op. cit., p. 153.

2. For a painstakingly complete account of this tragedy see Thomas P. Anderson, *Matanza: El Salvador's Communist Revolt of 1932*, (Lincoln: University of Nebraska Press, 1971).

3. There has always been a dissident faction within the church which has sought more recognition of the rights of the poor. Fray Bartholomé de Las Casas, a Spanish friar who came to the Americas in the early stages of the Conquest exemplifies this group. Las Casas is known for his passionate, though clearly limited, defense of the rights of the indigenous people of the continent.

4. For a wonderful fictional rendering of this transformation and the response of "the authorities" see Manilo Argueta, *One Day of Life*, (New York: Vintage Books, 1981).

5. Even pro-government popular organizations and government officials associated with the agrarian reform and other policies opposed by the extreme right tasted the repression of the early 1980s. Two U.S. land reform experts associated with the American Institute for Free Labor Development (AIFLD) and the Salvadoran Director of the agrarian reform were murdered in San Salvador in 1980.

6. Important sources on the popular movement include: Segundo Montes, *Estructura de clases y comportamiento de las fuerzas sociales* (San Salvador: IDHUCA, 1988) and *Problemática urbana, movimiento popular y democracia en el area metropolitana de San Salvador, 1986-1988*, Documento de Trabajo (San Salvador: Coordinación Universitaria de Investigación Científica, UES, 1988).

7. Salvadoran activists created an enormous number of organizations in the late 1980s but it must be remembered that these involved only a small segment of the population.

8. The existence of three or four organizations in the same sector—family members of the disappeared, for example—was not uncommon.

9. The bombing served as the immediate cause of the offensive but the FMLN had clearly been preparing such an action for months.

10. Mary Jo McConahay, "No Political Space Left," *Pacific News Service*, November 20, 1989.

11. Uclés, *Los Obstáculos . . .* , op. cit., p. 165-7.

12. Centro de Estudios del Trabajo (CENTRA), *La transformación del movimiento sindical salvadoreño en el proceso de transición*, (San Salvador: CENTRA, 1994).

13. The same CENTRA study finds that only 1,024,883 Salvadorans possess "formal" non-agricultural jobs. At least 75,000 of those workers are public sector workers who cannot form unions.

14. For the most complete history of the labor movement, see William Bollinger, "El Salvador," *Latin American Labor Organizations*, Gerald Greenfield and Sheldon Maran, eds. (Westport: Greenwood Press, 1987).

15. U.S. Embassy, San Salvador, "Update of Investment Climate," July 13, 1988.

16. United Nations, *Acuerdos...*, p. 87.

17. For a summary of the pre-1989 record on this point, see David Slaney, "Thinking Globally: Labor Rights Legislation and El Salvador," *Dollars & Sense*, May 1989.

18. "El Salvador: GSP Benefits Extended," *Central America Reports*, January 28, 1994.

19. Although the Labor Code changes recognize the rights of rural workers to organize in certain, narrowly defined, conditions, they do not improve the overall climate of organizing. In what was considered a major setback, public workers were not accorded the right to organize unions to replace the less-protected employee associations in which they are currently organized.

20. Interview with labor analyst Mark Anner in San Salvador, January 1995.

21. The same CENTRA report quoted above found a tremendous lack of local leadership and organizational structure in the union movement. For example, in 1993, 91 of 117 local unions in El Salvador were without elected executive boards, and only 6 of the 182 shops in the four construction unions had elected shop-level leadership.

22. For a more complete discussion of the Platform, see CIDAI, "La plataforma unitaria sindical en el nuevo contexto nacional," *Proceso*, June 7, 1994.

23. The unions have been unable to make significant inroads in the *maquila* plants, and the recent actions were apparently not directly related to union organizing drives. When officials of FENASTRAS arrived to address the women who had shut down the San Marcos free zone, the women reportedly gave them a cool reception.

24. "Urgent Action Alert" from Charles Kernaghan of the National Labor Committee requesting support for the workers of Mandarin International, May 1995.

25. See David Browning, *El Salvador: Landscape and Society* (Oxford: Clarendon Press, 1971) for an exceptionally detailed investigation of this process.

26. The repression in the western area of the country was so great that even at the height of the civil war, campesinos in the parts of the country that suffered most from the *matanza* remained fearful of organizing. The western provinces were never a fertile ground for FMLN organizing.

27. The repression of the late 1970s around Aguilares is dramatized in the film *Romero*.

28. The Salvadoran military committed several massacres during this period as part of its strategy to move civilians out of the war zones. Mark Danner, *The Massacre at El Mozote*, (New York: Vintage Books, 1994) tells the story of the best known of these massacres, while EPICA, *Condoning the Killing*, (Washington, DC: 1990) offers a broader overview of a systematic policy on the part of the Salvadoran military.

29. The Jesuit Development Service has published a collection of stories, songs, and interviews that offer first-person information about the resettlement experience. JDS, *Tiempo de recordar y tiempo de contar* (San Salvador: JDS, 1994).

30. Less than thirty thousand campesinos repatriated from the refugee camps in Honduras and elsewhere. Perhaps another twenty thousand moved into the conflictive areas from other areas of El Salvador as part of the return movement. These people, by deciding to return to conflictive areas while the war was in progress, had a political significance far beyond their numbers.

31. CRIPDES, CNR, CCR, CRCC, CORESA, CODECOSTA, PADECOES, PROGRESO, CDR, and UCRES were among the best known of this network of community organizations formed between 1986 and the end of the war.

32. This displacement resulted from the presence of an insufficient number of people to purchase all of the land that had been occupied in the last stages of the war. Facing that reality, the ERP decided to concentrate it supporters on *Hacienda La California* and its valuable salt works and shrimp ponds.

33. Murray, et. al., *Rescuing...*, op. cit.

34. The 1994 march by campesinos from Chalatenango to demand progress on the Land Transfer Program might be a singular exception. In contrast, demobilized members of the security forces and civil defense units grouped in ADEFAES carried out militant

street actions including the occupation of the Legislative Assembly on three occasions to insure their inclusion in reconstruction programs.

35. The cooperatives with coffee land did much better than the others as long as the price of coffee stayed relatively high.

36. An international aid organization representative observed that all joint cooperative development projects ceased after the May 1 debacle in the Assembly.

37. Caryn Kewell, "Women's Groups in El Salvador—Organizing for a Change," *The Upstream Journal*, December 1994.

38. Quoted in "Gender in Focus: Adjusting Development Strategies for Gender," *El Salvador Information Project*, San Salvador, September 1994.

39. Kewell, op. cit., p. 3.

40. The MAM takes its name from the leader of the Salvadoran teacher's union who became the second most influential leader in the FPL. Melida Anaya Montes was murdered in Managua in 1983, apparently by men working for FPL leader Cayetano Carpio.

41. For an exceptional assessment of the importance of the Montelimar conference, see Norma Stoltz Chinchilla, "Women's Movements in the Americas: Feminism's Second Wave," *NACLA*, July/August 1993.

42. Ibid.

43. This paid ad in *El Diario de Hoy* was quoted in *Central America Report*, November 19, 1994.

44. *El Salvador Information Project*, "Gender...," op. cit.

45. Quoted in Jeffrey, op. cit.

46. This demand actually originated with the popular movement and was later taken up by the FMLN as it became clear that a negotiated solution was the only practical way out of the conflict.

47. Here it is important to note that the FMLN was not alone in this pattern of relation to the social movements. The PDC clearly dominated the social organizations more closely identified with its project during the 1980s. ARENA also spawned a network of social organizations closely connected to its structures.

48. This observation is the product of numerous interviews with local leaders, especially in rural areas, during and after the electoral period in 1994.

Part 7: Ecology and Environmentalism

1. Katherine Yih, *Water and Human Ecology in El Salvador: A Review*, (PRISMA, 1994), p. 20.

2. For a well-documented discussion of the environmental degradation caused by the war, see Bill Hall and Dan Faber, "El Salvador: Ecology of Conflict," *Earth Island Journal*, Summer 1989.

3. Mac Chapin, *El Salvador's Environment: Problems and Institutional Responses* (Cambridge: Cultural Survival, August 1990), p. 20.

4. "Degradación Ambiental y Gestión de Desarrollo en El Salvador," *PRISMA*, October-December 1994, p. 2.

5. Chapin, *El Salvador's Environment*, op. cit.

6. In a public opinion poll conducted by the UCA's Public Opinion Institute (IUDUP) and quoted in Chapin, no reference was made to the environment among those problems that respondents identified as El Salvador's most serious problems in 1987-88. War, economic crisis, and unemployment were named as the three most pressing difficulties.

7. AID, *Environment and Natural Resources: A Strategy for Central America*, March 1989.

8. At one time or another, almost every public figure of note entered the debate over El Espino. For example, Joaquín Villalobos created a stir by engaging in direct negotiations with the Poma family—the potential developers—over a possible "deal" for land.

9. CIDAI, "El parque de los pericos: algo más que una polémica," *Proceso*, December 14, 1994, pp. 13-14.

10. According to this argument, the forest cover increases the ability of the ground to absorb water from the torrential rains falling between May and November. Without the forest cover, most of the rain would run off (as it does in other areas of the country like the Upper Lempa basin) and ground water would greatly diminish.

11. Yih, "*Water and Human Ecology...*," op. cit., p. 33.

12. ANDA is one of the semi-autonomous organizations which control the nation's basic services. During the war, ANDA used the excuse of electrical sabotage to explain their inability to expand water and sewage systems—or even adequately serve the existing system. Since the war, however, the general public has become more aware that poor planning and corruption underlie the water shortage. As a result, the government's plans to privatize ANDA leave many people hopeful that service may improve under a private water authority.

13. Interview with Mark Smith in San Salvador, January 1995.

14. There are no serious efforts at reforestation on a national level, but the government and local NGOs are attempting small-scale programs that confront these same problems.

15. FUNDALEMPA, "El Río Lempa: Una crisis que puede ser ireversible antes del año 2000," (published as an insert to *Tendencias*), p. 4.

16. Hall and Faber, "El Salvador: Ecology ...," op. cit., citing Howard E. Daugherty, *Man-Induced Ecological Change in El Salvador* (Ph.D. dissertation, University of California, Los Angeles, 1969), and Ernesto López, *Ecological Impact of Cotton Cultivation in El Salvador: Example of Jiquilisco* (York University, April 1977).

17. Ernesto López Quesada, et. al., *Agroquímicos Usados en el Cultivo del Algodón*, Department of Biology, University of El Salvador, 1986.

18. Chapin, op. cit., p. 13.

19. López Quesada, op. cit.

20. Quoted in Chapin, op. cit., p. 14.

21. "El Problema del Desarrollo Urbano en San Salvador," *Alternativas para el Desarrollo*, (FUNDE, February 1993).

22. In the campaign against the Christian Democrats in 1988, ARENA made trash disposal a major municipal issue, and Calderón Sol as mayor insisted on regular trash pick-ups in some neighborhoods.

23. "Toxic Mudslide Kills 25," *Mesoamerica*, July 1993, p. 4.

24. CIDAI, "Recuperación ambiental y desarrollo económico social," *Proceso*, December 21, 1994, p. 7.

25. The bulk of that money was designated to support economic projects, but some was also intended to support child survival projects.

26. *Update on the "Initiative for the Americas" Fund*, (ESIP, December 1994).

27. Ibid.

28. CIDAI, "Recuperación...," op. cit., p. 8.

29. Carlos Restrepo, "Medio ambiente y desarrollo sostenible," *Tendencias*, October 1994.

30. "Economía de mercado amenaza a la ecología advierte Ministro," *La Prensa Gráfica*, February 15, 1992.

31. "*Update on the ...*," op. cit.

Part 8: U.S.-El Salvador Relations

1. Deborah Barry, "Una herencia de AID en El Salvador: Andamiaje institucional empresarial en la sociedad civil," *PRISMA*, October, 1993, p. 1.

2. Benjamin C. Schwarz, "American Counterinsurgency Doctrine and El Salvador: The Frustrations of Reform and the Illusions of Nation Building," (RAND Corporation, 1992), p. 2. Schwarz arrives at the figure by combining official aid, unsubsidized credits, and covert assistance.

3. Sen. Mark Hatfield, Rep. Jim Leach, and Rep. George Miller, *U.S. Aid to El Salvador: An Evaluation of the Past, A Proposal for the Future* (February 1985) and *Bankrolling Failure: United States Policy in El Salvador and the Urgent Need for Reform: A Report to the Arms Control and Foreign Policy Caucus* (November 1987).

4. U.S. State Department, "El Salvador: The Battle for Democracy," *Department of State Bulletin*, January 1989.

5. Thomas Long & Frank Smyth, "How the FMLN Won the Peace," *Village Voice*, February 18, 1992, p. 19.

6. For an in depth consideration of the origins and regional application of LIC Strategy in Central America, see Tom Barry and Deb Preusch, *The Soft War: Uses and Abuses of U.S. Economic Aid in Central America*, (New York: Grove Press, 1988).

7. U.S. State Department, "U.S. Policy Toward El Salvador," (undated), p. 1.

8. Robert Elam, *Appeal to Arms: The Army and Politics in El Salvador* (Ph.D. dissertation, University of New Mexico, 1969).

9. Philip l. Russell, *El Salvador in Crisis* (Austin: Colorado River Press, 1984), p. 120.

10. *New York Times*, May 8, 1978.

11. K. Larry Storrs, "El Salvador: New Challenges for U.S. Policy," *CRS Review*, February 1989.

12. Anjali Sundaram, "Taking Center Stage: The Reagan Years," *A Decade of War*, (New York: Monthly Review Press, 1991), pp. 150-1.

13. Tommie Sue Montgomery, *Revolution in El Salvador: From Civil Strife to Civil Peace*, (Boulder: Westview Press, 1995), p. 221.

14. That same month, *Proceso* called for a clear signal of U.S. support for the negotiations.

15. Journalist Frank Smyth reported that he was given that view by the head of U.S. MIL-GROUP on the morning of November 11, 1989. That evening, the same officer was forced to barricade himself in his home in Colonia Escalón where he remained until he left the country in the general evacuation of U.S. personnel on Tuesday, November 14.

16. Teresa Whitfield, *Paying the Price...*, op. cit., p. 171.

17. William M. Leogrande, "After the Battle of San Salvador," *World Policy Journal*, No. 1-2, 1989/90, p. 343.

18. *New York Times*, January 25, 1990

19. Quoted in Long & Smyth, "How the FMLN...," op. cit.

20. Quoted in Leogrande, "After the Battle...," op. cit., p. 352.

21. Ironically, as support for military aid in Congress quickly disappeared, many Salvadorans, including some leaders in the FMLN, began to argue in favor of continued military aid as a stabilizing factor during the country's transition to peace. Carlos Ramos, "El Salvador en la agenda Clinton," *Tendencias*, December 1992-January 1993.

22. Van Gosse, "Active Engagement: The Legacy of Central American Solidarity," *NACLA, Report on the Americas*, March/April 1995, pp. 22-29.

23. Clifford Krauss, "U.S., Aware of Killings, Kept Ties to Salvadoran Rightists, Papers Suggest," *New York Times*, November 9, 1993.

24. CRIES, *Proceso de paz en El Salvador: La solución política negociada*, (Managua, 1992), p. 49.

Reference Notes

25. See, for example, Montgomery, *Revolution in El Salvador...*, op. cit., p. 228.

26. The delay was due largely to bureaucratic snags regarding the nomination of Michael Cusack as ambassador, but such delays would not have been tolerated or allowed to slow diplomatic appointments during the 1980s.

27. Montgomery, *Revolution in El Salvador...*, op. cit.

28. Quoted in *Centroamérica*, August 1993, p. 5.

29. See Danner, *The Massacre...*, op. cit., for a disturbing consideration of this case.

30. Ibid.

31. CIDAI, "Estados Unidos pretende lavarse las manos," *Proceso*, July 28, 1993, p. 2.

32. Schwarz, *American Counterinsurgency...*, p. *vii*.

33. Ibid., p. *xii*.

34. Krauss, "U.S., Aware of Killings...", op. cit.

35. Quoted in Arthur Jones, "El Salvador Revisited: A Look at Classified State Department Documents," *National Catholic Reporter*, September 23, 199, p. 17.

36. Cynthia Arnson of Human Rights Watch, quoted in ibid.

37. Ross Gelbspan, "The New FBI," *Covert Action Information Bulletin*, Winter 1989, p. 11.

38. Alberto Arene, "Relaciones EU-El Salvador: ¿De la máxima prioridad al casi olvido?, *Tendencias*, December 1992-January 1993, p. 7.

39. Reported by Lee Winkleman, a CISPES activist living in El Salvador, November 1992.

40. Arene, "Relaciones EU-El Salvador...".

41. Current trade patterns suggest a concentration of world trade among the economic superpowers that stand at the center of the emerging trade blocs. Whereas Japan, the United States, and the European Union accounted for 55 percent of all international trade in 1981, that number had increased to 76 percent by 1990. Most of the rest of world trade involves exchange between the giants and a handful of the largest of the remaining countries. The participation of small economies like El Salvador is negligible and getting rapidly smaller. Héctor Casanueva Ojeda, "El GATT y la cooperación internacional," *Tendencias*, April 1994, p. 27.

42. CIDAI, "Perspectivas Latinoamericanas en la próxima Cumbre de las Américas," *Proceso*, December 7, 1994, p. 13.

43. The economic proposal advanced by the Salvadoran government in early 1995 reflects an understanding of this limitation of the free trade model, and, in response, seeks to encourage more direct foreign investment.

44. "U.S. Extends Stay of Refugees," *Mesoamerica*, December 1994, p. 3.

45. CIDAI, "La aprobación de la propuesta 187," *Proceso*, November 16, 1994, p. 12.

46. U.S. State Department, "U.S. Policy...," op. cit.

47. Ibid.

48. Through the ESF mechanism, the U.S. government provides the Salvadoran central bank with dollars. Those dollars are then "sold" to Salvadoran businesspeople in exchange for local currency. The private sector uses the dollars for international transactions—thus relieving pressure on the balance of payments—and the local currency funds government programs. A useful comparison can be made with Nicaragua, where the United States directed its efforts toward the destabilization of the economy. Shortages and runaway inflation contributed to the electoral defeat of the Sandinista party, and the country's economy continues to be undermined by interest payments on its massive foreign debt.

49. The clearest example of this shift is AID's changing attitude toward the agrarian reform. After writing the agrarian reform program and insisting on its implementation, AID quietly backed away from any insistence on the program's completion. By the late 1980s, the agency was supporting legislation designed to allow the ARENA government to subdivide the cooperatives and sell them off to individual campesinos.

50. Allan Austin, Luis Flores, and Donald Stout, *CONARA Impact Evaluation* (Research Triangle Institute, AID Contract PDC-0000-I-00-6169-00), September 20, 1988.

51. While support for the PRN became AID's largest program, the agency was still involved in projects supporting the Ministries of Planning, Public Works, Health, Education and Agriculture. In addition, support for the American Institute for Free Labor Development (AIFLD) through a six-year project for $16.4 million continued. Among the ongoing projects folded into the PRN were the Public Services Improvement Program ($22.5 million), Maternal Health and Child Survival (PROSAMI) ($9 million), and the Caribbean and Latin American Scholarship program (CLASP) ($5 million).

52. The government created the SRN by executive decree on January 31, 1992, the night before the Chapultepec Accord took effect.

53. See Sollis, *Reluctant Reforms...*, for a discussion of the SRN's failure to build a consensus in the critical period immediately after the war.

54. *Evaluation of the Peace and National Recovery Project (519-0394) El Salvador*, (Development Associates, Inc., January 1994).

55. Bryan Atwood, *Statement before the Subcommittee on International Economic Policy, Trade, Oceans and the Environment*, Washington, July 14, 1993.

56. Memo from AID El Salvador Desk Officer Kathleen Barrett to Debra Preusch, The Resource Center, January 4, 1994.

57. Ibid.

58. Interview with Mark Scott, Tom Hawke, and John Sullivan in San Salvador, January, 1995.

59. By 1994, each of these multilateral institutions had become a more important actor in El Salvador, in financial terms, than AID.

60. See Popkin, et. al., *Justice Delayed...*, op. cit., pp. 13-14.

61. All of the AID reorganization proposals being discussed in Congress in 1995 involved some sort of folding of AID into the institutional structure of the State Department. Such a reorganization would make the agency even more an instrument of the short-term policy goals of those in control of the executive branch.

62. This amount does not include the cost of U.S. military advisers and all U.S. intelligence personnel attached to the military and the CIA.

63. Schwarz, "American Counterinsurgency..." op.cit., p. 2. Based on an interview with a U.S. diplomat conducted by Charles Lane for his 1989 article in the *New Republic*, "The War That Will Not End."

64. According to Col. Juan Orlando Zepeda, former director of military intelligence: "The DNI receives most of its aid from the Central Intelligence Agency. The CIA provides some support to the C-2 [Intelligence Division of Combined General Staff], such as direct training. But the whole product, the handling of sources, such as communications, traffic analysis, and equipment, is handed over to the DNI." *El Salvador at War: An Oral History*, Max G. Manwarring and Court Prisk, eds. (Washington, DC: National Defense University Press, 1988).

65. *NACLA Report on the Americas*, July 1989.

66. Bacevich, et. al., "The Case of El Salvador," op. cit.

67. Phone interview with U.S. State Department Desk Officer for El Salvador, March 1995.

68. Quoted in "Strong resistance '94," *Central America Report*, September 24, 1993, p. 284.

69. Ibid.

Acronyms

ADEFAES	Association of Demobilized Members of the Salvadoran Armed Forces
ADC	Democratic Campesinos Association
AID	U.S. Agency for International Development
AIFLD	American Institute for Free Labor Development
AMES	Salvadoran Women's Association
AMPES	Association of Progressive Women of El Salvador
ANSESAL	Salvadoran National Security Agency
ANSP	National Academy of Public Security
ARENA	Nationalist Republican Alliance
CCE	Central Electoral Council
CCTEM	Coordinating Council of State and Municipal Workers
CD	Democratic Convergence
CENTRA	Center for Labor Study
CEPAL	Economic Commission for Latin America
CERPROFA	Armed Forces Center for Professional Rehabilitation
CESTA	Salvadoran Center for Appropriate Technology
CGT	General Confederation of Workers
CIA	U.S. Central Intelligence Agency
CIDAI	University Center for Documentation and Information

CIREFCA	International Conference on Refugees in Central America
CISPES	Committee in Solidarity with the People of El Salvador
CGS	Salvadoran General Confederation of Unions
CNJ	National Judicial Council
COACES	Salvadoran Federation of Cooperative Associations
COMADRES	Salvadoran Committee of Mothers and Family Members of the Disappeared
CONADES	National Commission for Aid to the Displaced
CONAMUS	National Coordination of Salvadoran Women
CONARA	National Commission for the Restoration of Areas
CONFRAS	Confederation of Salvadoran Agrarian Reform Federations
COPREFA	Press and Public Relations Committee of the Armed Forces
CPDN	Permanent Committee for National Debate
CRIPDES	Christian Committee of the Displaced
DIA	U.S. Defense Intelligence Agency
DNI	National Intelligence Directorate
EDUCO	Education with Community Participation
ERP	Revolutionary People's Army; People's Expression of Renewal
EU	European Union
FAES	Armed Forces of El Salvador
FAL	Armed Forces of Liberation
FDR	Democratic Revolutionary Front
FEASIES	Federation of Associations and Independent Unions of El Salvador
FECCAS	Federation of Christian Campesinos
FEDECOOPADES	Salvadoran Federation of Agricultural Cooperatives
FENASTRAS	National Federation of Salvadoran Workers
FES	Economic and Social Forum
FESACORA	Federation of Salvadoran Agrarian Reform Cooperatives
FESINCONSTRANS	Federation of Construction Industry Unions

FIAES	Enterprise for the Americas Fund
FIS	Social Investment Fund
FMLN	Farabundo Martí National Liberation Front
FPL	Popular Liberation Forces
FUNPROCOOP	Cooperative Development Foundation
FUSADES	Salvadoran Foundation for Economic and Social Development
GDP	Gross Domestic Product
GN	National Guard
IDB	Inter-American Development Bank
IDHUCA	Human Rights Institute of the UCA
ILYD	Freedom and Democracy Institute
IMF	International Monetary Fund
IPSFA	Social Provision Institute of the Armed Forces
ISSS	Salvadoran Social Security Institute
ISTA	Salvadoran Institute for Agrarian Transformation
IUDOP	University Public Opinion Institute
MAC	Authentic Christian Movement
MAM	Melida Anaya Montes Women's Movement
MIA	Municipalities in Action
MILGROUP	U.S. Military Group
MIPLAN	Ministry of Planning
MNR	National Revolutionary Movement
MPSC	Popular Social Christian Movement
MRSC	Social Christian Renovation Movement
MSM	Salvadoran Women's Movement
MSN	National Solidarity Movement
MU	Unity Movement
NAFTA	North American Free Trade Agreement
ONUSAL	United Nations Observer Mission in El Salvador
ORDEN	National Democratic Organization
PCN	National Conciliation Party
PCS	Communist Party of El Salvador
PDC	Christian Democratic Party

PDH	Ombudsman for Human Rights
PH	Treasury Police
PLD	Liberal Democratic Party
PN	National Police
PNC	Civilian National Police
PRN	National Reconstruction Plan
PROMESA	Salvadoran Environmental Protection Project
PRTC	Central America Revolutionary Workers Party
PSD	Social Democratic Party
PTT	Land Transfer Program
RN	National Resistance
SABE	Solidifying Salvadoran Primary Education
SEMA	Executive Secretariat for the Environment
SENCO	National Communications Secretariat
SINCOMCOOP	Integrated Cooperative Marketing System
SLD	Democratic Labor Sector
SRN	National Reconstruction Secretariat
TSE	Supreme Electoral Tribunal
UCA	Central American University
UDN	Democratic Nationalist Union
UDP	Democratic Popular Party
UES	University of El Salvador
UNDP	United Nations Development Program
UNOC	National Union of Workers and Campesinos
UNTS	National Unity of Salvadoran Workers
UPR	United to Reconstruct
USCEOM	U.S. Citizens Elections Observer Mission

Bibliography

The following periodicals are useful sources of information and analysis on El Salvador:

Carta a las Iglesias, UCA (San Salvador), bi-weekly, Spanish.

Central America Report, Inforpress Centroamericana (Guatemala), weekly, English.

ECA: Estudios Centroamericanos, UCA (San Salvador), monthly, Spanish.

Primera Plana (San Salvador), weekly, Spanish.

PRISMA, Salvadoran Development and Environment Research Program-PRISMA (San Salvador), monthly, Spanish.

Proceso, University Documentation and Information Center (CI-DAI), UCA (San Salvador), weekly, Spanish.

Realidad Económico-Social, UCA (San Salvador), bimonthly, Spanish.

Report from El Salvador, Fundación Flor de Izote (San Salvador), weekly, Spanish-English

Tendencias (San Salvador), monthly, Spanish.

The following articles and papers are useful sources of information and analysis on El Salvador:

Ltc. A.J. Bacevich, et. al., "American Military Policy in Small Wars: The Case of El Salvador." (John F. Kennedy School of Government) Cambridge, MA, March 22, 1988.

Daniel Bausch, "From the Trenches: Post-War Health Care." *Links*, Summer 1992.

Gianni Beretta, "Todos Contra ARENA." *Pensamiento Propio*, August 1989.

Morris J. Blachman and Kenneth E. Sharpe, "Things Fall Apart: Trouble Ahead in El Salvador." *World Policy Journal*, Winter 1988-1989.

Alfredo Guerra Borges, "Desarrollo e Integración en Centroamérica: Del Pasado a las Perspectivas." *Cultura Popular* 1988.

CENITEC, "Propuesta de un Programa Económico-Social de Consenso para El Salvador." *Política Económica* March-April 1993.

Norma Stoltz Chinchilla, "Women's Movements in the Americas: Feminism's Second Wave." *NACLA* July/August 1993.

"El Salvador estremece a los vecinos." *InterPress Service*, February 3, 1995.

El Salvador Information Project:
"Environmental Funds: Update on the Initiative for the Americas Fund," November 1994.
"Free Trade Zones and Textiles: Abuses Against Women and Labor Rights," February 1995.
"Gender in Focus: Adjusting Development Strategies for Gender," September 1994.
"Land Transfers: 'Til Debt Do Us Part?" March 1994.

"El Salvador: Picking Up the Pieces." *Links*, Summer 1992.

Van Gosse, "Active Engagement: The Legacy of Central American Solidarity," *NACLA: Report on the Americas* March/April 1995.

Lindsey Gruson, "Salvador TV Dares to Tell the News," *New York Times*, September 27, 1988.

Bill Hall and Dan Faber, "El Salvador: Ecology of Conflict," *Earth Island Journal*, Summer 1989.

Michael Hoffman, "Update on Land Issues in El Salvador," SHARE Foundation, October 1994.

Paul Jeffrey, "Salvadoran women work for new revolution," *Latinamerica Press*. September 2, 1993.

Arthur Jones, "El Salvador Revisited: A Look at Classified State Department Documents," *National Catholic Reporter*, September 23, 1994.

Caryn Kewell, "Women's Groups in El Salvador: Organizing for a Change," *The Upstream Journal*, December 1994.

Clifford Krauss, "U.S., Aware of Killings, Kept Ties to Salvadoran Rightists, Papers Suggest," *New York Times*, November 9, 1993.

William M. Leogrande, "After the Battle of San Salvador," *World Policy Journal*, 1989/90.

Tom Long and Frank Smyth, "How the FMLN Won the Peace," *Village Voice*, February 18, 1992.

Carlos Orellana Merlos, "El Nuevo Modelo de Integración Centroamericana y la Armonización Regional de Políticas Macroeconómicas," San Salvador: CENITEC, 1993.

Joel Millman, "El Salvador's Army: A Force Unto Itself," *New York Times*, December 10, 1989.

Mike O'Connor, "A New U.S. Import in El Salvador: Street Gangs," *New York Times*, July 3, 1994.

Trish O'Kane, "Central America still eating bitter fruit," *Latinamerica Press*, March 24, 1994.

Gene Palumbo, "Paying Tribute to Rivera y Damas," *Latinamerica Press*, December 22, 1994.

"Report exposes renewed death squad violence." *National Catholic Reporter*, August 12, 1994.

Juan Hernández Pico, "La seguridad, la impunidad, la justicia," *Envio*, July 1994.

Margaret Popkin, "El Salvador: A Negotiated End to Impunity?" *Impunity and Human Rights in International Law and Practice* (New York and Oxford:Oxford University Press, 1995).

América Rodriguez, "Inversión en Recursos Humanos y Nuevas Modalidades de la Política Social en El Salvador: El Programa EDUCO," *Política Económica*, July-August 1993.

David Slaney, "Thinking Globally: Labor Rights Legislation and El Salvador," *Dollars & Sense* May 1989.

Frank Smyth, "Salvadoran Abyss," *Nation*, January 8/15, 1990.

William Stanley, "Demilitarization in El Salvador: Harbinger or Exception?" International Studies Association Meeting, Acapulco, Mexico, March 23-28, 1993.

K. Larry Storrs, "El Salvador: New Challenges for U.S. Policy," *CRS Review*, February 1989.

Mario Lungo Uclés, "Los Obstáculos a la Democratización en El Salvador," *El Salvador en Construcción*, August 1993.

Knut Walter and Philip Williams, *The Military and Democratization in El Salvador*, Latin American Studies Association Congress, Los Angeles, September 24-27, 1992.

The following books and reports contain valuable background information on many issues important to understanding El Salvador:

U.S. Agency for International Development (AID), *Environment and Natural Resources: A Strategy for Central America* (Washington, DC: AID, 1989).

Americas Watch, *Accountability and Human Rights: The Report of the United Nations Commission on the Truth for El Salvador* (New York: Americas Watch, August 1993).

Darkening Horizons: Human Rights on the Eve of the March 1994 Elections (Washington, DC: Americas Watch, 1994).

El Salvador's Decade of Terror: Human Rights Since the Assassination of Archbishop Romero (New Haven: Yale University Press, 1991).

Nightmare Revisited (New York: Americas Watch, 1988).

Thomas P. Anderson, *Matanza: El Salvador's Communist Revolt* (Lincoln: University of Nebraska Press, 1971).

ANSAL, *La reforma de salud: hacia su equidad y eficiencia* (San Salvador: ANSAL, 1994).

Manilo Argueta, *One Day of Life* (New York: Vintage Books, 1981).

Cynthia Arnson, *Crossroads: Congress, the President, and Central America* (Pennsylvania State University Press, 1993).

Tom Barry and Deb Preusch, *The Soft War* (New York: Grove Press, 1988).

Raymond Bonner, *Weakness and Deceit: U.S. Policy and El Salvador* (New York: Times Books, 1984).

James R. Brockman, *Romero: A Life* (Maryknoll: Orbis Books, 1990).

Frank Brodhead and Edward S. Herman, *Demonstration Elections: U.S.-Staged Elections in the Dominican Republic, Vietnam, and El Salvador* (Boston: South End Press, 1984).

David Browning, *El Salvador: Landscape and Society* (Oxford: Clarendon Press, 1971).

Beth Cagan and Steven Cagan, *This Promised Land, El Salvador: The Refugee Community of Colomoncagua and Their Return to Morazán* (New Brunswick: Rutgers University Press, 1991).

Alejandro Cantor, ed., *Visiones Alternativas sobre la Transición* (San Salvador: Editorial Sombrero Azul, 1993).

CCR-CIDEP, *La Educación Popular en Chalatenango: Un Diagnóstico* (San Salvador: CCR-CIDEP, 1993).

CEPAL, *Centroamérica: el Camino de los Noventa.* LC/MEX/R.386 (SEM 53/2), January 1993.

Bibliography

Mac Chapin, *El Salvador's Environment: Problems and Institutional Responses* (Cambridge: Cultural Survival, 1990).

Mauricio Chávez, *Fin del Siglo* (San Salvador: Editorial Arcoiris, 1993).

Hernan Darío Correa, *Neoliberales y pobres* (Bogotá: CINEP, 1993).

Roque Dalton, *El Salvador* (Monografía) (San Salvador: Editorial Universitaria, 1979).

    Miguel Mármol (Trans. Kathleen Ross and Richard Schaaf) (Willimantic: Curbstone Press, 1987).

Mark Danner, *The Massacre at El Mozote* (New York: Vintage Books 1993).

Martha Doggett, *A Death Foretold* (Washington, DC: Lawyer's Committee for Human Rights, 1993).

W.H. Durham, *Scarcity and Survival in Central America* (Palo Alto: Stanford University Press, 1979).

Ecumenical Program on Central America and the Caribbean (EPICA), *Condoning the Killing: Ten Years of Massacres in El Salvador* (Washington, DC: EPICA, 1990).

Cristina Eguizábal, et.al., *Humanitarian Challenges in Central America: Learning the Lessons of Recent Armed Conflicts* (Providence: Thomas J. Watson Jr. Institute for International Studies, 1993).

Alberto Enríquez, et. al., *Diagnóstico Socio-económico y Propuesta de Desarrollo Sostenible para el Municipio de Tecoluca, San Vicente* (San Salvador: FUNDE, 1995).

Equipo de Maíz, *El Salvador y el Crecimiento Económica* (San Salvador: Equipo de Maíz, 1994).

European Economic Community, *Informe Final ALA 92/18: Usulután* (San Salvador: EEC, 1994).

Patricia Weiss Fagen and Joseph T. Eldridge, "Salvadoran Repatriation from Honduras." *Repatriation Under Conflict in Central America*, Mary Larkin, et. al., eds. (Washington, DC: Center for Immigration Policy and Refugee Assistance, 1991).

Albert Fishlow and Stephan Haggard, *The United States and the Regionalism of the World Economy* (Paris: OECD, 1992).

Fuerzas Populares de Liberación/FMLN, *Plataforma para la Transición Democrática: Propuesta a la Nación Salvadoreña* (San Salvador: FPL/FMLN, 1993).

Grupo Conjunto Para la Investigación... *Informe del Grupo Conjunto para la Investigación de Grupos Armados Ilegales con Motivación Política en El Salvador* (San Salvador: 1994).

Sen. Mark Hatfield, Rep. Jim Leach, and Rep. George Miller, *U.S. Aid to El Salvador: An Evaluation of the Past, A Proposal for the Future*, February 1985.

Bankrolling Failure: United States Policy in El Salvador and the Urgent Need for Reform: A Report to the Arms Control and Foreign Policy Caucus, November 1987.

IDESES/CRIES. *Proceso de paz en El Salvador: La solución negociada* (San Salvador and Managua: IDESES/CRIES, 1992).

IDB and UNDP, *Reforma Social y Pobreza: Hacia una agenda integrada de desarrollo* (New York: United Nations, 1993).

Stewart Lawrence, *Postwar El Salvador: An Examination of Military Issues Related to Reconstruction* (Cambridge: Unitarian Universalist Service Committee, 1991).

Lawyer's Committee for Human Rights, *El Salvador's Negotiated Revolution: Prospects for Legal Reform* (New York: Lawyer's Committee for Human Rights, 1993).

Los escuadrones de la muerte en El Salvador (San Salvador: Editorial Jaraguá, 1994).

Max G. Manwarring and Court Prisk, eds., *El Salvador at War: An Oral History* (Washington, DC: National Defense University Press, 1988).

Michael McClintock, *The American Connection: State Terror and Public Resistance in El Salvador, Vol. 1* (London: Zed Books, 1985).

Segundo Montes, *Estructura de Clases y Comportamiento de las Fuerzas Sociales* (San Salvador: IDHUCA, 1988).

Tommie Sue Montgomery, *Revolution in El Salvador: From Civil Strife to Civil Peace* (Boulder: Westview Press, 1995).

Aquiles Montoya, *La nueva economía popular: una aproximación empírica* (San Salvador: UCA Editores, 1994).

La nueva economía popular: una aproximación teórica (San Salvador: UCA Editores, 1993).

Kevin Murray, et. al., *Rescuing Reconstruction: The Debate on the Post-War Economic Recovery in El Salvador* (Cambridge, MA: Hemisphere Initiatives, 1994).

Organization of American States, Inter-American Commission on Human Rights, *Report on the Situation of Human Rights in El Salvador* (OEA/Ser. L/V/II.85, Doc. 28 FCU, February 11, 1994).

Oxfam America, *The Impact of Structural Adjustment on Community Life: Undoing Development* (Boston: Oxfam America, 1995).

Bibliography

Joaquín Arriola Palomares and José Antonio Candray Alvarado, *Derechos Prohibidos: Negociación Colectiva y Sindicatos en El Salvador* (San Salvador: UCA, Ciencias Sociales y Humanidades, 1994).

Margaret Popkin, et. al., *Justice Impugned* (Cambridge: Hemisphere Initiatives, 1993).
Justice Delayed: The Slow Pace of Judicial Reform in El Salvador (Cambridge: Hemisphere Initiatives, 1994).

James Roush, et. al., *Evaluation of the Peace and National Recovery Project (519-0394) El Salvador* (Arlington: Development Associates Inc., 1994).

Benjamin Schwarz, *American Counterinsurgency Doctrine and El Salvador: The Frustrations of Reform and the Illusions of Nation Building* (Washington, DC: The RAND Corporation, 1992).

Secretaria de Reconstrucción Nacional, *Plan de Reconstrucción Nacional: Evaluación e Informe de Avance, Agosto de 1994* (San Salvador: SRN, 1994).

Mitchell Seligson, et. al., *El Salvador Agricultural Policy Analysis Land Tenure Study* (Washington, DC: AID, 1993).

Servicio Jesuita para el Desarrollo "Pedro Arrupe", *Tiempo de Recordar y tiempo de contar: Testimonios de comunidades repatriada y reubicadas de El Salvador* (San Salvador: SJD, 1994).

Minor Sinclair, ed., *The New Politics of Survival: Grassroots Movements in Central America* (Washington, DC and New York: EPICA/Monthly Review Press, 1995).

Peter Sollis, *Reluctant Reforms: The Cristiani Government and the International Community in the Process of Post-War Reconstruction* (Washington, DC: Washington Office on Latin America, 1993).

Jack Spence, et. al., *El Salvador: Elections of the Century* (Cambridge: Hemisphere Initiatives, 1994).
A Negotiated Revolution?: A Two Year Progress Report on the Salvadoran Peace Accords (Cambridge: Hemisphere Initiatives, 1994).
The Salvadoran Peace Accords and Democratization (Cambridge: Hemisphere Initiatives, 1995).

William Stanley, *Risking Failure: The Problems and Promise of the New Civilian Police* (Cambridge: Hemisphere Initiatives, 1993).

Anjali Sundaram and George Gelber, eds. *A Decade of War* (New York: Monthy Review Press, 1995).

Marilyn Thomson, *Women of El Salvador* (Philadelphia: Institute for the Study of Human Issues, 1986).

United Nations, *Acuerdos de El Salvador: En el Camino a la Paz.* San Salvador: United Nations, 1992.

De la Locura a la Esperanze: la Guerra de 12 Años en El Salvador (New York & San Salvador: United Nations, 1993).

Report of the Director of the Human Rights Division of ONUSAL, covering the period for March 1 to June 31, 1994 (San Salvador: United Nations, July 1994).

USCEOM, *Free and Fair?: The Conduct of El Salvador's 1994 Elections* (Washington, DC: USCEOM, 1994).

U.S. Department of Agriculture, *El Salvador: Agricultural Situation Report* (Washington, DC: Foreign Agricultural Service/USDA, 1989).

José Ignacio López Vigil, *Rebel Radio: The Story of El Salvador's Radio Venceremos* (trans. Mark Fried) (Willimantic: Curbstone Press, 1994).

María López Vigil, *Piezas para un Retrato* (San Salvador: UCA Editores, 1993).

Alistair White, *El Salvador* (San Salvador: UCA Editores, 1987).

Teresa Whitfield, *Paying the Price: Ignacio Ellacuría and the Murdered Jesuits of El Salvador* (Philadelphia: Temple University Press, 1995).

World Bank, *World Bank Development Report 1994* (Washington, DC: World Bank, 1994).

Danielle Yariv and Cynthia Curtis, *After the War: A Preliminary Look at the Role of U.S. Aid in the Post-War Reconstruction of El Salvador* (Washington, DC: Foreign Aid Monitoring Project, 1992).

Katherine Yih, *Water and Human Ecology in El Salvador: A Review* (PRISMA: San Salvador, 1994).

Chronology

1525	Area of El Salvador conquered by Pedro de Alvarado, becomes part of Captaincy-General of Guatemala.
1700	San Salvador second most important city of region.
1786	El Salvador raised to status of intendency, equal to Honduras and Nicaragua.
1811	First Central American pro-independence revolt, led by Salvadorans.
1821	Declaration of independence of Central America; the United Provinces of Central America continues to exist until 1838.
1822	Revolt against attempt by Mexican emperor Augustín Iturbide to dominate Central America.
1838	Independence of El Salvador, but pro-Conservative interventions from Guatemala and pro-Liberal interventions from Honduras continue; interparty conflict, assassinations, revolutions.
1886	Stability under Conservative rule for next 45 years. Communal lands privatized. Coffee becomes dominant crop, and coffee oligarchy consolidates into "14 families."
1913	Presidency alternates between Meléndez and Quiñónez families until 1927.
1922	Formation of the National Guard.
1924	Formation of the Regional Federation of Salvadoran Workers.
1930	Formation of the Communist Party of El Salvador (PCS).
1931	
March	First honest elections; no clear popular winner; Congress elects Arturo Araujo, who begins reformist government.
	Depression wipes out market for coffee.
	Popular agitation led by PCS under charismatic Augustín Farabundo Martí.
Dec.	Coup led by Minister of War Gen. Maximiliano Hernández Martínez. His dictatorship continues until 1944.
	Martí organizes revolt but is captured first. Revolt occurs, especially among Indian peasants, easily put down.

Up to 30,000 peasants rounded up and massacred in *matanza*. Martí and PCS leadership publicly executed, PCS outlawed.

Union organizing outlawed until 1944.

1944 Hernández Martínez overthrown by sit-down (Fallen Arms) strike.

Salvadoran Trade Union Reorganizing Committee (CROSS) builds underground union movement.

1945 Gen. Salvador Castañeda Castro elected president.

Major strike by Railway Workers Union.

1948 Revolt by reformist junior officers.

1950 New constitution promulgated.

Government party (PRUD) organized.

Presidential elections won by PRUD's Lt. Col. Oscar Osorio. Over next six years, unions are legalized, social security, public housing, and electric power projects are begun.

1952 CROSS outlawed; increased anticommunism.

1956 Lt. Col. José María Lemus of PRUD becomes president after rigged elections. Repressive rule; repudiated by Osorio.

1960 Coup by reformist officers.

Leftwing parties legalized.

1961 Conservative countercoup led by Lt. Col. Julio Rivera. New government Party of National Conciliation (PCN, renamed from PRUD) wins all seats in Constituent Assembly.

Formation of National Democratic Organization (ORDEN), a rural paramilitary network of informers and enforcers, by Gen. José Alberto Medrano of military intelligence.

Formation of Christian Democratic Party (PDC).

1962 Rivera elected president on pro-Alliance for Progress platform. Opposition parties boycott elections.

New constitution adopted.

1964 Opposition PDC and Party of Renovating Action (PAR) win over 40 percent of votes in honest election for Legislative Assembly.

José Napoleón Duarte of PDC elected mayor of San Salvador.

Formation of Federation of Christian Campesinos (FECCAS).

1965 Formation of the National Revolutionary Movement (MNR).

American Institute for Free Labor Development (AIFLD) begins educational seminars for farmworkers.

1967 Col. Fidel Sánchez Hernández of PCN elected president.

1968 Formation of the Salvadoran Communal Union (UCS).

1969 "Soccer War" with Honduras (over mistreatment of Salvadorans in Honduras and related issues) lasts four days.

Formation of UNO and the Nationalist Democratic Union (UDN).

1970 Formation of Popular Liberation Forces (FPL).

1971 Formation of People's Revolutionary Army (ERP).

1972	Duarte and Guillermo Manuel Ungo of UNO apparently elected president and vice president, but results altered by electoral commission; Col. Arturo Molina of PCN elected by Legislative Assembly. Nixon administration declines to use influence to assist Duarte.
	Revolt led by reformist younger officers put down with 200 deaths. Duarte arrested, tortured, exiled.
1974	Fraudulent legislative elections, all PCN candidates win.
	Formation of Unified Popular Action Front (FAPU).
1975	Murder of Roque Dalton.
	Formation of second mass organization, Popular Revolutionary Bloc (BPR), linked to FPL.
	Formation of Armed Forces of National Resistance (FARN), linked to FAPU.
1976	President Molina attempts moderate land reform, abandoned when landowners threaten armed resistance.
	Formation of Salvadoran Institute of Agrarian Transformation (ISTA).
1977	Monsignor Oscar Arnulfo Romero becomes Archbishop of El Salvador.
	Assassination of Jesuit Father Rutilio Grande by death squad apparently sponsored by security forces, the first of seven priests killed in next two years.
	Gen. Carlos Humberto Romero elected president in fraudulent election; over 200 peaceful protesters killed. Catholic Church boycotts inauguration.
	Assassinations of several prominent government figures, including Foreign Minister Mauricio Borgonovo Pohl, by guerrillas.
1978	Third popular organization formed: People's League of February 28 (LP-28), linked with ERP, favoring more direct action than FAPU and BPR.
1979	Escalating violence: kidnappings, assassinations, building seizures, and hostage-taking by guerrillas; repression and killings by government forces. Over 600 political killings during year. Shafik Handal of PCS says armed revolt now necessary.
Oct.	General Romero overthrown by junior officers. First junta formed, including Guillermo Ungo and Lt. Cols. Majano and Gutiérrez. Progressive cabinet; Col. José García Defense Minister.
	United States begins increase in military and economic assistance.
1980	
Jan.	First junta and cabinet resign, charging military noncooperation; Ungo goes into exile. Second junta formed, with Majano, Gutiérrez, and Christian Democrats.
	Formation of Revolutionary Coordinator of Masses (CRM).
Feb.	Banks nationalized and land reform decreed. Death squad killings escalate.

	Archbishop Romero writes letter to President Carter requesting halt of aid.
March	Archbishop Romero assassinated while saying mass.
	Third junta formed; includes Duarte.
May	Coup organized by Roberto D'Aubuisson fails. D'Aubuisson organizes Secret Anticommunist Army to coordinate death squad activities.
	Formation of the Farabundo Martí National Liberation Front (FMLN) to coordinate guerrillas; formation of the Democratic Revolutionary Front (FDR) to coordinate leftist political opposition, which links up with FMLN; six FDR leaders killed.
	Attempt by U.S. Ambassador Robert White to negotiate peaceful settlement.
	Gutiérrez narrowly elected commander-in-chief by officers over more progressive Majano. War escalates.
	Military occupy National University campus.
Dec.	Four U.S. churchwomen raped and killed; U.S. military aid cut off.
	Third junta disbanded; Duarte becomes provisional president.
1981	Reagan takes office; U.S. military aid resumes.
	FMLN launches "final offensive."
	Head of land reform institute and two U.S. advisors assassinated.
	D'Aubuisson organizes Nationalist Republican Alliance (ARENA).
1982	
March	Elections for Constituent Assembly, boycotted by left. Rightwing majority, though PDC largest single party.
	Four Dutch journalists killed.
	Alvaro Magaña elected president after United States blocks D'Aubuisson, who becomes president of Assembly.
	Foreign Ministers of Costa Rica, El Salvador, and Honduras form the Central American Democratic Community.
1983	Military insubordination forces García to resign as Defense Minister, replaced by U.S. protege Eugenio Vides Casanova.
	Salvador Cayetano Carpio suicide in Managua.
	Massacre at Las Hojas.
	Contadora group meets for first time to develop dialogue and negotiation in Central America; parties to the peace accords include Costa Rica, El Salvador, Guatemala, Honduras, and Nicaragua.
	New constitution promulgated.
	Cumulative total of political killings reaches 45,000.
1984	Kissinger Commission report: fight, but win hearts and minds.
	Presidential elections: Duarte beats D'Aubuisson in May run-offs, inaugurated in June.

Duarte attempts peace talks with FMLN without prior consultation with United States, but FMLN power-sharing demands are unacceptable to army and United States.

Nicaragua agrees to sign Contadora treaty, but Costa Rica, El Salvador, and Honduras refuse to sign.

1985   PDC success in municipal elections credited to peace overtures.

Four U.S. marines killed by FMLN in San Salvador restaurant.

Duarte's daughter kidnapped, released in exchange for guerrilla prisoners.

1986   New military strategy to clear and hold areas one by one is unsuccessful.

Formation of National Unity of Salvadoran Workers (UNTS).

New round of peace talks sabotaged by military violation of ground rules.

Third revised Contadora treaty presented, Costa Rica, El Salvador, and Honduras refuse to sign.

Oct.   Disastrous earthquake in San Salvador: 1,500 killed, 10,000 families displaced, $1.5 billion damage.

PDC passes taxes on wealthy.

1987

Feb.   Costa Rican President Arias takes leadership role in regional peace initiatives, meets with representatives from El Salvador, Guatemala, and Honduras in Esquipulas, Guatemala.

Aug.   Presidents of Costa Rica, El Salvador, Guatemala, Honduras, and Nicaragua sign Esquipulas II Peace Accord. Duarte tries to make parallels between Nicaraguan contras and Salvadoran rebel groups.

Oct.   Formation of National Reconciliation Commission, as required in peace plan; FMLN-government talks begin.

Duarte proposes amnesty for political prisoners; Herbert Anaya of nongovernmental Human Rights Commission speaks out against amnesty and is killed in death squad fashion. Some political parties withdraw from National Reconciliation Commission and FMLN talks broken off as a result.

Duarte bows and kisses U.S. flag during visit to United States.

Guillermo Ungo and Rubén Zamora return from exile to enter overt political activity; Zamora kisses Salvadoran flag.

Mass repatriation of refugees from Mesa Grande camps in Honduras.

1988   Tensions increase with prospect of presidential elections in El Salvador and United States.

Death squad killings rise; FMLN increases military actions, sabotage, assassinations (especially of local officials).

Hardline Col. René Emilio Ponce replaces Gen. Adolfo Blandón as army chief of staff.

PDC and ARENA split over presidential candidacies.

Honduras requests UN peacekeeping force to patrol borders with El Salvador and Nicaragua.

Catholic Church initiates National Debate for Peace; over 60 organizations participate.

1989

Jan.   FMLN offers to participate in elections if they are postponed six months, dropping demand for prior participation in government and new military force.

Pressure from new Bush administration induces PDC and ARENA to send representatives to Mexico discussions: FMLN asks reduction in size of military, civilian control, prosecution of assassins; rejected by army.

Feb.   Esquipulas peace talks held in Costa Del Sol, El Salvador after four postponements. On same day as peace summit, Armed Forces of El Salvador (FAES) attacks FMLN field hospital, raping female doctor and paramedics, killing them and wounded guerrillas.

March   Presidential elections won by Alfredo Cristiani (ARENA) with 53%, PDC gets 37%, only 3.2% for Ungo (Democratic Convergence). FMLN ambiguous: calls for boycott, or spoiling ballot, or voting for Ungo. Turnout low.

New Cristiani administration pro-free market, privatization. Split between "total war" and "hearts and minds" strategies.

Sept.   New FMLN offer of truce if U.S. stops military aid; new talks in Mexico.

Oct.   FMLN calls off talks with government after bombing of FENASTRAS, country's largest labor federation.

Nov.   FMLN launches major military offensive.

Six Jesuit priests (including rector) of University of Central America assassinated by elite Atlacatl Battalion of FAES.

1990

Jan.   President Cristiani announces detention of military men accused of Jesuit assassinations.

May   FMLN and Salvadoran government sign "Caracas Agreement" establishing agenda and ground rules for peace negotiations.

June   Agreement signed in San José, Costa Rica, establishing human rights guarantees and giving monitoring role to UN.

Oct.   U.S. Congress votes for 50% cut in military aid to El Salvador.

Dec.   In face of FMLN "mini-offensive," President Bush orders expedited release of $48.1 in aid to FAES.

1991

Jan.   FMLN downs U.S. helicopter, killing two crew members, President Bush orders release of $42.5 in military aid frozen by Congress.

March   Voters elect new Legislative Assembly and municipal governments, including nine members of leftwing parties.

April	In Mexico, peace negotiators reach agreement on key set of constitutional reforms and establishment of Truth Commission.
July	UN observer mission (ONUSAL) officially established in San Salvador.
Sept.	Government and FMLN sign "New York Agreement" solving outstanding issues regarding military and PNC.
	Jury finds two Salvadoran officers guilty of one count of murder in Jesuit case and acquits rest of accused members of Atlacatl Battalion.
Nov.	Congressman Joseph Moakley releases evidence implicating several members of military High Command in planning of Jesuit murders.
Dec.	Negotiators, including Cristiani, reach understanding assuring cessation of hostilities and opening way for final agreement.

1992

Jan.	Government and FMLN meet in Chapultepec, Mexico, to sign final Peace Accords.
Feb.	Chapultepec Accord takes effect, ending civil war in El Salvador.
March	World Bank Consultative Group meeting in Washington responds to National Reconstruction Plan with over $800 million in pledges, including nearly $300 million from U.S.
Aug.	In Mexico, El Salvador signs free trade agreement designed to make Central America a free trade zone by 1996.
Sept.	Ad Hoc Commission presents results of investigation of human rights records of past and current officers of FAES.
	World Court makes decision in case involving territorial dispute between El Salvador and Honduras.
Oct.	Government and FMLN accept UN proposal of process to carry out land transfers dictated by Peace Accords.
Dec.	FMLN formally disarms last 20 percent of guerrilla force.
	Supreme Electoral Tribunal approves application of FMLN for recognition as legal political party.

1993

Feb.	First members of new National Civilian Police graduate from National Academy of Public Security.
March	Truth Commission releases report on most celebrated cases of human rights violations from El Salvador's civil war era.
	Legislative Assembly passes broad amnesty law covering war-related crimes.
May	National Police attacks demonstration of disabled war veterans in San Salvador, killing at least one and wounding six others.
	Secret arms cache of FMLN explodes in Managua, Nicaragua.
July	Command changes in FAES remove last of officers named in Ad Hoc Commission report.
Sept.	First contingent of U.S. troops arrives in El Salvador for initiation of *Fuertes Caminos*, program of military exercises.

	United Nations verifies final destruction of arms by FMLN.
Nov.	State Department makes public over 12,000 classified documents related to U.S. policy in El Salvador.
	Sixth Latin American Feminist Conference in Costa del Sol, El Salvador.
Dec.	Assassination of ex-FMLN commander Mario López marks third murder of high-level FMLN official in six weeks.

1994

Jan.	With detonation of last ten landmines, El Salvador is declared officially free of mines.
March	Salvadorans go to polls for simultaneous presidential, legislative, and municipal elections.
April	In run-off election for presidency, ARENA candidate Armando Calderón Sol handily defeats Rubén Zamora, candidate of leftist coalition led by FMLN.
July	After long debate, Legislative Assembly elects new Supreme Court.
Aug.	Special Joint Commission established to investigate persistence of illegal armed groups in El Salvador presents its report.
Oct.	Conservative columnist Kirio Waldo Salgado shakes political establishment with charges of corruption against past and current government officials.
Nov.	Army, called in to reinforce PNC, attacks demonstration of bus owners in San Miguel, killing three and wounding sixteen demonstrators.
	Monseñor Arturo Rivera Damas, Archbishop of San Salvador, dies of heart attack.
Dec.	ERP and RN withdraw from FMLN.

1995

Jan.	Association of Demobilized Members of the Armed Forces (ADEFAES) occupies Legislative Assembly for third time to demand severance and other benefits.
	Calderón Sol government announces new economic plan emphasizing accelerated privatization and radical opening of Salvadoran economy to foreign investment and competition.
April	Fernando Sáenz Lecalle, ultraconservative auxiliary bishop of Santa Ana, becomes new Archbishop of San Salvador.

SOURCES: *El Salvador Election Factbook* (Washington: Institute for the Comparative Study of Political Systems, 1967); Thomas P. Anderson, *Politics in Central America* (New York: Praeger, 1982); *Conflict in Central America* (1987); Jan K. Black, *Sentinels of Empire* (Westport: Greenwood Press, 1986); *Crisis in Central America* (Boulder: Westview, 1988); *Labor Organizations in Latin America*, Gerald Greenfield and Sheldon Maran, eds. (Greenwood Press, 1987); *Central America Report*, 3 March 1989; *Central America Bulletin*, April 1989; *Proceso*, December 1990, December 1991, December 30, 1992, December 30, 1993, December 28, 1994.

Appendix 4

For More Information

Resources

CISPES
Box 1801
NY, NY 10159   (212) 229-1290

Hemisphere Initiatives
608 Franklin St.
Cambridge, MA 02139   (617) 354-1896

Human Rights Watch
485 Fifth Ave.
NY, NY 10017-6104   (212) 972-8400

Lawyers Committee for Human Rights
330 Seventh Ave., 10th Floor
NY, NY 10001   (212) 629-6170

U.S. NGOs

American Friends Service Committee
1501 Cherry St.
Philadelphia, PA 19102

Lutheran World Relief
390 Park Avenue South
NY, NY 10016   (212) 532-6350

Oxfam America
26 West St.
Boston, MA 02111-1206   (617) 482-1211

Project Salvador
Box 300105
Denver, CO 80218   (303) 964-8606

The SHARE Foundation
Box 192825
San Francisco, CA 94119 (415) 882-1540

Unitarian Universalist Service Committee
78 Beacon St.
Boston, MA 02108   (617) 742-2120

Delegations and Volunteers

The Center for Global Education
Augsburg College
2211 Riverside Avenue
Minneapolis, MN 55454   (612) 330-1159

CRISPAZ
1135 Mission Rd.
San Antonio, TX 78210   (210) 534-6996

EPICA
1470 Irving Street NW
Washington, DC 20010   (202) 332-0292

Mennonite Central Committee
Mesoamerica Desk
PO Box 500
Akron, PA 17501

Advocacy Groups

El Salvador Policy Project
Box 29355
Washington, DC 20017   (202) 319-4465

Latin America Working Group
110 Maryland Ave, N.E.
Box 15
Washington, DC 20002   (202) 546-7010

Transition to Democracy
Box 16 Cardinal Station
Washington, DC 20064   (202) 319-5540

Washington Office on Latin America
400 C Street N.E.
Washington, DC 20002   (202) 544-8045

The Resource Center

The Interhemispheric Resource Center is a private, nonprofit, research and policy institute located in New Mexico. Founded in 1979, the Resource Center produces books, policy reports, and other educational materials about U.S. foreign policy, as well as sponsoring popular education projects. For more information and a catalog of publications, please write to the Resource Center, Box 4506, Albuquerque, New Mexico 87196.

Board of Directors

Become an RC member!

Yes! I want to support your efforts to make the U.S. a responsible member of the world community.

☐ **$25 Basic Membership:** You receive one year (four issues) of our quarterly *Resource Center Bulletin.*

☐ **$50 Amiga/Amigo Membership:** You receive subscriptions to the *Bulletin*, bimonthly *Democracy Backgrounder*, monthly *BorderLines*, and all our special reports.

☐ **$100 Compañera/Compañero Membership:** You receive all our periodicals, special reports, and a 33% discount on RC books.

☐ **$250 Comadre/Compadre Membership:** You receive all the benefits of a compañera membership as well as all new RC materials free.

☐ **$1,000 RC Sustainer:** You receive all new publications, and you may take your pick of existing materials from our catalog.

Charge my   ☐ VISA   ☐ MasterCard

Account # _____

Expiration date _____ Daytime Phone ( )_____

Name_____

Street Address_____

City_____ State_____Zip_____

The Interhemispheric Resource Center is a 501(c)3 nonprofit organization. All donations are tax deductible to the extent allowable by law.

☐ Please do not trade my name with other organizations.

To receive our catalog, write us or give us a call:

Interhemispheric Resource Center
P.O. Box 4506
Albuquerque, NM 87196
phone: (505) 842-8288
fax: (505) 246-1601

Central America

GUATEMALA
1992   308 pp.
ISBN 0-911213-40-6
$11.95

BELIZE
1995   200 pp.
ISBN 0-911213-54-6
$11.95

HONDURAS
1994   200 pp.
ISBN 0-911213-49-X
$11.95

COSTA RICA
1995   200 pp.
ISBN 0-911213-51-1
$11.95

EL SALVADOR
1995   304 pp.
ISBN 0-911213-53-8
$11.95

PANAMA
1995   160 pp.
ISBN 0-911213-50-3
$11.95

NICARAGUA
1990   226 pp.
ISBN 0-911213-29-5
$9.95

Everything you need to know about each nation's economy, politics, environment, and society.

ZAPATA'S REVENGE

Free Trade and the Farm Crisis in Mexico

by Tom Barry

The past and future collide in this compelling account of the drama unfolding in the Mexican countryside. Visions of a modernized and industrialized nation competing in the global market clash with the sobering reality of a desperate peasantry and falling agricultural production. These crises in Chiapas are the same ones confronting most of Mexico and the third world.

Barry views the crisis that confronts Mexico as alarming evidence of the incapacity of today's neoliberal and free trade policies to foster broad economic development. He explains that such strategies have resulted in reduced food security, environmental destruction, increased rural-urban polarization, depopulation of peasant communities and social and political instability.

This book offers personal interviews, investigative research, and analysis that goes to the heart of the development challenge faced by Mexico and other Latin American nations.

South End Press, 1995
ISBN 089608-499-X

250 PAGES
$16.00 paper

$35.00 cloth